# EUROPE
## IN THE XIX CENTURY
## (1815–1914)

T0382372

# EUROPE

## IN THE XIX CENTURY

## (1815–1914)

by

### JOHN E. MORRIS

D.Litt. (Oxford), Litt.D. (Manchester)
formerly Assistant Master in Bedford School

Cambridge:
at the University Press
1928

# CAMBRIDGE
## UNIVERSITY PRESS

University Printing House, Cambridge CB2 8BS, United Kingdom

Cambridge University Press is part of the University of Cambridge.

It furthers the University's mission by disseminating knowledge in the pursuit of education, learning and research at the highest international levels of excellence.

www.cambridge.org
Information on this title: www.cambridge.org/9781107585751

© Cambridge University Press 1928

First edition 1916
Second edition 1920
Third edition 1928
First paperback edition 2015

*A catalogue record for this publication is available from the British Library*

ISBN 978-1-107-58575-1 Paperback

# PREFACE TO SECOND EDITION

My purpose has been to give such details of the great events since Waterloo that the general reader and the student may be able to attach some value to such names as Navarino, Magenta, Sadowa, Sedan, Plevna. After experience of a great war it should be needless to apologise for writing about past wars, the success which attends determination and preparation, the feebleness of alternate bluff and non-interference. But I trust that the importance of *les idées* has not been lost. The First French Revolution tried to express "the rights of man"; the Republic at first defended and then sought to spread, in defiance of all crowned heads, these same "rights"; very soon the "idea" of conquest and glory for France's own sake eclipsed all else. Even so the "ideas" of National Unity and of Self-Determination, though the word was not yet invented, dominated Europe in the middle of the 19th century; yet "glory" still played its part. Therefore to see how ideas can be realised it is necessary to show how they have been realised, namely by war.

I maintain against some critics that I have rightly written "Napoleon III's Second Decade" to Chapter VI. Bismarck is, of course, the central figure, but he had his chance just because Napoleon was so feeble. It was not so much what the one did as what the other failed to do that influenced Europe. We see this now very clearly. We believe in Self-Determination, and Napoleon's mind swung between the *idée* of glory and the *idée* of helping those who would be free, so that the man who believed solely in the *idée* of German Unity under the coercive power of Prussia was able to crush each power that wanted to determine its own future.

Since 1914 I have been much struck by the present generation's ignorance of Carlyle's influence. Yet he is almost worshipped to-day in Germany, and Hertling quoted him recently as justifying Germany's retention of Alsace and Lorraine. It is impossible to deny that his was the mind that, at the same time when Palmerston was finding out Napoleon and unwilling to cooperate with him, made us pro-Germans in those critical sixties; at least he influenced educated minds, and in that decade blind uneducated jingoism was not a strong factor in the political world. There was, indeed, much excited talk against Prussia in 1864 and 1866. But Carlyle wrote that it "will go altogether as soon as knowledge of the matter is had," and it did go. So we grew to admire the strong man. Too late we saw that a new strong man, developed on Carlylean lines, really meant something when he talked about "the mailed fist."

So we come back to our main fact. The Crimean *entente* faded away because we could not trust Napoleon III; we looked on France with distorted vision after 1870; and it was only after a long period of blind anti-Russianism, while France and Russia were drawing near together, that we learnt the wisdom of a better *entente* with the Third Republic. And even then neither statesmen nor people knew enough Latin to translate *si vis pacem para bellum.*

In this edition a few pages have been added to carry the reader from the Berlin Congress to the murder of

the Crown Prince of Austria in 1914. Throughout I have
aimed at preserving chronological sequence, so as to show
how German Unity and Italian Unity and other movements
advanced together; if each movement has its own chapter
the mind is apt to lose the sense of cause and effect as between
different nations.

J. E. M.

BEDFORD,
 *February* 1919.

# CONTENTS

## MAPS

## PEDIGREES

# CHAPTER I

## EUROPE AFTER WATERLOO

After Napoleon's first collapse in 1814 the Powers of
Europe sent their representatives to a Congress at Vienna
to rearrange the map. The Waterloo campaign did not
materially influence the final settlement. The Congress
expressed the right of the Great Powers to exercise a
general control and inaugurated the Concert of Europe.

It will be useful first to see what the Republic and the
Empire had done, so as to understand what the Allies
considered should be undone. In 1792 Louis XVI, still
king in name, was forced to declare war against Austria;
then in the same year when Austrians and Prussians
poured into France, when the Duke of Brunswick issued
a manifesto denouncing the French who had made their
king a slave and driven the nobles into exile, the country
roused itself, back to the wall, and the invaders recoiled
from the position at Valmy. The Republic was established,
and the war-cry was for the defence of Liberty, Fraternity,
and Equality. Almost at once a new cry was raised; the
Republic would retaliate by invading countries under
monarchical rule so as to give them the blessings of republicanism and the rights of man. It was a propagandist
Republic in arms to force its gospel upon Europe. And
a third cry was heard very soon; the Republic wanted the

natural boundaries of France to be hers, namely the Rhine and the Alps. Prussia, deserting the Allies, recognised the Rhine frontier in 1795, for the French armies had actually won it.

Bonaparte's campaigns of 1796 and 1797 in north Italy took the French arms far beyond the natural boundaries. His tremendous victories in 1805–07 laid all central Europe at his feet. He, as Emperor, was heir to the Republic in so far as he broke down all out-of-date medieval survivals and feudal inequalities. Where he annexed lands to France, the north-west coast of Germany, north Italy, and the Dalmatian coast, an element of personal freedom was introduced for the first time on a wide scale such as would satisfy republican ideals. Saxony and Poland may be quoted as ardently attached to him. But whether the Belgians and Dutch, the Bavarians and Westphalians, or the Italians, were so ardent, it would be hard to say. The burden of Conscription was laid upon them. They were unable, under his Continental System, to obtain British manufactured goods. In fact they were treated in the Napoleonic scheme as victims to the honour and glory of French military might, compelled to fight the battles of France and to abstain from trade, rather than as peoples liberated from monarchies by a generous and chivalrous race of crusaders. The glitter of Napoleon's imperial court, and of the minor kingly and ducal courts which mimicked it, did not blind them to the truth.

Two countries in particular, Prussia and Spain, saw that even in theory they were not invaded for their own good. The Spaniards were the first to show that peoples as well as kings were the enemies of France. The Tyrolese were not far behind them in patriotism, but were few in numbers and, being far from the coast, had no assistance from

Britain. Then, after the retreat from Moscow, the Prussians as a people led the uprising of Germany, forcing their king in the early days of 1813 to league himself with the Russians; and indeed the Moscow disaster was brought about by the Russian peasants co-operating with their Tsar, destroying their property, and retreating before the French so as to starve them out.

Thus various problems were placed before the Congress at Vienna in 1814, while Napoleon was at Elba. Was he alone to be punished, or France as well? Were the old dynasties to be restored to the old positions, or were popular rights to be acknowledged? How were the countries most liable to be invaded by the French to be saved from future invasion? In answer to the first question the Allies treated France generously; she was not to suffer. But after the Waterloo campaign a certain amount of humiliation was inflicted, for, if she had not unanimously welcomed Napoleon back from Elba, at least a great many of her sons had welcomed him. As to the others, the chief and immediate need was to strengthen Europe against any possibility of renewed war. The various monarchs wanted compensation after the hardships they had suffered from Napoleon. The Congress could not formulate schemes of self-government for each nation saved from France; it could only restore dynasties, or award to them new lands left kingless. Monarch and people in each case had to settle popular questions at home. The result was disappointment and brooding over wrongs up to the year 1848. In fact 1792–94 were too near to 1814–15. All that the Spaniards and Tyrolese had done, all that the Prussians had suffered, could not make rulers forget that the crisis through which Europe had passed had its origin in the republican fury twenty-two years back. Liberty seemed to be synonymous with Jacobinical excess. And, even had such a thought not been natural, one can hardly picture any statesman at Vienna solemnly proposing the creation of a Parliament and popular franchise for each country. It is a hard truth that a nation must win its own salvation.

The crown of France was restored to Louis XVIII, brother of the guillotined Louis XVI; "Louis XVII" was reserved for the young dauphin who had perished during the early days of the Republic. At one time there was a possibility that the French ex-Marshal Bernadotte, adopted heir of the King of Sweden and Regent for him, and declared enemy of Napoleon after the Moscow disaster, might be chosen. There was some feeling that the Bourbons should not be restored, and it may be that Tsar Alexander, who for a time supported Bernadotte, wanted to show that the Powers in crushing Napoleon had no wish to humiliate France and therefore ought not to force upon her the old dynasty. But, as at the time of our own Restoration, it must have been clear that the king *de jure* should have his chance; should the Bourbons, like the Stuarts, misuse it, then the French nation would take matters into its own hands and none would pity them. In the meanwhile *la légitimité* would stand for peace, whereas Bernadotte might prove to be ambitious and restless. France needed peace such as the true king, restored by the Allies, would find it to his interest to maintain. Moreover it was a new France over which Louis XVIII was to preside; a France of peasant pro- prietors and small estates, where the law of succession was as laid down in the *Code Napoléon*; a France to which the Revolution had given liberty and to which, though curtailing the liberty which had become licence and brought anarchy and bankruptcy in its train, Napoleon had given stability;

a France which, in spite of conscription and absence of
self-government, enjoyed personal freedom. The *émigrés*,
those nobles and royalists who had fled in 1789 and subsequent years, some of whom were irreconcileables and had
hounded on the Austrians and Prussians in 1792, and some
of whom were less bitter and returned to France on
Napoleon's invitation, did not regain their old privileges;
they might hope to secure remission from taxation, as in
the good old days before 1789, and to occupy all the highest
positions in Church and State, but they had against them
the solid weight of a peasantry that had become free and
prosperous. The Bourbon dynasty without a privileged
nobility was not really dangerous.

Whether the men of 1814 consciously argued in this
manner, or whether we with a century's experience attribute
to them our thoughts, is immaterial. Something of this
kind, a confidence in the legitimist dynasty as the best
shield against civil war and a new revolution which would
bring in again a military despot, and as the best guarantee
of peace for a France drained of men by long wars, must
have been in the mind of the wily Talleyrand who represented *la légitimité* to the Powers.

In 1814 the Allies looked upon Napoleon rather than
upon France as the enemy. But, after "the hundred days"
of 1815, it was necessary to punish the country that had
welcomed Napoleon back from Elba. A fine of forty
millions of our money was imposed. An allied army of
150,000 men, under Wellington's chief command, was to
occupy certain positions. Works of art carried off from
conquered countries to adorn the Louvre were to be
restored[1]. Blucher and the Prussians, who indeed had

[1] For instance the bronze horses of St Mark, the restoration of
which to Venice caused much excitement; yet the Venetians had

suffered more than any other nation from Napoleon's severity, wanted to plunder in revenge, and in particular to blow up the "Jena" bridge in Paris; their bitterness was shown also in much destruction and wanton defilement of private property on their march after Waterloo into France. But Wellington set his face steadily against the reprisals of mere revenge, and our own soldiers, behaving decently in France, certainly set a good example.

It was Wellington also who protested strongly against the re-annexation of Alsace and Lorraine to Germany. Louis, he argued, would not be safe on the French throne if the provinces won by his ancestors were given up. They had been recognised as belonging to France by international treaties[1]. The inhabitants, from whose ranks had come many famous Frenchmen, wished to be French, for they had learnt under France the meaning of freedom and the Revolution had created a large class of peasant proprietors, who might lose their advantages if handed back to Germany. The Tsar supported Wellington, and Austria did not care to make this a vital question. The Prussian desire for annexation was not pressed, although the argument that

carried them off as loot from Constantinople at the time of the Fourth Crusade. The French bitterly resented the loss, and probably the modern Huns justify their thieving instinct because the French of Napoleon were fond of loot.

[1] The French first obtained Alsace, less a few patches of land, in 1648 by the Treaty of Westphalia; Louis XIV seized Strasburg, hitherto a free German city, in 1681 by a mixture of fraud and force, but the Treaty of Rastadt in 1714 recognised it as his. Three bishoprics of Lorraine, Metz, Verdun, Toul, became French by the Treaty of Cateau Cambrésis in 1559; the last Duke of Lorraine, Francis, gave up the rest of the duchy in 1737 when he married Maria Theresa, and received Tuscany in exchange; it then fell to a dethroned King of Poland, and on his death to France.

German lands ought to form part of Germany appealed
to Prussian minds most of all; for Prussia was directly
aiming at obtaining the lead in Germany, and it was a
sentimental ambition, as well as a military need in view
of any future war against France, that demanded restoration, and how could the British and Russians who lived far
away from Strasburg and Metz understand German senti-
ment?    However France retained her old boundaries as in
1789.    Indeed she had one actual gain, for the little papal
state of Avignon, joined to her early in the Revolution,
remained French.    Just a scrap of Lorraine and a scrap of
Savoy, recognised as French in 1814, were taken away in
1815.

Napoleon's Europe was as follows.    Belgium, Holland—
except for a short time when Louis Bonaparte was king,—
all Germany west of the Rhine, a piece of north Germany
touching the North Sea and extending to a point on the
Baltic at Lubeck, Savoy, north-west Italy extending down
the coast to Rome, and the Dalmatian coast of the Adriatic,
were parts of France.    North-east Italy was the Kingdom
of Italy with Napoleon himself as king, wearing the old
iron crown of Lombardy, and his stepson Eugène as
viceroy.    Murat, his brother-in-law, was King of Naples.
Central Germany, composed of four kingdoms, Westphalia
under his brother Jerome, Saxony, Bavaria, and Wurtemberg under German kings created by him and allied to
him, and several duchies, formed the Confederation of
the Rhine.    Poland, reconstituted as the Grand Duchy of
Warsaw, was under the King of Saxony.    Austria, stripped
of the Tyrol and neighbouring territory which he gave to
Bavaria, and of the land behind Trieste incorporated with
France, was nominally independent.    Prussia was reduced
to little more than East and West Prussia, Brandenburg,

and Silesia, but a French garrison held Dantzig.  Denmark
was his ally.  One point is clear; by abolishing the medieval
survivals in Germany, the Holy Roman Empire, the
electorates, the secular power of archbishops and bishops,
the lay bishoprics in those parts of Germany where the
Protestant Reformation had given church lands to prince-
bishops, and by creating the Confederation of the Rhine,
he gave a great impetus to the German ideal of union;
similarly in Italy, by creating three main divisions and
abolishing all foreign rule except his own, he first suggested
a possible unity.

Of the immediate neighbours of France the question of
Belgium was the most important and touched the English
most nearly.  The Austrians had been in occupation from
1714 to 1793, the French from 1793 to 1814.  To our
statesmen it was a fixed idea that no strong Power should
hold Antwerp so as to create there during peace a naval
base from which it could menace our shores;—Napoleon
had wished to do so, and our ill-fated expedition of 1809
which occupied the island of Walcheren was aimed against
the shipping of Antwerp, but throughout the long war our
naval blockade of the mouth of the Scheldt made Antwerp
useless to him.  Now the Austrians had no ambition to
regain a country so far from them; they coveted rather
access to the sea by way of Venice and Trieste.  No one
thought of a free and independent Belgium as coming
within practical politics; the mixed races, the Flemings of
the western part, the French-speaking Walloons of the
east, the Liégeois who used to be governed by prince-
bishops, the Brabanters and Hainaulters lying between,
had no bond of union, except an affection for France.
Now this affection, which speaks volumes for her decency
and ability to secure the loyalty of even those whom she

had conquered, was quite sufficient in itself to make the Allies callous towards Belgian feeling. At Vienna the statesmen of the moment cared only to promote the interests of their own countries, not those of the people concerned, least of all those of small states. So the Roman Catholic Belgians were handed over to and incorporated with the Calvinistic Dutch under the House of Orange to form the Kingdom of the Netherlands. Such a strange union seemed to be the only solution then possible.

Holland had been practically part of France between 1794 and 1814. Napoleon had indeed made his brother Louis king for a short time, but he had enrolled both Belgians and Dutchmen in his armies as if they had been Frenchmen. The House of Orange was restored in 1814. But after a French régime old and now meaningless titles were dropped. "Stadholder" disappears, and a "king" of the Netherlands appears for the first time in history. In 1815 Belgian and Dutch regiments fought against France under the Prince of Orange, the new king's son and heir, and at Quatre Bras they held their ground in a way which materially helped Wellington's plans. Yet the union was unnatural. Not only was there a religious difficulty, but also, ever since the days of Philip II and Parma, the Dutch had been free, the Belgians in turn under the yoke of Spain and of Austria; the Dutch were sailors and merchants, the Belgians in pre-Spanish days had been manufacturers and bankers; the Dutch had held both banks at the mouth of the Scheldt, and had killed the commerce of Antwerp. Of course the twenty years of connection with France would do something to bring the two races together. Also, when under the same crown, the Belgians would be able to navigate the Scheldt freely, which meant that Antwerp would enjoy a commercial prosperity that she had never known since 1585[1]. But all the traditions of Belgium were opposed to Dutch traditions.

At the other end of the French frontier the House of Savoy was restored to its old dominions as in 1792, namely the Duchy of Savoy, which lay south of the Lake of Geneva and west of the Alps; Piedmont, lying around the upper Po and enclosed on two sides by Alps and on the third by Apennines; the territory of Nice; and the island of Sardinia, from which the Duke took the title of King of Sardinia. To these were added the old rich republic of Genoa, and the strip of coast known as the Italian Riviera which had been conquered by Genoa[2]. It was a compact little kingdom, strong out of proportion to its size because it contained the Alpine passes between France and Italy, and now stronger than of old because of the addition of Genoa. The object of the Allies was to erect a strong barrier against any future attempt of France to reconquer Italy, either by the inland passes or the coast road. As a matter of fact the Riviera is a very difficult country for an army on the march; the mountains in places fall sheer to the sea, and landslides are frequent, so that even to-day both the road and the single-track railway have to be often repaired. But Napoleon had invaded Italy in 1796 along this coast. Genoa had republican sympathy with France. Therefore the land had to be annexed to Savoy and Sardinia.

The restored dynasty had no leaning towards con- stitutional government. But the Savoyards and north- western Italians had enjoyed personal freedom, as had the

[1] The year when Alexander of Parma besieged and took Antwerp.

[2] Many a Riviera town has to-day an old fort erected by the Genoese to overawe, not to protect it; the old "freedom" of Genoa carried with it freedom to enslave.

Belgians, during the score of years of French régime; probably also, like the Belgians, they felt that the burden of conscription imposed by Napoleon had been balanced by their share of military glory. Thus a yearning for popular government was openly shown. Genoa lamented her lost republic, and from her came Mazzini the ardent conspirator and dreamer. Nice was the birthplace of Garibaldi. And ultimately the dynasty, by no means liberal in 1814, caught the ideas of democracy from their subjects and became the champions of a liberal monarchy.

The Emperor of Austria, Francis II, looked to Italy and the Adriatic for his reward after years of war against France and Napoleon. It has been the fate of Austria to expand towards non-German lands, for France was her hereditary enemy in the west, Bavaria supported by France tried constantly to undermine her ascendancy in south Germany, and Prussia was her youngest and strongest rival in north Germany. For centuries she was the bulwark of Europe against the Turks, gaining Hungary and much Slavonic land in consequence. In 1814 she recovered the Tyrol, which Napoleon had given to Bavaria, and thereby held the Brenner Pass and the Adige route into Italy. She recovered Lombardy, which the Spaniards had ceded to her in 1714 and Napoleon had conquered in 1796. She obtained Venetia, both the late republic of Venice[1] and all

[1] It is interesting to compare modern Venice with modern Genoa. The one has a magnificent hinterland for trade, the Po valley, and access to the transalpine routes to Germany; but the shallow water of the lagoon prevents the approach of the large ships of commerce which the conditions of modern trade demand. The other is shut in by a triple amphitheatre of mountains; but the deep-sea harbour can admit large ships. The art of the engineer has been unable to deepen the lagoon, but has been able to drive roads and railways over the Apennines. Hence the trade of Genoa

the hinterland that Venice had conquered, and the Dalmatian coast downwards from Trieste to Ragusa and Cattaro.
Thus Austria, by way of compensation for the loss of
Belgium which, indeed, she never cared to hold, secured
the string of harbours and inlets on the flank of Turkey
where she was able to create a navy; the effect of this was
felt in 1914-18. Next, the protectorate over the Ionian
Islands was entrusted to us, and Malta was definitely
acknowledged as ours.

South of the Po the Duchy of Parma was allotted to
Marie Louise, Napoleon's Austrian wife, for her life; a
new Duchy of Lucca was created for the Bourbon Duke of
Parma, who, when Marie died, was to have Parma back
again, and then Lucca was to go to Tuscany. The Duchy
of Modena was restored to a junior Hapsburg line. The
Grand Duchy of Tuscany, which since the extinction of
the famous Medici family in 1737 had been held by a
Hapsburg, was restored to the Emperor's brother. The
Pope regained not only full authority over Rome and the
Patrimony of St Peter, but also the Marches which stretched
from the Apennines to the Adriatic, and the Legations of
Bologna and Ferrara which touched the lower Po. The
Bourbon king of Naples recovered Naples, and Sicily, owing
to British aid, he had never lost. Thus the overthrow of
Napoleon simply meant the re-establishment, and in the
cases of Genoa and Venice the establishment, of foreign
rulers whose one idea was to be despots and who had no

is great, and that of Venice, whether under Austrian rule or as a
city of free Italy, cannot be compared with what it was in her glorious
medieval days. Genoa before 1914 was being rebuilt and laid out
as a modern city with wide and prosaic streets, only a few of her
quaint narrow ways remaining and still flanked by her old palaces,
and her citizens had largely forgotten the past in their more recent
prosperity. Venice is substantially unaltered.

consideration for national feeling. Austrian white-coated soldiers garrisoned the territories actually governed by Austria, and were ready at a moment's notice to march over the borders into the Roman or Neapolitan territories to maintain pope or king. This was done to prevent any possibility of a new French occupation. Liberalism was to be suppressed because it meant sympathy with French ideals. Of course there was no bond of union between Milanese, Tuscans, Romans, Sicilians, and the others. Italy was "a geographical expression." But all Italians must have had a feeling of community as long as the French régime lasted. Napoleon had broken up the artificial kingdoms and duchies of old days, the Allies had restored them, and educated Italians could not but grieve that they were handed over to the tender mercies of those who cared nothing for them.

Napoleon had destroyed the medieval Germany of 1792, a bundle of two or three hundred states, great and small, lay and clerical. Francis II was no longer Holy Roman Emperor but Emperor of Austria. There was no thought of reviving the electorates in 1814. Napoleon's example was followed, and the Germany of 1814 as constituted by the Congress of Vienna was in less than forty pieces.

The general position of the Emperor of Austria has already been indicated. He was King of Hungary and of Bohemia, he ruled over a considerable stretch of Slavonic country, he recovered the Tyrol which Napoleon had cut off from him, and he had no regret in giving up any claim to the Belgian Netherlands. He held comparatively little German land, and his ambition was to dominate Italy.

In strong contrast the ambitious dynasty of the Hohenzollerns aspired to dominate Germany. It was in 1701 that the " Markgraf " and Elector of Brandenburg first took

the title of King of Prussia, as ruler of the non-German
Prussians[1]. Many small pieces of central and western
Germany were absorbed by the dynasty. The reigning
Hohenzollern in 1795 made peace with the French Republic
and deserted the Allies; in 1805 he made no effort to help
the Austrians against Napoleon; and in 1806 he reaped
the reward of his base selfishness, and was goaded into war
by Napoleon and overwhelmed in the double defeat of
Jena—Auerstadt. Napoleon crushed Prussia ruthlessly.
Her resurrection dates from the early part of 1813, when
she forced her king to make alliance with the victorious
Russians and took the chief lead in the uprising of Germany.
Prussian statesmen demanded a large reward for her
devotion and services, the entire annexation of Saxony
which had been Napoleon's warmest ally; but to this
Great Britain and Austria could not agree, and indeed
there was even some danger that the Allies might split
into two parties and fight each other on the Saxon question.
Finally Prussia obtained about half of Saxony and a good
part of central Germany, including the great cities of
Magdeburg and Halberstadt; likewise Westphalia, and a
large stretch of land on the left bank of the Rhine, including
Köln and Trier[2]. This was more than a mere gain of
many square miles and much population. It was a recognition that Prussia, not Austria, was the leading German
power, worthy to hold and defend against any new French
aggression that Rhineland which was so dear to the German

[1] We are apt to forget that the genuine Prussians, not the
Brandenburgers, are Slavs. Hence pre-war talk of German Kultur
as a bulwark of civilisation against Russian Slavism was more than
a little illogical.

[2] That is the archbishopric-electorates of Köln (Cologne) and
Trier (Trèves). The third archbishopric-electorate of Mainz (Mayence)
was added to Hesse Darmstadt. See map on p. 188.

heart, which France coveted and had held so long, and over which a watch had to be kept[1]. Westphalia and Rhineland were Roman Catholic, and Lutheran Prussia was deputed to guard them. Thus the future of the Hohenzollerns was assured; they would be the champions of all Germany, Catholic or Protestant, west or east. Swedish Pomerania was also annexed to Prussia.

Prussian ambition also aimed at securing a good portion of Poland. In the old pre-Napoleonic partitions of Poland they had gained most of the Vistula and Warsaw with it; Napoleon had restored Poland, not as a kingdom, but as a Grand Duchy, and the Poles fought very well under him, especially as cavalry. But as Prussia received so much new land in Germany, the largest portion of Poland was now awarded to Russia, Warsaw included; Prussia's gain was the strip of West Prussia, filling the gap between Brandenburg and East Prussia, with the old free German city of Dantzig, and the fortresses Thorn and Posen; Austria obtained Galicia, including Lemberg, but Cracow was made an independent republic.

Saxony, Bavaria, and Wurtemberg, had been Napoleon's allies; but whereas Saxony remained true to him to the end, the Bavarians turned against him, and he even had to fight against them as he retired from the great battle of Leipzig. Therefore it was thought that whilst the Allies should punish Saxony they should leave the other two intact. The Allies finally accepted the King of Saxony as king, but only in command of half of his old dominions, that is, the present Saxony lying around Dresden and Leipzig. The Kings of Bavaria—minus the Tyrol—and of Wurtemberg retained their lands and titles. Hanover was entirely restored to George III of England, no longer as

[1] See p. 74.

Elector but as King of Hanover. The Grand Duchies of Baden, Hesse Darmstadt, Hesse Cassel[1], and the two Mecklenburgs, were constituted; and several Duchies, such as Saxe Weimar and Saxe Coburg[2], still remained to represent the little states which had formerly been a chief feature of Germany. Four only of the old free cities of Germany remained, Frankfort on the Main, Hamburg, Bremen, and Lubeck. Bavaria held a piece of the old Palatinate on the west bank of the Rhine. The old archbishopric-electorate of Mainz was added to Hesse Darmstadt.

A spirit of unity was abroad in Germany, yet the time had not come for a settlement of a definite union. The old jealousy between Austria and Prussia was quite sufficient in itself to prevent the scheme, and the question of ascendancy had first to be fought out between them. But a Bund or Confederation was formed: it embraced thirty-nine states, German Austria, Prussia, the four lesser kingdoms, five grand duchies, many duchies, four free cities, together with the King of the Netherlands by virtue of his position as Grand Duke of Luxemburg, and the King of Denmark who held the Duchy of Holstein. It was by no means an ideal confederation. In general terms one can say that the kings and dukes and others

[1] But, curiously enough, the Grand Duke was popularly styled "Elector."

[2] A former Elector of Saxony had two sons, Ernest and Albert. Luther's protector was of the Ernestine branch, but his nephew lost the electorate in 1547; the lands of their part of Saxony were split into fragments and shared by members of the family, such as Coburg, Gotha, Altenburg, Weimar, Meiningen. The Albertine branch got the electorate and the "march" of Meissen, which Napoleon formed into the Kingdom of Saxony, and of which the Congress awarded a large share to Prussia.

were members of it, rather than the countries over which they ruled. They nominated representatives who should attend the Diets. The presidency belonged to Austria, but neither Austria nor Prussia had more than one vote, and the pettiest duke had one. It would be impossible for the Diet to enforce its wishes upon its stronger members. Still it accustomed the German mind to entertain an idea of unity which might lead to something better later on. As in Italy, there had been hitherto no real bond between states as far apart as Mecklenburg and Baden, but Napoleon had forced all Germans to consider themselves in some sense as one nation, and therefore the new Confederation had in it greater possibilities than the old Holy Roman Empire.

In the old days the one great power of the Holy Roman Empire had been Austria. Jealousy of Austria had always prevented any scheme of reform which would tend to produce unity. The many second-rate states, Brandenburg before the creation of the Kingdom of Prussia, Saxony, Bavaria, the three Archbishop-Electors, were none of them strong enough alone to counterbalance Austria, and France had only to offer her aid to one of these to find a ready ally, through whom she could weaken Austria. But now there were two rivals for ascendancy; the one, which would prove herself within the next half-century strong enough to lead and detach from the other the minor states which held the balance of power, would win the unity of Germany. Meanwhile the mere fact that Prussia had obtained such a large portion of Roman Catholic Rhineland, whereas Austria had only gained accessions of territory in Italy, was a forecast of what would happen. Finally fear of France would produce the desired result when Prussian statesmen would be clever enough to exploit this feeling in her own favour.

As regards smaller nations, the King of Sweden lost both Finland and the small Swedish remnant of Pomerania: in return the Allies awarded to him Norway, compelling the Norwegians to submit by threat of armed force. Denmark lost Norway by her resolute devotion to Napoleon, whereas Bernadotte, the adopted crown prince of Sweden, had been clever enough to attach himself to the cause of the Allies in 1813.

Switzerland obtained the constitution which she enjoys now, except that the central government is to-day stronger in proportion to the governments of the cantons, and the bonds which unite the cantons have been tightened by the necessities of modern life.

Castlereagh obtained from the Congress a general condemnation of the slave-trade. France agreed to abolish it. But Portugal and Spain, in spite of all our services to them, refused and argued as if this was an instance of English hypocrisy. We did not abolish slavery till 1833.

Throughout the whole of Europe there were high hopes that some constitutional form of government would be adopted in each country, that popular rights would in some way be recognised. Tsar Alexander, proclaiming himself King of Poland, was going to introduce constitutional and national freedom. One of the clauses of the instrument which created the German Confederation assumed that each of the members would have a Constitution. But while the peoples had under French influence absorbed the idea of popular liberty, the restored monarchs could only remember that in France republicanism had produced licence and excess, that republican excitement had begun a long series of wars and led directly to Napoleonism. Even in England the fear that any much-desired reform would only prove the thin end of the wedge of revolutionary radicalism had effectually checked redress of abuses; between 1789 and 1815 the only remedial legislation that was carried in the face of a strong reaction against reform was the abolition of the slave-trade in 1807, and that was only possible after Pitt's death; also Sir Samuel Romilly by persistent effort was beginning to reform the criminal law, and brought about the abolition of hanging as a penalty for certain small offences. Therefore, if in our island Reform of Parliament had not yet been effected, there is little reason for surprise that continental nations which had never had a true parliament would receive one. "Liberalism" was in the air, but the word was used to imply an unjustifiable yearning after liberty and was used scornfully.

A great deal depended upon the personal influence of Alexander. He had high ideals and a generous nature, but he was ready to fall under the influence of whoever was the most masterful at the moment. Thus in 1805–07 he was Napoleon's enemy; in 1807, disappointed in receiving no direct help from the British, he met at Tilsit the master mind and became Napoleon's ardent ally; he accepted the continental blockade against British trade, but soon, finding that Russia could not get on without it, also insulted by Napoleon's proposal for his sister's hand and subsequent rejection of her for Marie Louise, he once more defied France and the result was the great Moscow campaign of 1812; thereafter he was the warm friend of the British, and was the most popular of the allied sovereigns who visited England in 1814. A man of moods, inclined to generosity and enthusiasm, then passionately resentful of real or imaginary insults, he was apt to run to one extreme and then to the opposite. In 1815 he suggested a Holy Alliance in defence of religion as against the excesses of the Jacobin atheism of the early days of the French Republic and the cynical toleration of the Catholic Church by Napoleon. "Holy Alliance" meant nothing, but the phrase is popularly used to express the political association of the sovereigns of Russia, Prussia, and Austria, when the clever Austrian Chancellor, Prince Metternich, obtained influence over them one by one and persuaded them to crush Liberalism.

Metternich moulded to his will the three potentates by warnings, and then by triumphantly pointing to a certain scene at Wartburg[1] in 1817 as a sure sign of the wickedness of unrestrained liberty. Students from the liberal university of Jena and elsewhere—under the Duke of Saxe Weimar freedom was real and Jena was the centre of liberal propaganda—met to celebrate the third centenary of Luther and the anniversary of the battle of Leipzig; they celebrated in good German style with religious services, and with feasting after service; a bonfire was lit, and into it were thrown, in imitation of Luther's burning of the pope's bull, writings which were in praise of despotism and various emblems of military brutality. Because of youthful rowdiness and the destruction of a pamphlet and a cane, Metternich condemned the Germans as a nation to forfeit all their rights to free speech and a free press. For the strongest as well as the noisiest freedom-lovers were, naturally enough, not the nobles who thought that they had a divine right to administer Germany under their

[1] In the castle of Wartburg Luther was sheltered by the Elector of Saxony in 1520; it stands above Eisenach in a detached fragment of Saxe Weimar some miles west of Weimar itself. Eisleben, Luther's birthplace, and Wittenberg, where he nailed up his theses in 1517, being in Prussian Saxony, were not so suitable for a centenary celebration.

respective princes, nor the dull and lately all but slavish peasants, but the keen student class.

Englishmen may find it difficult to understand why such an outburst of high spirits should be so bitterly punished, yet a very little reflection reminds us that the late war was after all the result of assiduous teaching in the universities and schools of Germany. But up to 1914 the Imperial campaign for the glorification of the German nation as supermen fit to govern the whole world was dictated from head-quarters; in 1817 the spontaneous outburst of a few liberal young men set the governments in alarm lest the ideas of freedom preached in the universities should penetrate through the nation.

There was also definite crime in honour of liberty; a student who had been at Wartburg was, in a fit of devout excitement, led in 1819 to murder a certain Russian journalist in Germany who was thought to have influence over the Tsar in the policy of tyranny, but this murder was done after the Tsar as well as the King of Prussia had already become reactionary. Alexander had already taken fright, and the high promises which he had made to the Poles that he would give them a free government, as well as his more vague aspirations towards the abolition of serfdom in Russia itself, had been abandoned.

The first of various conferences between the ministers of the Great Powers met at Aachen (Aix-la-Chapelle) in 1818. As regards France it was agreed to withdraw the Allied army of occupation, and even to consider Louis XVIII as a free sovereign and member of the Concert of Europe. Now it was that Metternich first began to exercise a real influence, bringing over Alexander to his view that the Concert should regulate the affairs of the other countries and repress liberty. Britain, represented

by Castlereagh and Wellington, was not a consenting party;
certainly at home our Tory government favoured repression
and considered every form of rioting and disturbance as
a crime: the massacre of Peterloo at Manchester took place
in 1818; yet ours was nominally a free country and there
was a strong Radical minority in the Commons, so that not
even Tories could face Parliament if they should bind
themselves to a union of European tyranny.   Our ministers,
however, were content to disapprove of Metternich's ideal;
they did not actively oppose him, and their mere non-
compliance was quite counterbalanced by Alexander's
change of front.   "Metternich has fairly enchanted them."

In Prussia there was no attempt to give a free parliament, and a vague idea expressed in the Congress of Vienna
that the new German Confederation should imply some sort
of constitutional freedom in each of the federated states
never came to fulfilment.   Metternich pointed out that
the Prussian kingdom, composed of seven provinces new
and old, had no common point of union; the Crown should
govern, and allow merely provincial diets to meet for local
business and assent to what the Crown proposed; as these
diets were composed of local magnates, they were not
centres of Liberalism.   Thus the Hohenzollern ideal of
doing everything for Prussians and nothing by Prussians
was carried out.   The Crown arranged a system of national
education and watched over the material prosperity of the
country as in the days of Frederick the Great.   The Crown
introduced the Prussian drill-sergeant into the annexed
provinces of Saxony and Westphalia.   Among lesser
princes the "Elector" of Hesse Cassel was a conspicuous
rough despot; on the other hand the King of Bavaria, the
Grand Duke of Baden, and the Duke of Saxe Weimar, were
liberals and granted Constitutions.   In 1819 Metternich

assembled at Carlsbad the ministers of eight German states
to secure a rigid censorship of the press throughout Germany,
and to enforce the Federal Diet to extend it to every state
in the Confederation; and in 1820 another meeting at
Vienna openly laid down the doctrine of the sovereigns'
supreme rights, which, if need were, should be enforced by
the Diet.

Outside Germany the state of affairs in Spain and the
Kingdom of Naples called for the intervention of the
Powers.  In Naples the restored Bourbon, Ferdinand I,
refused to allow any liberty or a Constitution; he even
cancelled what he had done, or promised to do under
British pressure, in Sicily; for when he had been maintained
in the island simply and solely by British help, he had in
1812 granted a Constitution.  But it was dangerous to
treat the Neapolitans as slaves, for under French rule they
had enjoyed at least justice and a fair administration.
The celebrated secret Society of the Carbonari, the Charcoal-
burners, had been formed before the expulsion of the
French, and was now enormously popular.  Neapolitans
who had served as soldiers of France either joined the
society, or came over to it when there was a rising.  General
Pepe put himself at the head of the movement; Ferdinand
was compelled to grant a Constitution and took a public
oath to observe it.  Now Metternich would have liked to
march Austrian troops at once to Naples, yet he preferred
to have the moral support of Russia and Prussia.  The
three sovereigns met towards the end of 1820 at Troppau
in Moravia.  Their Concert was popularly but wrongly
known as the Holy Alliance, being confused with the union
which Alexander had proposed, five years earlier, for the
maintenance of religion against republicanism.  There was
nothing religious in the meeting at Troppau, but only

a decision to take steps in concert against Naples. Britain and France stood outside, but it must be added that Castlereagh protested. Ferdinand was summoned to meet the sovereigns at Laibach in the south of Austria; he escaped from Naples after swearing to uphold the Constitution, openly declared after his escape that his oath was void, and arrived at Laibach. An Austrian army marched south and entered Naples in March 1821 without any trouble; unluckily for Liberalism, Neapolitans and Sicilians were quarrelling and even fighting in Sicily instead of making a united front; despotism was restored and the horrible prisons of Naples were filled. Austria was revealed to Europe as the power which imposed itself upon Italy by the frightfulness of its revenge.

Meanwhile there was a popular movement in Piedmont, and some conspirators against the Austrian yoke were plotting in Milan and hoped to obtain aid from Piedmont; both movements collapsed and the House of Savoy did not put itself forward to champion Liberalism or Italian nationality. The fortress-prison of Spielberg in Moravia, where the Lombard ringleaders were immured, has become in Italian literature a synonym for horrors worse because more refined than those of Naples.

Similarly there was a revolution in Spain, and as a fact it began in Spain before the outbreak in Naples. The restored Bourbon king was Ferdinand VII, who had been deposed by Napoleon, and he was a bigot and tyrant. It is wonderful to us that Spain should have submitted to him at all after all the heroic deeds of the nation in the war against the French, but Ferdinand was a good Catholic and the mass of the illiterate Spaniards were Catholics. His chief ambition was to conquer the rebel Spanish colonies of South America, but it was a task too great for him.

Conspiracy was first hatched at Cadiz among soldiers told
off to sail to America, the movement spread, and Ferdinand,
like his namesake in Naples, granted a Constitution under
compulsion.    But the Powers did not act against Spain so
quickly as against Naples.    The European Concert was
assembled at Verona late in 1822 ; Alexander wanted to
send a Russian army to Spain ; Wellington, who represented England—Castlereagh who committed suicide this
year, and Canning who succeeded him as Foreign Secretary,
were at one upon this point—resolutely opposed a joint
expedition against Spain.    Then Louis XVIII, who
strongly disliked the idea of allowing Russians to march
across French soil, took the task upon himself.    Neither
Canning nor Wellington felt it to be Britain's duty to use
armed force in Spain's defence.    Left to themselves, the
Spanish priests and peasants welcomed the French royal
armies, though they had fought Napoleon in a war to the
knife.    Ferdinand was restored in 1823.    The Constitution,
extorted from him by soldiers and townsmen, was cancelled.

Any discussion on the rival merits of Castlereagh and
Canning may seem to be out of place in a history of Europe ;
it is enough to say that Castlereagh was a man of decision
and coolness when once he was embarked upon a definite
policy, whether he made up his mind to resist Napoleon's
Peninsular ambitions to the bitter end, or opposed reform
at home.    Canning was much more Liberal, yet he too was
a Tory in domestic politics.    Whatever praise or blame is
due to Castlereagh during the years 1816–20 must be
shared by Canning, for during those years he was in the
Cabinet.    Had Castlereagh lived he might have taken a
step forward from mere disapproval of Metternich.    Had
Canning been Foreign Secretary at the earlier date he
might have confined himself also to mere disapproval,

before he took up the line of active opposition. But
Castlereagh was reserved, though he seems often to have
hidden behind a cold manner more generous thoughts, for
otherwise his consciousness of his unpopularity in England
would not have driven him to suicide. Canning took up
any policy hotly and spoke eloquently, but had at least
a reputation for belittling other politicians so as to surround
himself with a halo of glory. Yet even if we allow that
there was this element of meanness in Canning, that he
had not previously been more high-minded than Castlereagh,
and that now he was not more clever and liberally generous
in taking a next step, it remains that he, and not Castlereagh, took the next step. He acknowledged the revolted
colonies of Spain to be sovereign states. Spain herself
being overrun by French troops, he made the balance true
by a policy which made Colombia, Argentina, Chile, Peru,
and Mexico for ever independent.

The after history of Spain is exceedingly dreary.
Ferdinand died in 1833, leaving his widow Christina to
be regent for his daughter Isabella. His brother Charles,
known as Don Carlos, claimed the throne and waged a war
of "Carlists" against "Christinos" for many years; he was
a reactionary against any form of liberalism, and at one
time interfered on the reactionary and clerical side in
Portugal; his strength was greatest in the northern provinces, especially Navarre. Isabella was deposed in 1868.
In 1870 the offer of the crown to a Prussian precipitated
the Franco-German War. For a time a son of Victor
Emmanuel was King of Spain, but he soon resigned.
A second Carlist war, fomented by the grandson of the
previous Don Carlos, lasted from 1873 to 1876. A republic
was found to be impossible, for the extremists of the cities,
especially Carthagena, were communists after the example

of the mob of Paris. At last in 1874 Alfonso XII, son of
Isabella, was restored. In 1898 the United States interfered
to stop the long war between the Spaniards and the rebels
of Cuba; they annexed Porto Rico and the Philippines,
and made Cuba nominally free but practically dependent
on them. In recent years it had seemed that Spain, previously torn asunder by ultra-democrats and ultra-royalists,
had adapted herself to a sane form of Parliamentary
government. Now General Primo de Rivero is military
dictator under Alfonso XIII.

In 1807 the royal family of Portugal, fleeing from
Napoleon's army, went to Brazil, and throughout the
Peninsular War a Council of Regency ruled. In 1816 King
John governed Portugal, and his son Peter governed
Brazil. In 1826 on the father's death Peter granted a
Constitution to Portugal, himself abdicating in favour of
his infant daughter Maria da Gloria, and returning to Brazil
as Emperor. A rebellion was set on foot by Dom Miguel,
Peter's brother, who represented the ultra-royalist and
clerical party and received help from Spain. Canning,
in defiance of the sovereigns of Europe, sent armed help
in 1826 to the party in favour of the child and Constitutionalism so as to save England's old ally from civil war
and anarchy. But the death of Canning, just as we shall
see in the next chapter that it caused British aid to be
withdrawn from Greece, led to withdrawal from Portugal.
Wellington simply allowed Dom Miguel to seize the throne
in 1828, which was a triumph for anti-liberalism. He
governed badly and tyrannically. At last Peter came over
from Brazil, enlisted volunteers from England with Palmerston's connivance, destroyed with their help Dom
Miguel's navy, and after a formal treaty with England

and France drove him out. Maria then reigned constitutionally, and her two sons and a grandson after her down
to the murder of the latter in 1908.

Louis XVIII commenced his reign with the supple
Talleyrand, ex-republican and ex-Bonapartist, as his
minister. With him was Fouché, chief of police and secret
service under both republic and empire. It was Talleyrand's chief work for France that he had persuaded the
Powers to restore the legitimist dynasty. But it was
impossible to retain such men when the royalists were
restored a second time after Waterloo. Louis as early as
July 1815 issued an amnesty with certain exceptions to be
afterwards made; Fouché made a long list of exceptions
to gratify his grudges against his old colleagues and enemies,
and Louis got rid of the scoundrel. Then he called to his
service the royalist Duke of Richelieu, who enjoyed the
favour of the Tsar and had been, while in exile, engaged in
the administration of South Russia. Moderation was the
new minister's programme. But a royalist reign of terror
broke out, the *terreur blanche*, so called as it was done in
favour of the white Bourbon flag, and it was worst in the
south of France; this was an excitable country and had
seen many horrible deeds of bloodshed on both sides,
especially in 1793 when Marseilles and Toulon declared
against the Republic. Several Bonapartist generals and
others were murdered. At Nîmes vengeance fell largely
upon Protestants. Mostly the atrocities were due to mobs,
but there were government prosecutions also and summary
sentences. The execution of Marshal Ney was ordered by
the Chamber of Peers; certainly a word from Wellington
would have saved him, and the sentence seemed to be due
to petty spite and a somewhat weird popular idea that
there must be a scape-goat, like the feeling after 1660 in

England which sacrificed Sir Harry Vane; but it is clear that Ney, put into a position of trust and then deserting to Napoleon, had materially helped in bringing the latter to power again. Argument in such a case is, however, useless, and the verdict of feeling after Ney's execution was that he was unjustly killed.

Louis in 1814 issued a Charter. He alone was, by divine right, the source of law and head of the administration. But he acknowledged, what the revolutionists had persistently refused to acknowledge[1], that something could be learnt from England; he granted responsibility of ministers to Parliament. He created two Chambers; the Peers, nominated by him, some to be hereditary, some for life only; and the Representatives, chosen from the *éligibles* who paid 1000 francs a year in direct taxes, by *électeurs* who paid 300 francs. His first Parliament thus elected was ultra-royalist and inclined to persecution. His younger brother, Charles, Count of Artois, a very violent man who had been the head of the *émigrés* and instigator of foreign countries to destroy the revolutionists in 1789–92, was the acknowledged chief of the ultras, and thought Louis too backward. But the Tsar gave Artois a hint to be cautious and not stir up a civil war in France. Louis and Richelieu as moderate men saved the country from the white terror after the first fury was abated, dissolved the Assembly, and obtained a more moderate one in 1817. They had their reward in 1818 when at Aachen the Powers admitted France as a sovereign state to the Concert, and agreed to withdraw the army of occupation.

Moderation, indeed, did not last very long. As Metter-

[1] In answer to Mirabeau in 1790, when he offered to the National Assembly a pamphlet on English Parliamentary methods, they said "We are not English and want nothing English."

# THE BOURBON CROWNS

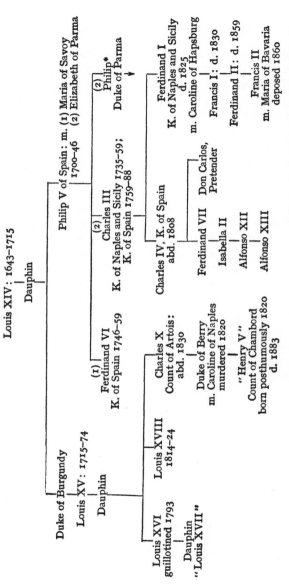

Louis XIV: 1643–1715

Philip V of Spain: m. (1) Maria of Savoy
1700–46        (2) Elizabeth of Parma

Dauphin

**Duke of Burgundy**

**Louis XV: 1715–74**

Dauphin

— Louis XVI guillotined 1793
  Dauphin "Louis XVII"

— Louis XVIII 1814–24

— Charles X Count of Artois: abd. 1830
  Duke of Berry m. Caroline of Naples murdered 1820
  "Henry V" Count of Chambord born posthumously 1820 d. 1883

(1) Ferdinand VI K. of Spain 1746–59

(2) Charles III K. of Naples and Sicily 1735–59; K. of Spain 1759–88

Charles IV, K. of Spain abd. 1808
  Ferdinand VII
    Isabella II
      Alfonso XII
        Alfonso XIII
  Don Carlos, Pretender

(2) Philip* Duke of Parma

Ferdinand I K. of Naples and Sicily d. 1825 m. Caroline of Hapsburg
  Francis I: d. 1830
  Ferdinand II: d. 1859
    Francis II m. Maria of Bavaria deposed 1860

* Descendant of this line dethroned in 1860

nich's influence prevailed and the Tsar swung round to intolerance, the ultras raised their heads again in France. In 1820 a fanatic murdered the Duke of Berry, the second son of Artois; both Louis himself and Artois' elder son were childless, and the object of the murder was to destroy the royal family. Murder is always stupid, as it gives to tyrants an excuse to tyrannise, witness the Serbian-Austrian crisis of 1914. Louis was ageing and could no longer resist the ultras. Richelieu resigned in 1822. When the Powers were holding conferences to suppress liberties in Naples and Spain, French king and ministers alike seized the opportunity to pose as anti-liberals worthy of Metternich, and, to prevent the Russian armies from having an excuse to march into western Europe, sent 100,000 French to restore Ferdinand VII. Louis died in 1824, knowing that ultra-royalism was dangerous and fearing for the future. On his deathbed he said of the baby born after Berry's murder: "May Charles X preserve this child's crown!"

Thus Artois, the no-surrender reactionary, came to the throne which he was to hold for six years. The ultras were unmuzzled. The *parti prêtre*, strengthened already in the previous reign by the return of the Jesuits and by the formation of a religious association called "The Congregation," obtained a law of strong penalties against sacrilege. The press was under a strict censorship. The nobles demanded a milliard (1,000,000,000) of francs as indemnity for their lands lost in 1789, which the new men would not give up except at the cost of a civil war; the money was raised on loan burdening France with an annual charge of thirty millions. Matters came to a crisis in 1829 when Polignac was minister. In the Assembly there was a solid opposition of 221; it was dissolved, and the new elections returned 270 opponents to 145 ministerials. A newspaper

campaign defied the censors, and among the writers were
the young historians, Thiers and Mignet. Prosecutions
and fines were ridiculed. Finally Charles issued four
*ordonnances*, extinguishing altogether the liberty of the
press, dissolving the Assembly, and pronouncing a new law
of elections which gave votes to only the large landed
proprietors, and thus destroyed the Charter of Louis XVIII.
He tried to distract the French from home politics by a
new colonial policy, the conquest of Algeria.

In July 1830 the crisis came to the culminating point.
Barricades were run up in the streets of Paris; it was still
the old Paris of mostly narrow and winding streets. Who
would be resolute to clear them with whiffs of grape-shot?
Marmont, Napoleon's old marshal, was in command. He
stormed some barricades and saw others rise; he failed to
concentrate his men, then fell back on the Louvre and
Tuileries. Regiments went over to the people, "*car les
baïonnettes aujourd'hui sont indépendantes,*" and only a
monarchy sure of its soldiers can afford to use soldiers, as
a comparison of the careers of Louis XVI and of Napoleon
abundantly shows. Thiers issued a proclamation calling for
the Duke of Orleans[1], who came to meet a provisional
government sitting at the Hôtel de Ville. Old Lafayette,
the "hero of the two worlds," who had fought for American
Independence and had been a leading figure in 1789, a
theatrical person and yet popular as an old-time revolutionary, publicly embraced Orleans, and Paris accepted
him for want of any better man. Charles X fled to England.

The meaning of the "July Revolution" is very plain.
The legitimist dynasty had had its chance; it behaved

---

[1] He was descended from the brother of Louis XIV; and was
son of the Duke who posed as a revolutionist in 1789, and was known
as Philippe Egalité.

well as long as Louis remained cool, but went over to revenge and absolutism under Charles. Even the Charter of Louis was insufficient, for it posited the divine right of Louis as the source of law in spite of responsibility of ministers and the existence of an Assembly. The men of July altered the Charter very considerably, taking these "rights" as belonging to them "essentially" and not as gifts of the crown; it was the same spirit which had made the men of 1789 reject the scheme of reforms of Louis XVI, and put forward their own. They accepted Orleans as "King of the French," not "of France." They were fortunate in the circumstances of their revolt and in their having a candidate, even an untried candidate, to bring forward. At least they were not revolutionaries. Thus they gave no excuse to the Powers to interfere.

*Note to Second Edition.* Perhaps it has not been sufficiently emphasised in the text (pp. 8, 10, 14) that the object of the Powers was to create a strong barrier against any future French aggression; therefore the Congress of Vienna deliberately united Belgium to Holland, awarded Rhineland and Westphalia to Prussia, and consolidated the kingdom of Sardinia. Also Metternich's policy of suppression of free speech and free press, however brutal it may now seem to our modern ideas, was dictated by a fear that all democratic licence was akin to French revolutionary fervour; therefore tongue and pen were to be restrained, lest talk about "rights" might breed a new sympathy with France and revolutionism.

# CHAPTER II

## THE INDEPENDENCE OF GREECE

The Turkish Empire has a great fascination for us. Yet we have to acknowledge that our ignorance about the Turks themselves, the proportion of their numbers to those of other Mohammedans, their history and past aims, even the spelling of names[1], is considerable. We may read expert historians[2], and yet remain doubtful whether we appreciate certain points. Where West and East clash there are, by the nature of things, rival explanations, because there are rival aspirations.

Herodotus first saw that there was a pendulum swinging between Europe and Asia; the Greeks besieged Troy and settled on the coasts of Asia Minor and on the islands; Croesus and then the Persian kings conquered here, next came the great invasion and repulse of Xerxes, followed by Greek reconquest which to him was the culmination of a world war. He would not have been surprised if some prophet had foretold the overthrow by Alexander of Macedon of the descendants of Xerxes, and the foundation

[1] Mŏhămmĕd or Mŭhammăd represents the Arabian pronunciation; Māhŏmet or Māh'mett is our approach to the Turkish variation. Salonīka ·is educated Greek, or even Thessalonika; Salonĭca is popular.

[2] *The Balkans* (Clarendon Press, 1915) by Messrs Forbes, Toynbee, Mitrany, and Hogarth.

of the first overlordship of Europeans in Asia. Now it is
self-evident that neither the Persians nor the Macedonians
could themselves alone govern the lands that they overran;
their numbers were quite insufficient. The Persians, though
stamping down national life and religion in some countries,
as in Babylon after revolt, yet had to employ local native
administrators; they favoured the tyrants in the Greek cities
of the Asiatic coast; they had the ships and men of Egypt,
Cyprus, Phoenicia, and these same Greek cities. Alexander,
posing at first as the champion of the Greek cause, soon
took up the rôle of liberator in Syria, Judaea, Egypt, and
Babylon, and appointed native officials; even when he
reached Persia he governed through Persian nobles. But
his life's work was, not so much mere conquest, as the
admission, through conquest, of the Greeks into Asia; his
Macedonian army was but his instrument, and the quick
Greeks profited by his wars and influenced thereby the
world's history, not the duller Macedonians. They settled
not only on the coasts, but also on the roads of the interior,
in the new cities such as Alexandria and Antioch and
Seleucia on the Tigris, and in the old cities such as Iconium
and Tarsus where Greek learning thus took root; the
brighter wits amongst the natives learnt the Greek ideas
and language, and we call them Grecians. Then came the
Romans as Alexander's heirs as far as the Euphrates.
So strongly did the Romans imprint on western Asia their
form of government that to-day the Turkish Empire is
"Rum."

The original Mohammedan conquerors, the Arabs,
swept through the southern provinces of the Roman Empire
in Asia and Africa. But the Eastern Emperors at Constantinople held Asia Minor, or Anatolia as it is also called
for convenience sake, as a strong bulwark in defence of

Christianity. A powerful dynasty of "Roman" Emperors was Anatolian by blood; the Anatolians remained a sturdy rustic and inland race and changed their character but little, whether their overlords were Macedonians or Romans of old Rome or Romans of Constantinople, and they were the defenders of the empire for some centuries; the Greeks of the coasts and of cities on the high-roads still gave a western touch to Anatolian civilisation. But the Turks came to reinforce Mohammedanism. Their home was in central Asia; they served first as mercenaries of the Caliphs of Bagdad, were converted to Islam, grew in numbers, and pushed on as adventurers to found dynasties, but never in such great numbers as to be more than a dominant military aristocracy. The thickest mass of true Turks to-day, we are told, is to be found in Persia, whence the true Persians fled and are to-day the fire-worshipping Parsees of India. The Seljuk Turks at last shattered the defence of the Eastern Roman Empire at the battle of Manzikert in 1071, and founded "Rum," their own Asiatic empire, with Iconium or Konieh as their capital. The advance of the Turks made the Crusades both necessary and possible; they upset the Mohammedan world, for they were not orthodox, and when the Mohammedans were disunited the Christians had a measure of success in the First Crusade. Saladin, a Kurd and the son of a captain of mercenaries, rising by sheer merit in the midst of confusion to be Sultan of Egypt, reunited the Mohammedans and foiled the Third Crusade.

Another tribe of Turks pushed into Asia Minor and conquered to the north of the Seljuks of Iconium. From one of their earlier leaders, Othman or Osman, they are known as the Ottomans or Osmanlis. They made Brusa, over against Constantinople, their capital in 1326. Their strength lay in their recognition of the Greeks and the

Anatolians, neither persecuting nor annihilating, but granting privileges which lasted for a time among the Greeks of Brusa but have disappeared, converting to Mohammedanism where they could, and raising a professional force of soldiers among Christian recruits. Later they imposed the tribute of Christian children, who, trained to war, and forbidden to marry, became the famous Janissaries. They looked across the Dardanelles at the shrivelled remnant of the Eastern Roman Empire, still centred round Constantinople with its navy and impregnable walls, while behind lay the main territories of the Balkans, held by Slavs and Bulgars. They crossed and conquered at the great battle of Kosovo in 1389 a confederacy of Slavs, who were terribly weakened by treachery and jealousy. But for a time the great city was yet safe, for a new peril came from the East.

The Tartar hordes of Jenghiz Khan and Timur came out of Asia as the next great swarm behind the Turks. They shattered the Seljuks of Iconium, but in the meanwhile the Seljuks covered the Ottoman attacks upon Europe. The Ottomans, when they had to face the Tartars in Asia, were already a European power. Thus, although their army was beaten and their Sultan taken prisoner at Angora in 1402, they were able from Europe to reassert themselves in Asia when the Tartar storm exhausted itself. They took into their empire most of the late Seljuk empire, and finally captured Constantinople in 1453, so that at last they had such a position both in Europe and in Asia with "second Rome" as their capital that they were the successors to Alexander and the Caesars, a dominant race with Greeks and Anatolians their subjects, contemptuously tolerant of Christianity, and not at all fanatical after the Arab type with a choice between Koran or sword. Their impetus carried them through the Balkan Peninsula in

spite of the resistance of the Venetians by sea and the
Hungarians by land. The Christians did not unite to
oppose them, but in their jealousy actually weakened
Venice by a league to win Venetia from her; Spain did
very little except occupy Tunis for a short time and take
a small share in the victory at Lepanto in 1571. It was by
land that the Turks at last found their masters when the
Austrians beat them from Vienna in 1529. In the other
direction they extended their power to Syria and Mesopotamia and Egypt, and nominally along the north of Africa
and in Arabia; but out on the extremities of their empire
they were not so well obeyed as at the centre. The Sultans,
after Selim 1512–20, had some glory as the successors of
the Caliphs of Bagdad, and as the protectors of the Holy
Places of Arabia, but received a grudged submission, for
they were not orthodox, but merely the strongest Mohammedans.

The decay of the Turkish Empire began when contact
with the steady Germans first stopped them. Every
conquering Eastern race has spent itself in time, the
Persians, Arabs, Seljuks, Tartars, Moguls, and like them
the Ottoman Turks in their turn. Only Christian jealousies,
which allowed them to penetrate so far west, prevented
their being turned out of Europe. When the Sultans
ceased to lead armies to war, but directed from their
palace; when the Janissaries as the strongest element in
the state took to pull down or to set up, and finally, by
extorting the right to marry, became a caste and intrigued
in the government; when corruption and persecution were
the results of pride and power, and the overswollen empire
of many different races was suffocated by the combination
of ignorant refusal to do things with ignorant persecution
of those who tried, so that the riches of Anatolia and

Mesopotamia and Egypt were allowed to disappear through downright stupidity; when the Turks ruined irrigation works, or as in the 20th century, greedy for bribes, thwarted whoever has tried to restore them, and over-taxed the farmers till Anatolia produced a tithe of what she yielded in the old Roman days; the Turkish peril was past. There was no interference in the horrible Thirty Years' War, 1619-48, when Germany was rent and exhausted. There was a revival of enterprise when the ambitions of Louis XIV made all Europe look westwards in self-defence, and the Turks attacked Vienna in the rear in 1683 but were repulsed. The Austrians retaliated and won back most of Hungary in 1699; again forced to fight against Louis XIV they slackened their efforts against the Turks until, after the Treaties of Utrecht and Rastadt, they took the offensive again and won more ground as far as Belgrad, where they halted in 1739 and left that city to the Turks.

Russia came late upon the scene as a champion of Europe, and her interest has been due to an anxiety to reach to the sea, to the Black Sea in the 18th century, to the Mediterranean in the 19th and 20th. Under the Tsarina Catharine, a Russian war resulted in the Treaty of Kainardji in 1774, by which she was acknowledged the defender of the Christians of Rumania, and obtained commercial rights in the Black Sea. Napoleon in 1807, making alliance with Tsar Alexander I at Tilsit, sanctioned so to speak Russian expansion at the expense of Turkey, but nothing came of it because Alexander broke with Napoleon too soon. The seeds of the jealousy between Austria and Russia were sown, though forgotten when they were allies against France, and later when they were allies against Liberalism in Europe under Metternich's guidance.

The Balkan peoples whom the Ottoman Turks brought

into their empire were various. The tribes conquered by
the Romans, the Roman and Greek settlers of the interior,
the Slavs who burst into the Roman Empire in the wake
of the Goths and Huns, the Tartar tribes from central
Asia of race akin to the original Turks themselves, in the
long period between 400 and 1400 fought each other and
partly coalesced with each other, fell apart and were
rearranged, while the Eastern Empire centred at Constantinople was weaker or stronger at intervals up to the *coup
de grâce* in 1453.

The Rumans are descended from the Dacians of the left
bank of the lower Danube, and from some few Romans
who entered as colonists after the Emperor Trajan conquered and annexed the country in A.D. 104. In the
thousand years of confusion they were conquered or fled
to the mountains to avoid conquest, yet maintained their
distinct nationality and their language, which is Latin
essentially with a mixture of Slav. Some Rumans were
caught into Hungary in the 18th century; until 1918 the
province of Bukovina was in the Austrian Empire. The two
chief districts, Moldavia and Wallachia, which paid tribute
to but were never directly governed by the Turks, had in
that same century Greek governors; Ottoman corruption
at the worst period in their history stooped to put up to
auction these governorships, and the ready Greeks bought
them[1]. But in 1774 the Russian protectorate over Rumania
was established, though the Russians themselves held
Bessarabia, and the Austrians had Bukovina, which was
*Rumania irredenta.*

The Serbs belong to the great group of Slav nations,
and have kept their blood pure; the original Bulgars were
Tartars of the same stock as the Huns and Turks. The Slavs

---

[1] See below, p. 47.

broke from the north across the middle Danube, the Bulgars
from the north-east across the plains of southern Russia,
into the collapsing Roman Empire in the 7th century.
Their modern historians claim, each for his own nation,
the right of priority of invasion. But it seems that the
Slavs, of whom the Serbs were the most numerous, were
by 650 settled between the Adriatic and the Aegean,
shortly before the Bulgars crossed the lower Danube.
The Eastern Roman Empire, defended by a navy and the
mighty walls of Constantinople, held them at bay, and
they were always bitterly jealous of each other, as they
contended for the middle debatable lands of Macedonia
and Thrace then as now. There were two short periods
of Bulgarian Empire, 893 to 972, and 1186 to 1258; and
then the Serbs had the supremacy, until, weakened already
by wars against the Hungarians, they collapsed before
the Turks. During these years the Serbs retained their
language and blood; Slavonic place-names have replaced
the old Greek and Roman names, except on the coast.
The Bulgars, on the contrary, attracted to themselves,
coalesced with and absorbed into themselves such Slavs
and, presumably, older inhabitants whom they conquered;
but, being adventurous and strong in physique, they
dominated when they absorbed, so that now they are a
hybrid race, largely Slav in blood, but with a high percentage of their old Tartar energy to counterbalance a low
percentage of Tartar nationality.

In the strong period of Turkish rule both Bulgars and
Serbs were "suffocated." Some families became Mohammedan, and colonies of Ottomans, or of other races converted
to Mohammedanism and generically styled Turks, were
planted. Where Christianity endured, the Orthodox Greek
Church maintained its sway, though in Bulgaria the

authority of the Patriarch at Constantinople was much resented. A Roman Catholic influence came from the Adriatic coast. As regards administration the Turkish hold was tightest over Bulgaria, and over Herzegovina and Bosnia where the Mohammedan element was strongest among the Slavs.

Then in the recoil of the 18th century the fortunes of these countries varied. The Slavs of Croatia and Slavonia were conquered by the Austrians and Hungarians, disliked the change of masters and would have wished the Turks back again, were forced into the Roman Catholic communion, revolted and were subdued, and some of them migrated into Russia; this tyranny was more Hungarian than Austrian, coming at a time when the aim of the Hapsburgs was to bribe Hungary into loyalty. Thus the majority of the Slavs in the Austrian Empire north of the Save were Roman Catholics, and cut off from the Orthodox Serbs.

One little ring of Serbs, being protected by their mountains, were governed by their prince-bishops without much interference from the Turks. They were the Montenegrins. Their bishop Daniel founded in 1700 a dynasty which reigned till modern times, and Peter I won practical independence by the end of the century, though the Turks still held Scutari[1]. Their kinsmen, the Serbs of the Serbia that we know, had a harder task; Austria did not wish to fight the Turks to liberate them; Russia was far away, and Russian treaties with the Turks only concerned Rumania; worse than that, the two families of Serbian patriots, the Karageorgevich and the Obrenovich, almost ruined the country by their rivalry in the 19th century. A revolt commenced in 1804 by Kara George (Black George)

[1] Scŭtări.

was, owing to Russian inability to help, put down by the Turks in 1813. Then Milosh Obrenovich renewed the war in 1815, and was chosen as prince at Belgrad in 1817, though he soiled his name by the murder of Kara George. Meanwhile there is nothing to record as regards Bosnia and Herzegovina, with their large Mohammedan population, on the one hand, or Bulgaria on the other; and the Turks still controlled Macedonia and Thrace with their mixed Serbian and Bulgarian population and Mohammedans interspersed.

The mountaineers of Albania, converted to Mohammedanism, are aboriginals, and represent to us that strong and manly race which contributed men to the armies of Alexander and Philip, and under Pyrrhus were a danger to Rome herself. They were rugged and independent. Alternately they have been Turkey's best soldiers and, though Mohammedans, dangerous rebels. Early in the 19th century, when the Sultan's governors in outlying provinces were making themselves independent in the manner of great medieval feudals defying their suzerain, such as Mohammed Ali in Egypt and Jezzar at Acre, the famous Ali Pasha ruled Albania. His capital was Yannina[1] (Janina), and he utilised the services of the Greeks in his administration. His sons governed Thessaly and the Morea as pashas, and in fact his power was such that the Sultan's rule seemed to be extinct.

Along the Adriatic coast from Albania northwards to Trieste the population is Slav. But in the middle ages, naturally enough, Venice extended her power over the islands and inlets, for she could not afford to allow pirates to threaten from them her commerce. Pola, Zara, Ragusa, became Venetian dependencies; they were Slav cities, and their hinterland was Slav, but naturally enough they were

[1] Yannĭna.

Italianised to a greater or less degree as they were nearer
to or further from Venice.   To-day we are told that the
inhabitants, when in the cities they are Italians, in the
immediate neighbourhood are Slavs, and even in the cities
many who speak Italian as the language of Adriatic trade
are by blood Slavs.   The Turks in their heyday conquered most of this coast.   They left self-government to
the cities, and Ragusa in particular thrived as a trading
republic, paying tribute to the Sultan and never even
trying to revolt.   Venice regained part of the coast in the
18th century, including the Bocche (mouth) di Cattaro in
Montenegro.   But the most important fact in the history
of the Adriatic is the award by the Allies at the Congress
of Vienna; Venice and Venetia were given to Austria,
and thus from Trieste, which was Austrian already long
before, down to Ragusa and Cattaro every harbour of
importance fell to the Hapsburgs as an inheritance from
Venice.   The Slavs of Serbia and Montenegro were thereby
shut out from the sea, Austrian ambition to secure the
Balkans at the expense of the natives was encouraged, and
the Austrian navy, when once built up, had a strong line
of bases.   To-day the Italian kingdom is regarded by all
Italians as the heir to Venetia, so that there is rivalry
between Italian and Slav for this coast, a rivalry which up
to 1918 benefited Austria alone.   The Ionian islands, Corfu,
Zante, and the others, Napoleon wished to make an outpost
of French influence in the Mediterranean; the British
wrested them, all but Corfu, from him; the Congress put
them under a British protectorate.

There remain to be discussed the Greeks, and this is
no light task.   In classical days the Hellenes prided themselves on their pure blood, distinguishing themselves from
all other nationalities who were Barbarians.   But with

the conquest of the Persian Empire by Alexander they
entered on a new sphere of activity.   They profited where
Alexander's Macedonians conquered.   No longer confining
themselves to the sea and coasts as in those classical days,
they poured along the great high-roads of western Asia
and settled in cities, whether the older cities such as Tarsus,
or the new foundations such as Antioch and Alexandria.
When Rome conquered, there she found Greeks or Grecians,
citizens, civil servants, traders, scholars, philosophers,
proud of their race and yet cosmopolitans, citizens of the
world, at heart.   When the Roman Empire was split into
halves, the Eastern Empire was Roman in administration
but Greek in character; the Orthodox Greek Church and
the Catholic Church fell apart, even as Constantinople and
Rome were apart.   Thus the Greeks were ready to accept
the Ottoman Empire, "Rum," the Asio-European agglo-
meration of races and tongues.   The Greek blood must by
that date have been more than a little diluted by Slav
blood, yet the Greek strain was dominant, and ever in the
worst days of subjection there was a consciousness of Greek
superiority.   Othman, the founder of the empire, saw that
these Greeks were useful, whether the landowners of north-
west Asia Minor to whom he gave privileges, as mentioned
above, or the children whom he demanded and turned
into Mohammedan soldiers.   The Orthodox Church sur-
vived the capture of Constantinople, being "spared by the
Ottoman government to facilitate its own political system—
by bringing the peasant, through the hierarchy of priest,
bishop, and patriarch, under the moral control of the new
Moslem master whom the ecclesiastics henceforth served[1]."
It was useful to the Turks that the seat of the Patriarch
should be in Constantinople.

[1] A. J. Toynbee, p. 182; Hogarth, pp. 325–6.

Yet the Ottomans only used the Greeks where and as they were necessary for the empire. In Greece proper the landowners and peasants were trodden under foot; in Constantinople and other cities Greek residents were in the position of hostages, and they might be turned out at any time if, for instance, the Sultan wished to give asylum to the persecuted Jews of Spain. There is now a very large Jewish population in the cities of the coast which otherwise seem to be entirely Greek in character, Salonica in particular.

Venice, the rival of Greek trading communities and of the "Greek" Empire in her days of strength before the Ottomans advanced, did her best in her own defence to save Greece. Crete was not conquered till 1669, and a new Venetian offensive in 1699 resulted in the possession of the Morea for some years. Genoa held the island of Chios up to 1566, and Venice kept the Ionian Islands. But whatever position the Greeks won in the Ottoman administration they won, not as the protegees of the fast decaying sea-republics of Italy, but by their own adaptability.

The most remarkable of the Greeks of the end of the 18th and the first years of the 19th century were the islanders, the men of Chios and Psara near the Asiatic coast, of Hydra and Spetza near the Morea. The Chians are particularly praised by all writers as a self-governing and self-respecting race, prosperous and unmolested by the Turks. The Hydriots and the others had, we are told, a strong intermixture of Albanian blood, yet they were recognised as Greeks; Byron's heroes were mostly islanders, fine dashing fellows, a blend of the pirate and free adventurer which appealed to the readers of his day. They entered on a new sphere of activity as Venice fell to decay. The coasting trade of the Levant was theirs and brought them much profit. Sometimes they traded under the Russian flag so as to secure the benefit of the Treaty of Kainardji of 1774. But what gave the strongest impetus to their trade was Napoleon's great continental blockade; all the efforts of the British to retaliate against Napoleon were so far confined to the western seas, that these Greeks had their chance. The men who profited by the Russian foundation of Odessa in 1792, and controlled the trade in South Russian corn, were Greeks. The Turks simply demanded a certain number of sailors for their own navy, but there were hundreds of other islanders to man the small trading ships which they armed and were ready to use. Hence the Greek island communities won self-government for themselves, and this practically meant government by an association of shipowners. They formed a strong contrast to the peasants of the Morea, who lived at the mercy of Turkish officials and Mohammedan landowners.

Another class of Greeks were those who won their way into the Turkish administration in this period when the energy of the Ottoman race seemed to have sunk so very low. Clever men won positions as "dragomans" or secretaries in the civil service. We have seen how some of them bought the position of "hospodars" or governors in Moldavia and Wallachia, where indeed their rule was much disliked; yet the mere fact of Christians being admitted to such office, even by bribery, was a step towards the possibility of native Rumans holding it. Such Greeks are known as Phanariots, so named from Phanari, the quarter of the lighthouse at Constantinople. The Ottomans could not get on without the Greeks, who thus had in their hands more than a little of local administration, whether in outlying parts of the Turkish Empire, or in such districts as Albania which were in revolt against the Turks, as well as of local trade.    Greek prosperity in some respects was pronounced just when the grip of the Ottoman was being relaxed.

"The age of the French Revolution and of the Napoleonic wars had silently wrought in the Greek Nation the last of a great series of changes which fitted it to take its place among the free peoples of Europe.    The signs were there from which those who could read the future might have gathered that the political resurrection of Greece was near at hand.........    The history of France, no less than the history of Greece, shows that it is not the excess, but the sense, of wrong that produces revolution.    A people may be so crushed by oppression as to suffer all conceivable misery with patience.    It is when the pulse has again begun to beat strong, when the eye is fixed no longer on the ground, and the knowledge of good and evil again burns in the heart, that the right and the duty of resistance is felt[1]." We sum up that many causes produced the Greek revolt, the sense of unity given by the wide power of the Orthodox Church, the tradition of ancient glory, the revival of Hellenism, the high hope that a new Greek Empire would arise to take the place of the Ottoman as the legitimate heir to the Eastern Roman Empire, the new development of Greek trade, the prosperity of Greek merchants at Odessa and Salonica, the cleverness of the race which made itself indispensable to its Turkish masters.    If Rumans had Phanariot governors, and Serbs were winning local independence, if Jezzar at Acre, Ali Pasha in Albania, and Mohammed Ali in Egypt could defy the Turks, the Greeks

---

[1] Fyffe, *Modern Europe*, chapter xv, pp. (popular edition) 525 and 544.

in their turn could not remain still. They were striving
to educate themselves to be true Hellenes, reviving the
name and the speech of ancient Hellas, and no longer
submitting to be called "Romaioi" speaking the Romaic
language as if they were mere provincials. They could
look to their brothers in the Ionian Islands, free as they
had never before been free, under the British Protectorate.
Byron familiarised to the Western world the dream that
"Greece might yet be free"; but Byron, though he afterwards died for the cause, wrote with a sneer, for they were
"light Greeks carolling by," "hereditary bondsmen,"
"silent still and silent all," unable to show themselves
worthy of Leonidas and his Three Hundred. Shelley had
a warmer heart and the New Hellenism meant more to him.

> "The World's great age begins anew,
>     The Golden years return...
> Another Athens shall arise,
>     And to remoter time
> Bequeath, like sunset to the skies,
>     The splendour of its prime."

He dedicated his *Hellas* to Alexander Mavrocordato, whose
family were Phanariots connected with Rumania.

Unfortunately a Greek rising in Greece was only too
certain to endanger the safety of the Greeks in Constantinople and other parts of the Ottoman Empire, who, scattered
in their various pursuits, or living as a despised minority
surrounded by Mohammedans, were hostages at the mercy
of their lords. Moreover there was the Concert of Europe
to be considered. The statesmen at Vienna had no thought
for national aspirations when they settled the fate of
Poland, Norway, Belgium, Genoa, and Venice. Metternich
had captivated the minds of the sovereigns of Prussia and
Russia, and would not regard Greece more favourably than

Naples and Spain. "Russia," writes Shelley, "desires to possess, not to liberate, Greece." We are accustomed to an Eastern Question the difficulty of which is that each Western Power is too jealous to allow any other to settle the fate of Turkey. In those days it was not mutual jealousy, but the solidarity of the three Great Powers, which stifled nationality and liberalism.

The first impetus towards rebellion was furnished by the " Philike Hetairia," the Society of Friends, which was founded in 1814. The first scene of their activity was Rumania, and they hoped to interest the Tsar in their fortunes, through one of the Phanariots, now the Tsar's minister, by name Capodistrias; but he was against any rash exploit. Then they won over Alexander Hypsilanti, a descendant of a previous Phanariot governor of Wallachia and an officer in the Tsar's army. The plan was to create a rising in Rumania in 1821. But everything went wrong. The Tsar was against the movement, being at that very moment engaged heart and soul in preparations against the Italian revolt. The congress at Laibach condemned the Greeks as much as the Italians and the Spaniards. The Sultan, Mahmud, forced the Patriarch at Constantinople to excommunicate the insurgents. The Rumans of course had no sympathy with the Greeks from whom they had suffered much tyranny under Phanariot governors. The Turks soon crushed the rising.

But the excitement of the time produced different results in the Morea. There the Turks and other Mohammedans were in the minority; there was a general rising in April, accompanied by massacre in the open country. The Turks were driven to a few fortresses such as Patras, Tripolitza, and Nauplia. Similarly north of the Gulf of Corinth the Greeks carried everything before them, and massacred in the country around Missolonghi. But both in Thessaly and along the coast they had no success. Then it was seen how fatal was such a movement to the Greek hostages in the Sultan's power. Greeks were massacred where they were helpless in both European and Asiatic Turkey. On Easter Sunday the Patriarch himself at Constantinople, and the Archbishops of Adrianople, Salonica, and Tirnovo, were executed. This was the moment when the Tsar might possibly have interfered. The hearts of the Russians were roused by the news of the massacre of their co-religionists and most sacred leaders. But still the influence of Metternich prevailed. The Tsar could not bring himself to support rebels, even persecuted Orthodox rebels, and the influence of England was thrown on the side of non-intervention; the terrible European war had been terminated only six years previously, and Castlereagh shrank from taking any part in what might lead once more to a war of all the nations. The most powerful argument that could be used in favour of non-intervention was that the British have been themselves since the middle of the 18th century a Mohammedan power, and it would be wrong for our statesmen to enter upon a crusade against Islam as Islam while there were so many Mohammedan subjects of our Empire in India. The atrocities committed on the Christian as well as on the Mohammedan side doubtless did much to alienate sympathy.

But in the Morea the Greeks carried all before them. Demetrius Hypsilanti, brother of Alexander, was one of the earliest leaders. With him was Alexander Mavrocordato, also the descendant of a Phanariot governor of Rumania, the first President of the Assembly which the Greeks formed in the early years of the war, and the man to whom Shelley dedicated his poem. Of a different type was

Kolokotrones, who in his previous life had been at one time a gendarme, at another time a brigand or "klepht," a man of low type but said to have been a born soldier. The Greeks pushed on. They captured Navarino, and massacred there. They invested Tripolitza, and fearing to lose their booty when they saw that negotiations for surrender were going on, they burst into the place and surpassed themselves in a massacre worse than that at Missolonghi.

In 1822 the Turks were more free in the north, and equipped large and regular forces to crush the rebels. Early in the year they at last captured Yannina and killed Ali Pasha. Two main armies were dispatched, the one against Missolonghi, the other against the Morea. The Greeks of Missolonghi held out successfully. The Greeks of the Morea, either by design or by happy accident, seizing the right moment after the Turks had pushed through the Isthmus into the interior, rose on all sides and Koloko-trones seized the mountains in their rear. Afraid to advance, deserted by the Turkish fleet, and in danger of starvation, the Turkish general, who in his plight might be compared to some French marshal in the Peninsular War cut off from France and harassed by Spanish guerilla bands, had to fight his way back towards the Isthmus; he himself died, and his army was annihilated. Such a collapse is often seen in Turkish history; demoralisation sets in just when matters seem most favourable, and usually has as its immediate cause some gross carelessness in connection with supplies. The outlying Turkish fortresses in the Morea now fell; next Athens was taken.

Meanwhile this same year a series of naval operations was taking place, the Turks victorious here, the Greeks there. Certainly the most energetic of the Greeks were the

Islanders who formed an association of shipowners, such as the Hydriots and the Spetziots from their islands near the Morea, and the Psariots, whose home lay close to Samos. But the fleet of the Islanders was not at hand when an army of 7000 Turkish regulars and a horde of irregulars were landed at Chios; in no part of the Greek world was there such an enlightened community, which had been self-governed and free from Turkish tyranny; now helpless before the Turks they suffered for the savagery of their kinsmen in the Morea, and were cut down or sold as slaves in thousands. Too late to save Chios, the Greek fleet under the command of Kanaris of Psara at last appeared. Kanaris himself steered a fire-ship by night up to the Turks' flag-ship and destroyed it.

In 1823 there was no fighting on a large scale, and the Greeks had time to consolidate their position. But promptly they fell out and fought against each other. Islanders were jealous of the men of the mainland. Kolokotrones, the rough brigand, could not act with the landowners, and therefore there was the unedifying spectacle of civil war almost in the very presence of the enemy. A breathing space was thus allowed to the Turks, and meanwhile Mahmud applied for help to Mohammed Ali[1] of Egypt, nominally his vassal, in reality independent and the master of a considerable fleet and army.

The year 1824 opened under new conditions. Ibrahim Pasha, Mohammed's adopted son, brought across a force to Crete. The plan of campaign was to attack outlying islands, with the idea that the wrangling Greek government in the Morea would be unable to send help so far in time; the Greeks were strong in their navy of fire-ships, but a speedy joint attack by Turks and Egyptians, if the Greek

[1] See pp. 71 and 72.

ships were on the wrong side of the Aegean and neglected the islands from which they could watch and blockade the Dardanelles, might be successful, and of course lessen in proportion the Greek offensive naval power. First Crete was overrun. Then a Turkish fleet from the Dardanelles attacked Psara, the home of the sailor-hero Kanaris, and it was surprised even as Chios had been. Too late the Greek ships arrived at Psara, though they paralysed the action of the Turkish-Egyptian fleets for the rest of the year. Then the Greeks returned to the Morea, and Ibrahim fell back unmolested to Crete.

In 1825 Ibrahim transported his army from Crete to Morea, and nothing shows more strikingly the weakness of the Greeks than this repeated inability to understand the true need of a small naval power, the need to strike, like Drake, on the enemy's coast. The Egyptians now were planted in the Morea. They made their base at Navarino bay, and swept through the interior. Tripolitza was deserted. Meanwhile a Turkish army under Rashid Pasha, the conqueror of Ali of Yannina, laid siege to Missolonghi from April 1825 to April 1826. At first the Greeks held out heroically, especially as on the lagoons the light Greek ships materially helped in the defence; but with the new year Ibrahim came across from the Morea and at last secured control of the lagoons with gunboats. The defenders made a desperate sortie with all their women and children, and a mere remnant cut their way through. In spite of the help of foreigners such as Sir Richard Church, whose life had been spent in the Ionian Islands, and who was an ardent sympathiser with Greek liberty, Athens was blockaded; an attempt to relieve the city from the sea came to nothing, for the Greek ships deserted and returned to Hydra, and Athens fell in June 1827.

Relieved from the worst of his anxieties by Egyptian help, Mahmud carried out in 1826 a policy which he must have long meditated. The celebrated force of Janissaries, which was now an hereditary militia, not well trained enough to take the field, yet capable of thwarting the Sultan's wishes at Constantinople, was attacked and destroyed by a force of Anatolians, the Sultan's devoted adherents in Asia Minor. From this may be dated the renewal of the Turkish military power. Mahmud was now able to train an army of Mohammedans from the districts loyal to him, though they were not by any means all of them pure-blooded Turks. The mountaineers of Albania on the one side and Anatolia on the other were henceforward recruited into the Sultan's ranks without the interference of a jealous corps at the capital.

The unspeakable atrocities of Turks and Egyptians, however much they may have been inspired by similar atrocities of Greeks when the revolt began, aroused at last the attention of the Great Powers. The conditions in Europe were undergoing change. Alexander I died in December 1825, and even he had been beginning to understand the need of the intervention of civilised force. The heart of Russia was being aroused. His younger brother and successor, Nicholas I, was ready to break the bonds by which the Russian freedom to act was hampered by Metternich. In England Canning had been Foreign Secretary since Castlereagh's suicide, and the voice of England was raised at last in April 1826, when Wellington himself, who made it the corner-stone of his military policy to prevent Russia from becoming strong in the Eastern Mediterranean under cover of protecting Christians against Turks, went as ambassador to Petrograd on the new Tsar's accession. It was agreed that Great Britain and Russia should co-operate to save the Greeks. The idea was that Greece should be tributary to the Sultan, yet with local self-government on the Rumanian model. But the Turks rejected mediation.

In April 1827, owing to the illness of Lord Liverpool, Canning became Prime Minister, and thus was able to put the last touch to his rapidly maturing policy of intervention; let it be remembered that he was Foreign Minister from 1822 onwards, that he could have made a stronger stand on behalf of Greece at an earlier date, or at least have resigned if Liverpool had made this a test question; yet it remains that he seized the opportunity now when he had full power, and when the conscience of Great Britain, however late, was at last fully aroused. It was too late to save thousands of Greek lives and infinite misery and desolation, yet not too late to prevent worse things. The conscience of France was also aroused, and Charles X, though an absolute sovereign, was a good Christian and ready to take up the rôle of the ancient crusading kings of France. A formal treaty was made at London between Great Britain, France, and Russia, July 1827, on the basis of the Petrograd agreement. Canning died in August, but orders had already been given to the fleets.

The aim of the Allies was to stop the war, not to make Greece independent. The Turks refused to submit. Ibrahim continued to ravage and destroy in the Morea. The three united fleets, under the command of our admiral, Codrington, as senior officer, entered Navarino bay, where lay the Turkish and Egyptian fleet. Ibrahim was absent on his fiendish task, and the wanton fire of Turks on a boat, followed by fire on even Codrington's flag-ship when he tried to stop a general engagement, forced the sailors' hands. The Egyptians were destroyed, October 20.

The Sultan was still defiant. But the stop-gap ministry of Lord Goderich withdrew from further action; it is notorious that, Canning's influence removed, our statesmen regarded Navarino as "an untoward event." Their purpose is somewhat difficult to understand. The one great argument for our share in the Treaty of London was the need to prevent the Russians from taking the Eastern Question into their own hands; therefore absolute inaction for fear of Russia obtaining too much power over the Balkans was illogical. Yet this was done. The French landed an army to clear the Morea. The Russians declared formal war on the Turks in 1828, while we took no further part.

The military power of the Turks had sunk very low, and the Russians enjoyed a tremendous reputation as fighters since 1812. But the campaign of 1828 was not decisive. Certain features appeared which were to be seen again in 1853–55 and 1877–78. It was no easy matter to bring an overpowering Russian army, or sufficient supplies for it, from a great distance; and there seems to have been bad administration in high places, even corruption. The Turks fought stubbornly from their bases in Bulgaria, the fortresses of Silistria, Shumla, and Varna. Then the unexpected happened, as often has happened when the Turks seem to have the upper hand. In 1829 they accepted battle, were defeated, and collapsed. The Russians advanced on Adrianople, their wings spread out from the Black Sea to the Aegean, but they were not in very large numbers, and their position was anything but secure. The Turks, however, were as much demoralised as in 1878. Kars and Erzerum had fallen in the further east. So the Sultan came to terms, and accepted the Treaty of Adrianople by which the independence of Rumania was practically acknowledged under Russian protection, and the Bosphorus and Dardanelles were opened to the commerce of all nations. In fact, after all, the Tsar gained very little for himself.

The Independence of Greece was settled in London earlier in 1829. Her northern boundary was drawn when the Turkish resistance to the Russians collapsed. Under cover of the Russian invasion of Bulgaria, the Greeks regained Missolonghi and saw the departure of Ibrahim. But it must have been a sore disappointment to the Greeks that neither Thessaly nor Epirus was included, nor any of the further islands, Crete or Samos or Chios, and that their co-religionists of Salonica and so many other towns of the Turkish Empire were still unfree. At first a republican form of government was set up with Capodistrias as President. But he was accustomed to the ways of the Russian court, when he had been minister under Alexander I, and believed in a centralised administration or bureaucracy, wisely, it may be, because the Greeks had proved to be unable to live in harmony among themselves and were hardly fit for a democracy; moreover in Europe in general, even in Great Britain before 1832, there was no real democracy. An aristocracy of "primates" or of Hydriot ship-owners might have caused civil war at any moment, and would have been unacceptable to the peasants. The crown of Greece was offered by the Powers to Leopold of Saxe Coburg, who first accepted and then refused it; then to Prince Otto of Bavaria, who entered into possession in 1833 with a staff of German officials. Meanwhile Capodistrias, trying to rule by Russian police methods, had to suppress a Hydriot revolt, and was assassinated. Thus modern Greece did not begin well. Government on Russian lines by a spy-supported autocrat was the only alternative to lawless freedom, until German methods were introduced. The 20th century had yet to reveal fully what a German king can do in a country of non-Germans; but in the 19th century it was clear enough already that he would crush individuality.

Two facts stand out when we study Balkan problems.

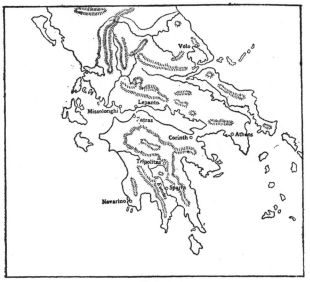

Greece.

Firstly, as with the Jews so with the Greeks, there are those of the home-land and those of the dispersion, and always were during the twenty centuries before the Turks arrived. Secondly, settlements of Turks everywhere from Crete to Bosnia complicated the question of national rights. If the inhabitants of a country have the right to say how they should be governed, who are the inhabitants who count?

# CHAPTER III

## FRANCE UNDER LOUIS PHILIPPE

Louis Philippe, chosen by the July Revolution, was a bourgeois King of the French. Being son of Egalité and owing his throne to a revolution, he tried in vain to be legitimist. The French nobles of the *ancien régime* never acknowledged him as a body, though some few pretended to "rally" to his cause. There were but few conspiracies against him; even two efforts made by Louis Napoleon had no chance of success. Legitimacy being dead and Bonapartism not yet having raised its head again, it remained that he had to be a constitutional sovereign. He was amiable and modest; Frenchmen had no fault to find with him except that he had no commanding presence, and was nicknamed King Pear; but he was under the taint which his father's action had attached to the name of Orleans, the taint of dallying with revolutionism in order to obtain the crown from the legitimate Louis XVI. He had had a life of poverty; but during his reign of eighteen years he amassed a considerable fortune which was invested in foreign countries, so that, when he in his turn was expelled, his family as well as himself, and it was a very large family, were well off.

M. Adolphe Thiers was minister, and for a short time Prime Minister, in this reign; he was also one of the ablest

French historians and wrote the history of the Republic, Consulate, and Empire. The thoughts of Frenchmen under the Orleanist régime can be understood from his work. The bourgeois government meant that policy could be neither revolutionary nor truly royal. There was a feeling of satisfaction that "we were governed by our middle-class equals," but this was not enough for the French *idée* of honour and glory; "it is necessary, according to an old writer, that the Fatherland should be not only prosperous but also sufficiently glorious." Hence came the yearning after distinction. Thiers thought that the most glorious period in French history was that of the Directory 1796–97, when "France at the height of her power was mistress of all the soil which extends from the Rhine to the Pyrenees, from the sea to the Alps...when no eye, however piercing, could see in that generation of heroes any who would commit crime or stifle liberty." Therefore, when he was Prime Minister himself, he had his programme of glory. He longed to see the Orleanist dynasty as glorious as the best of the Bourbons or Napoleon himself, or, better still, as glorious as was the Directory before Bonaparte stifled liberty. Of course such an ideal was impossible. The bourgeois king at a critical moment failed to respond, and this yearning after military honour, which the writings of Thiers did so much to encourage, only gathered strength later under Napoleon III. In fact the historian-premier created the Napoleonic legend, that is to say encouraged Frenchmen to believe that the glories of Napoleon were far greater than his crimes, but was unable to create an Orleanist glory.

In domestic affairs it is but natural to find that constitutionalism was established in a thoroughly middle-class manner. Membership of the Assembly was, by the electoral

law, open to those who paid 500 francs in direct taxes;
qualification as an elector was fixed at 200 francs, or at
100 francs for officials and professional men, which gave
a voting strength in all France of about 200,000 citizens.
Therefore respectability and consequent capacity to vote
was a matter of money or profession; and we are irre-
sistibly reminded of Disraeli's policy of what John Bright
styled "fancy franchises." Similarly, by the municipal
law, the same type of men elected town councillors, from
whom mayors were chosen by the government. The same
men again composed the National Guard, providing arms
and uniform at their own expense.

Foreign policy, of course, had to proceed on middle
lines. Louis Philippe could not possibly support Metternich
and the autocrats of Russia and Prussia. If Thiers, like
the older Whigs of William III and Anne, stood for a bold
foreign policy, he also resembled them as advocate of
parliamentary government; his was the party of the
left centre. Guizot, another historian-minister, who had
already held office under Charles X, was rather of the
type of the constitutional Tories of the same period; he
was a parliamentarian, yet preferred to see a pronounced
influence exercised by the king himself; and thus he
belonged to the right centre. Extremists were the right
and left wings of the Chamber, Legitimist Royalists and
avowed Radicals respectively.

Events in several foreign countries immediately tested
the capacity of the new government. It was impossible
for Paris to have its July Revolution without the governments of neighbouring countries being also shaken.
Naturally enough Belgium followed suit in the autumn of
the same year 1830. The Belgians declared in their
"Proclamation of Independence" that though they were

in a majority over the Dutch by about five to two millions, they were outvoted in the States General; that the National Debt of Holland was much greater than theirs before 1814, yet they paid taxes higher out of all proportion; that almost all officials were Dutch, and the official language was Dutch; and that mercantile policy favoured the Dutch, for with their possibilities as a manufacturing nation they wanted some form of protection, whilst the shipowning Dutch were in favour of free trade. Beyond all this Belgium was largely Roman Catholic, though with a free-thinking element, and a sense of unity between Flemings and Brabanters and Walloons had been growing up during French rule; the Calvinistic Dutch had in other periods been bitterly opposed to France, and their sense of nation-ality did not go so far as to acknowledge the Belgians as their equals. The outbreak took place at Brussels suddenly on August 25. A small Dutch army, advancing to the suburbs of the capital, was driven back on September 21–27. A National Congress met on November 16 to proclaim independence. In February 1831 the second son of Louis Philippe was chosen to be king, for the middle-class Belgians had no liking for a republic. But then Britain intervened, for on no account might a cadet of any Great Power hold the country which lies nearest to the mouth of the Thames. In June the choice fell upon Leopold of Saxe Coburg, late king-elect of Greece; he accepted the crown, and was recognised by the British government. He was a straightforward and honourable king, and we know that his grandson has preferred to pursue the path of honour, though another Coburger and other Germans called to govern non-German countries and their German relations have subordinated national needs to the interests of Germanism. The French, not

taking it amiss that their candidate was rejected, supported
the new government. When King William of Holland
refused to surrender Antwerp, a French army under
Marshal Gérard—he had commanded an army corps at
the battle of Ligny, and had tried to persuade Grouchy to
march to the sound of the guns at Waterloo—came to
besiege Antwerp and marched across the field of Waterloo
on the way; an English squadron blockaded the mouth
of the Scheldt, and Antwerp was surrendered December

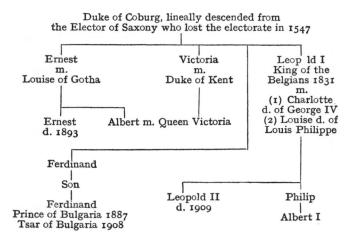

1832. The Dutch finally retained most of Luxemburg and
the fortress of Maestricht. Yet King William did not
give way to a final settlement till 1838, and the Treaty of
London guaranteeing Belgian Neutrality was not signed
till April 1839; the guarantors of this scrap of paper
were Austria, France, Great Britain, Prussia, and Russia.

In one particular the Belgians lost considerably by
cutting their connection with Holland. The Dutch, holding

both banks of the mouth of the Scheldt, could prevent ships from passing to and from Antwerp. Therefore the great port was useless to free Belgium. It was not till 1863 that free navigation was bought from the Dutch, and the Antwerp that we knew in 1914 is the creation of quite modern days.

Poland also had her insurrection. Tsar Alexander I had in 1815 intended to govern constitutionally with a Chamber as King of Poland. He put in as Viceroy his brother Constantine, who married a Polish princess. When he became a reactionary, Poland of course suffered; freedom of speech and freedom of the press disappeared, and military colonies of Russians were introduced. Consequently secret societies were formed, for if any country aspired to freedom, especially after enjoying a period of enthusiasm for Napoleon, that country was Poland. The insurrection burst out at Warsaw November 1830. Probably the Poles took off the attention of Nicholas from Belgium and attracted it to themselves, thereby helping a distant country to their own loss. Both French and British sympathised, and Palmerston and Grey gave offence to the Russians by what they said, but they were too far away to send any help ; thus, while they held out for Belgian independence, no autocratic power interfered to help Holland, but, while they only talked, the Russian autocrat crushed Poland.

In Italy the Carbonari were still active. Since their failure ten years back their head-quarters were at Paris, from which some attempt was made to knit together the threads of revolutionary feeling. Yet when they tried to raise the standard of revolt, profiting by the impetus given by the July Revolution, the risings in 1831 were but feeble and isolated. The kings and dukes of Bourbon and Hapsburg blood in Italy were not at all attached to Austria, nor even was the Pope, which fact explains why

Italian conspirators constantly looked to some monarch in their own midst to be their ultimate saviour. However when there was a rising at Modena in February 1831, the Duke had no place to which to flee but Austrian soil. At once there was a similar movement in Parma whence Marie Louise fled, in Bologna, in Ravenna and the other cities of the Papal Legations, in Ancona and all the Marches up to the Apennines. A National Assembly was summoned to Bologna. The collapse was as rapid as the outbreak. As soon as ever it was seen that Louis Philippe's ministry would not interfere, the Austrian troops overran Parma and Modena without any trouble, and proceeded, in spite of a check before Ancona, to reduce the papal provinces as well. Ministers of the Great Powers then met at Rome, where the British and French at least pressed upon the Pope the need of a generous measure of reform; some vague promises were given, but probably no one was surprised that nothing was ever done. Again there was a rising at Bologna. This time papal troops crushed the revolt, and plundered some of the towns with ruthless severity, so that Bologna itself preferred to admit the Austrians rather than submit to papal atrocities. Now Louis Philippe sent a French contingent to occupy Ancona. The Austrians garrisoned Bologna and the French Ancona for half a dozen years, and then were withdrawn by mutual consent. The episode marks a re-entry of France into Italian politics, and was a presage of what might happen later when France and Austria would be rivals in defence of the temporal power of the Papacy.

In Germany there were insurrections in Brunswick and Cassel. A measure of liberty of the press was granted in Hanover and Saxony. There was a rising in 1833 at Frankfort, which was immediately suppressed by Prussians.

Metternich, as before, made use of the Federal Diet to
pronounce against Liberalism in Germany, entrusting to
the individual sovereigns of the Federal States the task
of suppressing liberty. There was the same outcry as
before against the licence of the press and the university
professors. Yet even before 1830 a new policy was being
carefully nursed and developed by Prussia; this was the
policy of commercial union, from which grew imperceptibly
the idea of political union under the lead of Prussia. The
Zollverein or Customs Union, by which the states one by
one were united to admit goods duty-free across their
common frontiers, was founded by Prussia, and from the
very first Austria was left outside.

In England we had the question of the great Reform
Bill. The influence of France was seen over here in the
reluctance of our new King William IV to take a strong
attitude on the side of reformers, for he inherited the idea
that was so rife in his father's reign, namely that, when
Revolution appeared in France, Reform ought to be checked
in England for fear of similar consequences. But when it
was clear that the excitements attending the rejection of
the Reform Bill by the Lords were not merely the revolutionary outbursts of rioters, but that a general popular
wish for a bill could be no longer resisted, and when
Wellington failed to create an anti-reform Tory ministry,
William consented to swamp the House of Lords by the
creation of new peers. The Reform Bill was passed, and
was at once seen to be anything but revolutionary; in
fact to the Radicals it was but a step towards a wider
measure. In the Whig ministries 1830 to 1834, and then
again in 1835, the Foreign Secretary was Lord Palmerston.
He it was who made so decided a stand on the question
of Belgium, acknowledging the new kingdom as fully

independent and guaranteeing its neutrality, whilst at the
same time opposing the candidature of Louis Philippe's
son.    The new King Leopold of Coburg was uncle to both
Victoria and Albert; it is impossible to read our late
Queen's letters without seeing the strength of her affection
for him, and his election was obviously considered to be
a happy solution of the difficulties in the Netherlands.
In Portugal British and French influence got rid of Dom
Miguel.    But further afield Palmerston's influence on the
Polish question had no weight, and his attempt to press a
scheme of reform upon the Pope came to nothing.    He was
beginning to lay a foundation of the reputation which he
afterwards enjoyed of being a sympathiser with revolution.

The chief work of Louis Philippe, which had the most
lasting results for France and for which he is best known,
was the conquest of Algeria; yet it had first been taken
in hand by Charles X.    We have to go a long way back
in history to understand Mediterranean politics.    When
Venice and Genoa began to decline, when the Turks
extended their control along the coast of North Africa in
a thoroughly Turkish manner, that is to say sometimes
regarding the chieftains as the Sultan's vassals, and sometimes as independent corsairs whom the Sultan could not
or would not control, there was no one naval power strong
enough to cope with the Mohammedan peril by sea.    In
the 16th century the Emperor Charles V sent unsuccessful
expeditions to the African coast more than once, and held
Tunis for a comparatively short time.    But Spain never
properly took up the task of saving Christians from the
horrors of slavery.    Christian merchants had either to sail
armed in company or to make terms with the Mohammedans.
Here we see the justification of certain spasmodic efforts
of our Stuart kings to protect our trade, including the

dispatch of our "Ship Money" fleet, the temporary occupation by Charles II of Tangier, also of Cromwell's policy when Blake bombarded Tunis. The new navy which Colbert gave to Louis XIV and our own occupation of Gibraltar did much to help Christian trade. As late as 1816, Great Britain being then in a position to enforce the wishes of the Congress of Vienna with respect to slavery as she was now protectress of the Ionian Islands, Lord Exmouth was sent with a fleet to demand the release of Greek slaves; further than that he demanded the freedom of all slaves. Tunis and Tripoli submitted, Algiers gave up Greek slaves and sold for ransom Italians. Opinion in England was not satisfied, and, when some Algerians again attacked Christian ships, Exmouth was ordered to take strong measures. A thorough bombardment of Algiers destroyed the harbour and batteries and ships. On another occasion United States ships had to interfere.

It is clear then that there was no need to argue in defence of French interference. The question first came up in 1827, when a French consul was struck by a dey of Algiers, and a French ship entering the harbour to demand satisfaction was fired upon. In July 1830, the very month when he was dethroned, Charles X sent an expedition under General Bourmont—he is otherwise known in history as the French general who deserted Napoleon just before the battle of Quatre Bras—which besieged and captured Algiers. The work was carried on for Louis Philippe by Marshal Clausel, who as general had won a considerable reputation in fighting against Wellington in the later years of the Peninsular War. Several places were captured on the coast east and west of Algiers. The ministry probably meant at first to occupy only the coast. But the excited Arabs of the interior, especially the Kabyles under the

command of Abd-el-Kader, resented so strongly the French
attack that, just as has been the case of our government in
India, it was absolutely necessary to conquer the hinterland.
In 1836 Clausel advanced on Constantine, 50 miles from
the coast at a point half-way between Algiers and Tunis.
He reached the place, found that he was unable to batter
it, as it stood on an inaccessible rock, without heavy guns,
and had to retreat with heavy losses amidst a swarm of
Arab horsemen. Next year another expedition with abun-
dant heavy artillery was more successful. Constantine
was breached and stormed, and a fearful number of Arabs
were hurled to death over the precipices of the southern
face. The resistance of Abd-el-Kader was gradually worn
down. Natives were enrolled in the French service,
Turcos on foot, Spahis mounted ; and a corps of French
dressed in native style in baggy knickerbockers and short
jackets, with shaven heads and wearing the fez, took the
name of Zouaves from one of the local tribes. The Arab
hero continued a desultory warfare of raids and did not
finally surrender till 1847. The permanent occupation of
Algeria was therefore not complete till the end of the reign,
and spasmodic fighting went on much later. The army of
occupation was at least 100,000 strong, and after Clausel's
failure was commanded by Bugeaud. Here Cavaignac,
Canrobert, Pélissier, and MacMahon learnt the art of war.
Turcos and Spahis were brought over to fight for France
in 1870 and again in 1914.

The success of the French in Algeria has been pronounced. French engineers have found there a country
where they could display their genius. Artesian wells have
brought fertility to barren places, and grapes and grasses
have been grown. Thus although there was at one time
a considerable outcry against the French occupation, and

it was more than insinuated that the methods of conquest
were brutal and that Abd-el-Kader and his Arabs were
national heroes, there is little doubt that it has tended
towards civilisation, not only suppressing piracy, but also
opening up the country, which in the days of the Romans
had been highly fertile, and which the Turks had blighted.
After 1871 many Alsatians who wished to remain French
were settled by the government on the more healthy
uplands of south Algeria.   In 1881 Tunis and its hinterland were added to the French Empire, and later the
hinterland of Senegal and the central region of Timbuctoo,
so that French ambition towards expansion has been
chiefly connected with Africa.

At the other end of the Mediterranean the affairs of
Egypt and Syria attracted the attention of Louis Philippe,
but he did not experience the same success.   The traditions
of France, dating from the Crusades, revived by Louis XIV,
and strengthened by Napoleon's efforts in spite of his
failure to hold Egypt or to conquer Acre, could not but
have a strong influence in attracting French thoughts to
the East.   It was in connection with Egypt and Acre
that Louis Philippe seemed likely to force France to the
front to obtain her "sufficiency of glory," and to show that
the Orleanist could defy Europe as well as Bonaparte.
Mohammed Ali, an Albanian by birth and an official of the
Sultan, had been made Pasha of Egypt in 1805.   He had
governed that country tyrannically but effectually; he
destroyed the Mamelukes, the hereditary caste of soldiers,
who were the counterpart of the Janissaries at Constantinople, and his action must have suggested to Mahmud
the idea of destroying the Janissaries; he conquered the
fanatical Arabs, the Wahabees, whose idea was to revive the
original Mohammedan programme of slaughtering infidels

if they refused to accept the Koran; he conquered up the
Nile and founded Khartum; he introduced cotton and
sugar-cane and extended the canal system of Egypt. All
this was connected with an oppressive method of government. The army and fleet which he sent under his son
to crush the Greeks in 1825–27 were composed of the
hardy Arabs and Sudanese of the interior rather than of
the peasant fellaheen, who, after centuries of oppression,
have little fighting force in them even to-day. Even after
the destruction of his hopes at Navarino, his ambition was
still high, his aim was to annex Syria of which he demanded
the governorship from Mahmud, and next he demanded
that his own position in Egypt should be that of hereditary
viceroy.

In 1831, at the time when the Sultan seemed to be in
the greatest difficulties owing to the Treaty of Adrianople,
Mohammed Ali sent Ibrahim to invade Palestine and lay
siege to Acre. Next year a Turkish army made an effort
to come to its relief, but was too late. Ibrahim, after the
fall of Acre, pushed northwards on Aleppo, routed the
Turks, and pursued them over the Taurus, followed after
a short pause and routed a second Turkish army at Konieh
(Iconium). The Turkish military power was so completely
broken down that Mahmud actually listened to offers of
help from Russia; but this alarmed the French, and under
French influence an armistice was arranged, by which the
Sultan granted to Mohammed the whole of Syria and
Cilicia south of Mount Taurus.

At this moment the strange friendship between Russia
and Turkey, unnatural and temporary, seemed however
likely to bear fruit. The Treaty of Unkiar Skelessi, July
1833, created a defensive alliance entirely in Russia's favour,
with a secret article that in case of war the Dardanelles

should be open to her but closed against other nations.
The chief result was that Louis Philippe made overtures
to Mohammed. A new complication soon gave the
opportunity that French statesmen required. There were
risings against Mohammed's heavy rule on the outskirts of
his newly annexed provinces. War broke out in 1839,
the Turkish army was once more routed at Nissib, and
Mahmud died suddenly before he had even received the
news of the defeat. Now was the time for Russian aid to
be given to the Turks, and in that case, with Thiers
resolutely supporting Mohammed with a view to making
France the paramount power in the Eastern Mediterranean,
an explosion would have been inevitable and the Crimean
War would have been anticipated. But Palmerston was
by no means ready then to allow Great Britain to enter
into the Eastern Question in the wake of either Russia or
France. He took his stand on the necessity of maintaining
the integrity of the Turkish Empire, and that could only
be maintained by the evacuation of Syria by Mohammed.
Russia and Great Britain were therefore ranged together
on the side of the Turks, and this thwarted Russia's policy,
because, if the Tsar were left alone as Turkey's friend,
whatever advantage might come from the humbling of
Mohammed would have been for Russia alone. Palmerston
went further and drew Austria and Prussia into his scheme.
The Quadruple Alliance was formed July 1840 to enforce
Egyptian surrender to the terms of Turkey; Mohammed
might hold Egypt by hereditary right, the four Powers
declared, but southern Syria only as an ordinary governor
under the Sultan.

Mohammed's defiance was a trifle. The crux of the
question was the exclusion of France from the Concert of
Europe. Was France then to be considered no longer as

a Great Power, but as the humbled and exhausted kingdom
of 1814–15 that had to look on whilst others arranged the
map of Europe to suit themselves? Had she not recovered
her position and right to have a voice in the Concert?
Twenty-five years had elapsed since Waterloo, and the new
generation was profoundly excited. Thiers had his chance
to show that a bourgeois Government could make France
sufficiently glorious and rival the deeds of Louis XIV or
Napoleon. A similar spirit was roused in Germany and
showed that there was a deep consciousness of the unity
of Germany, however diverse the individual governments
might be, whenever a threat of a French war should arise.
Now were written new patriotic war songs, Becker's "Sie
sollen ihn nicht haben den freien Deutschen Rhein," and
Alfred de Musset's answer "Nous avons eu votre Rhin
Allemand." The suddenness of the storm was remarkable;
Egypt and Syria were forgotten, France and Germany were
face to face. But whatever might be the ardour of the
historian of the wars of the old French Republic, and
however much he might yearn to see the French frontier
extended as in 1794 to the Rhine, or French arms victorious
as in 1796–97 down the valley of the Po, Louis Philippe was
forced to be cautious. A great European War might unlock
the floodgates of Revolution; therefore, when Thiers drew
up an uncompromising speech for the King to deliver to
the Chamber in the autumn of 1840, he refused to read it.
Thiers resigned. Guizot was called to form a new ministry
and submit to the will of Europe.

The artificiality of Mohammed's power was quickly
seen. A British fleet under Sir Charles Napier with an
Austrian contingent reduced Acre and appeared off
Alexandria. In the East the collapse of an apparently
powerful absolute monarch is a common enough feature.

Faced by the might of Europe, and deserted by the Syrians and Arabs, to whom he had been more strict than the old Turkish government[1], Mohammed had no choice but to accept the terms offered by Napier and sanctioned by Palmerston; he was to be content with the possession of Egypt to be held henceforth by heredity, and therefore he became the first Khedive. On the side of Turkey it was arranged that the Dardanelles should be closed to all ships of war, and therefore the Treaty of Unkiar Skelessi became null and void by implication. Palmerston's policy was from his point of view wonderfully successful; he had used Russia to bolster up the Turkish government, and now Russia had no special advantage.

Certainly the new Sultan had his chance to show that his country was not moribund. Palmerston's policy, which was a continuation of Wellington's, namely that by no means should the Russians be allowed to reach the Mediterranean, had as its corner-stone the idea that the Turkish Empire was not "a dead body or a sapless trunk." There were no troubles then in the Balkans; Greece was free, though hardly yet prosperous in her freedom; Serbia and Rumania were practically free; the Janissaries had been destroyed, and the Turkish army was being remodelled on modern lines, being now recruited from the sturdy Mohammedans of Anatolia and those of the southern parts of the Balkans who had no traditions of insubordination towards their Sultan. No outburst of fury occurred within the next several years to prove to Europe that the Turk was beyond reform.

[1] Kinglake tells in *Eothen* how, at the time of his visit to Palestine, the mere name of Ibrahim was enough to terrify the people. The Holy Places at Jerusalem were then, under the Egyptian government, controlled by Greek Orthodox clergy.

We return to France and the Guizot ministry. The new historian-premier during the next seven years pursued a dull and not very glorious policy. He declared openly that he had no wish for glory, only for the prosperity of France. For seven years he had an obedient majority in the Chamber, and governed it by methods which French writers compared to those of Sir Robert Walpole. He got into the Chamber officials and civil servants who were in the pay of the government; outside the government, posts and pensions and a share in government monopolies were granted to those who faithfully voted for his nominees. Meanwhile it was a period of prosperity, railways were being laid down, the colonisation of Algeria was going on well, the trouble with regard to England was removed for the time being, as the Whigs went out of power in England and Palmerston with them. He wished even to promote an *entente* with our government, and Louis Philippe and Victoria paid each other visits of state; but this was not popular in France. When Palmerston returned to the Foreign Office, he and Guizot fenced with each other on the question of the Spanish marriages. The marriage of Queen Isabella was considered a matter of high importance, and it was understood that a projected marriage between Isabella's younger sister Louisa and Louis Philippe's son, the Duc de Montpensier, should not take place until the young Queen herself was married and had children. The French King and Guizot hurried on the marriage of the Queen to her cousin Francisco, and the marriage of the sister to the French Prince at the same time. The good feeling with England therefore passed away, but what might have happened as the result of the Bourbon marriage it would be useless to argue, for the year of Revolution was approaching. Palmerston being a strong Liberal, Guizot in opposition swung more to the side of autocracy, and in 1847 troubles in Paris showed that he was so unpopular that he resigned.

The Revolution of 1848 had both immediate and underlying causes, as had that in 1789. There were no striking grievances, uneven taxes, grinding poverty of peasants, or restlessness of a people irritated by the haughtiness and contemptuousness of a privileged nobility. The utmost that could be complained of was that only the rich and bourgeois had votes, which were used in an unworthy manner by systematic corruption, and the reformers were simply demanding electoral reform. They organised in 1847 a series of political banquets, at which speeches were made in favour of reform. A certain banquet advertised for February 22, 1848 was forbidden by the government for fear of fierce oratory ; the result was rioting, and on the 23rd barricades appeared, though Guizot had already resigned ; some shots were fired by the soldiers, and a few civilians were killed. Louis Philippe apparently feared to trust the soldiers, and even the bourgeois National Guard was against him. Probably he had foreseen that, when a Revolution did occur, it would be safest for him to disappear at once rather than fight it out. On the 24th he abdicated in favour of his grandson, and left Paris. But the excited Parisians were not to be put off, and proclaimed a Republic at the Hôtel de Ville.

But an outburst of excitement cannot adequately explain the rapid downfall of the dynasty. The seeds of this Revolution were really sown by the writers and thinkers and even the amateur experiment-makers of the last twenty years. It was the result of modern conditions of life, of the new manufactures and railways, and the consequent emergence into political life of that very modern person the thoughtful working man, who was a townsman and not a peasant. In our own country, after the Manchester Massacre and the Six Acts, the Reform Bill of 1832 had been an answer to the demands of those who wished to have their voice felt in Parliament; and disappointed by it the same class had put forward the People's Charter. But in England there were many rival interests, middle-class and manufacturing as well as landowning interests, which opposed a barrier against extreme democracy. In the France of 1848 the bourgeois dynasty had been found wanting, and the extremists, and those who had been reading and thinking about political theories, rushed to the front.

Therefore, just as the great Revolution was caused, not so much by grievances and protests against noble privileges, as by talk and brooding over grievances; so the Second Revolution sprang, not so much from Guizot's corruption and a high electoral franchise, as from the brooding of working men over their wrongs and their poverty, their low wages and the new conditions of manufacturing life, and their impotence against the capitalists. As in 1789 the nobles, in 1848 the bourgeois were the enemy. As Rousseau had preached and prepared the way for 1789, so Louis Blanc and other socialists created the feeling which exploded in 1848. As in the one case inexperienced men who had never had any training in self-government rushed in to make amateur experiments in the art of parliament-making,—it is Burke's chief criticism of the National Assembly (1789–91) that the members were ignorant, therefore could only destroy and bring on bankruptcy, so that ultimately the greatest soldier would become master of France,—so in the present case the discontented workmen demanded universal suffrage and "the right to work,"

knowing their wrongs and ready to destroy capital, but
utterly inexperienced, as they could not but be, as this
problem of labour and capital was so new. They too, like
the men of 1792–94, were destined after a period of confusion
and bankruptcy to be overcome by military force. Therefore
we need not be surprised that the Revolution was against
the government of a mild bourgeois King, who had no
Bastille as the symbol of his despotism, whose nobles were
not privileged, and indeed whose new nobility was of an
upstart type not recognised by the old Legitimist aristocrats. The movement did not originate with the peasants,
nor was it popular with the peasants, who had gained by
the first Revolution all that they wanted and were now
distinctly conservative.

As far back as 1831 at the very beginning of his reign
there had been a rising at Lyons among the silk-workers,
who received miserably low pay and were liable to be
thrown out of work whenever the master spinners had
too much unsold stuff on hand. They had overpowered
the police, and had forced a minimum wage, but they had
been promptly overpowered by the soldiers. However, the
rights of working men were being preached. The pioneer
of the movement was Saint Simon, who died in 1825, and
his work was carried on by many enthusiastic men, even
bankers and professors and men of letters. Enfantin was
prosecuted and condemned to prison in 1832, but he lived
on to 1864, studying social questions in Algeria and in
Egypt, and dreaming of a great system of railways and
steam-boats and even of the Suez Canal, a world of useful
workers in which there would be no room for the lazy
capitalist who lived only on what had been left him by
industrious ancestors, of popular education also—which
indeed made great progress under Louis Philippe—and

liberty of thought. There were other schools of thought
after Saint Simon had provided the impulse. Fourier
preached Communism, and others a system of entire
freedom and anarchy. But Fourier was likewise dead, and
the chief living exponent of Socialism in the middle of the
century was Louis Blanc, whose main idea was to make
the State the one capitalist of the nation, and put the
means of production into the hands of everyone. "The
workers have been slaves; they have been serfs; they are
to-day wage-earners; we must make them partners—the
State owes to the citizen work." Therefore although the
organisers of the banquets made speeches against Guizot
and political corruption, demanding that public officials
should have no seat in the Chamber, and that the franchise
should be lowered, though the poet Lamartine made his
oration about traffickers and the vices of officials, Louis
Blanc appealed to a wider audience. Now nothing can be
easier than to sneer at the vagueness or the impossibility of
*le droit au travail*. But every one must acknowledge the
need of enthusiasm for some system in modern life which
is not based upon sheer selfish individualism. In England,
in spite of much suffering caused by machinery and life
in insanitary slums, there were yet alleviations, and about
this same time the conditions of the working men were
becoming better, as some of the worst evils were being
removed by the Factory Acts and Free Trade was being
established. But France had entered later than England
into the struggle for existence in the world of manufacture
and competition, and was now suddenly demanding that
experiments should be made on the lines of socialism.
The past history of England showed that rights could be
gradually extended, for our Constitution has been the work
of many centuries of slow development; our most socialistic

institution, the Post Office, was created a long way back, and has gradually taken to itself the Savings Bank, the telegraph and the telephone, and recently the payment of old age pensions. But France was not prepared by long experience and wanted in 1848 to set up Socialism at once.

# CHAPTER IV

## THE YEAR OF REVOLUTIONS

The Provisional Government was constituted on February 24, 1848 by the public voice of the Parisians. It included Lamartine and Louis Blanc. It decreed a general election by universal suffrage, together with absolute freedom of the press, and of public meetings. Of course there was no question of any alternative to a Republic, for there was no possible king of a more democratic type than Louis Philippe. The only question was whether it should be under the "red" flag or the tricolour, and Lamartine used all his powers of oratory against the "red" flag. At once the "Right to Work" was put into practice under a commission. *Les Ateliers Nationaux* were organised. Men were not put to work according to their capacity or training; they were organised on a military basis and then put to work, first to clear a space of ground for a new railway station, the Saint Lazare terminus, and then to dig up earth on a great open space and put it back again. In fact the Minister of Commerce deliberately meant to destroy the movement at once by ridicule. The pay was two francs a day. In the month of May 120,000 workmen were employed. The most unfortunate thing however was that these same men and others like them were admitted into the National Guard, which was thus no longer an armed force of the bourgeoisie, but of the most dangerous men, who of course were either being turned into loafers ready for riot, or into revolutionaries angry past endurance at the ridicule which was attached to a movement in which they had profoundly believed. In fact the National Workshops were deliberately created to caricature the ideas of Louis Blanc, and violence was the result.

When danger threatens France from the unbridled passions of the mob of Paris, it is usually found that the peasants, and especially since the first Revolution the small landed proprietors, are the counterweight. The feeling of provincial France in 1848 was strongly against so many Parisians being paid to do practically nothing. The new Assembly met on May 4; it was entirely in favour of a Republic, but was against Socialism. It created an executive of five, one of whom was Marie the organiser of the sham workshops. A mob rose to overpower the Assembly and create a new provisional government under Louis Blanc; it was dispersed at last and Louis fled. In the middle of June the workshops were declared closed, and as a natural result the majority of the disappointed workmen rushed to arms. June 23–26 were the days of the barricades. It must be remembered that Paris was still mostly the old city of narrow streets, and when we shall come to the story of barricades in Milan this same year we must think of an old city of streets narrower even than those of Paris, and therefore favourable to an armed mob. The Minister of War was General Cavaignac, who had seen service in Algeria, and, having dictatorial powers from the Assembly, was ready to use his guns just as Bonaparte did in 1795. By massing his men on certain points he brought up overpowering forces and carried the barricades, until he forced the revolutionaries into their last stronghold in the district of Saint Antoine, near where once stood the Bastille. Between 3000 and 4000 of the leaders were transported to Algeria and elsewhere without trial on the mere decree of the Assembly.

A new Constitution was created and came into effect in the autumn. It was proclaimed that "Sovereignty resides in the people and all powers emanate from the people"; voting was to be by the universal suffrage of all Frenchmen over 21; the Assembly was to sit for three years, and could not be dissolved nor prorogued except by its own vote; the head of the Executive was to be a President, elected for four years by the direct votes of the people, responsible to the Assembly, and not re-eligible for a second period of four years. Jules Grévy proposed that the Assembly should elect the President with power to depose him at need; another suggestion was that no member of a family that had reigned in France should be eligible; each amendment was lost. The result was that the peasants of France, frightened by the spectre of a Red Republic, which they took to mean a confiscation of property in land, and the majority of Roman Catholics and lovers of law and order of all kinds, even Royalists who despaired of a Bourbon being elected, and all those who forgot the despotism and the fatal results of the exhausting wars of the great Napoleon, but who had been excited by the "Napoleonic Legend" as read in the historians such as Thiers and Mignet, who showed how glorious France had been once upon a time in war even if the result had been fatal, voted for Louis Napoleon. He received $5\frac{1}{2}$ millions of votes; Cavaignac $1\frac{1}{2}$ millions; Lamartine a few thousands. Louis Napoleon was the son of Napoleon I's brother Louis, once King of Holland; he had already made two theatrical attempts to capture the loyalty of the army,

once at Strasburg and once at Boulogne; he had been
imprisoned and had been allowed to escape to England,
and, as no one seemed to take him seriously, the Republic
let him come back to France in 1848.

The Revolution in Paris was the signal for a Revolution
in Italy.  This too had been gradually prepared by much
talk and reading and brooding over Italy's sense of wrong
since the failures of 1831 and 1832; it was just the spark
from Paris that was required to explode the train of gunpowder that had been laid.  The soul of the new movement
was Mazzini, a Genoese, who had been imprisoned for
conspiracy in 1831, and was allowed to depart into exile.
From France or from Switzerland he poured forth his
doctrine of "Young Italy."  The Carbonari had failed
because their efforts had been too purely local or provincial.
It was necessary to have a new faith, to trust the young
and rising generation, to implant in them the feeling of
brotherhood and nationality, of republicanism and of
unity; then there would be some chance to be successful
against the Austrian yoke, when the heart of the whole
country was roused.  Mazzini's ideal of a successful rebellion
was taken from Spain rising against Napoleon, and to his
eyes Italy seemed equally adapted for that guerilla warfare,
in which the Italians of the mountains could harass the
Austrians and be themselves out of reach, while the canals
and rivers of the plain and the narrow streets of the old
towns would also play their part.  He had no faith in
dynasties, even though aware of the value of a regular
army, however small, that such a Prince as Charles Albert
might be able to bring against the trained troops of Austria.
Moreover it was not only against Austria that he wanted to
fight, or against the crime of forcing Italians into the Austrian
ranks to be drilled in the hated white uniform; it was

against all tyranny and officialdom, privilege and wealth, that he wished to arouse a New Italy as a land which ought to follow in the lead of Ancient Rome and of Dante and the republics of the middle ages, when the Lombard League defied the Emperors of the Swabian House. Shelley, when he foresaw a New Greece, quoted Milan as the city of medieval liberty; "Her unwearied wings could fan the quenchless ashes of Milan." The historian Sismondi, a Swiss who wrote in French, yet an Italian by birth and sympathy after his family had been for generations in exile, brought out a work which contributed to spread Mazzini's ideas; this was the *History of the Italian Republics*, the tale of Italy's greatness in art and in literature as well as in war, but of final ruin because the jealousy between State and State, or between party and party in each State, left her a prey to the French and Spaniards, and ultimately to the Austrians. There were many Italian nationalist writers who helped both to light up and to fan the new spirit.

But there were other influences than Mazzini's. One hardly can quite understand how there should have been such a persistent belief that Charles Albert would prove to be the coming champion, unless indeed the wish was father to the thought. Yet, when we judge him, we are prejudiced by our knowledge of his failure and his lack of stamina when the crisis came. He had become King of Sardinia in 1831[1], was suspected by Metternich who, indeed, wished to exclude him in favour of the Austrian Duke of Modena, and had no declared friend in all Europe; his was not a strong character, and between his wishes and his

[1] We have to go back two centuries to find the common ancestor of Charles Albert and Charles Felix who was the last of the senior line of Savoy.

natural fears he passed his life in anxiety and asceticism, knowing well that, if he took a strong line without support, he would do it at his peril. But men in those days hoped much from the House of Savoy, the only line of rulers not of Hapsburg or Bourbon blood, and therefore not condemned by fate to be despots. Similarly those who looked to Rome for a leader are not to be ridiculed, though after events showed how deeply they were deceived. The "New Guelfs" had aspirations towards papal guidance and a new Rome taking the lead against the modern Ghibellines; it was a fantastic ideal, yet the medieval Papacy, as was told by Sismondi, had been the ally of the old Lombard League. This explains why Pio Nono, raised to the chair of Saint Peter in 1846, was so fervently greeted. He started by giving an amnesty to all political offenders, and granting to Rome a Civic Guard. Also he protested against the Austrian occupation of Ferrara. Moreover it was but natural for a high-minded Pontiff to wish to be free from Austrian leading-strings. "Little was done; not much was actually promised; everything was believed."

Meanwhile the practical side of the 19th century could be seen in the scientific congresses held in 1839 and each year onwards to 1847 at Pisa, Turin, Florence, Padua, Lucca, Milan, Naples, Genoa, and Venice in turn. Railways were being projected, and even short stretches of line were being laid down. The tunnelling of the Alps was talked about. Therefore modern ideas as well as the thoughts of Italy's past glory were preparing men's minds for a revolution, not only against Austria but against the disunion of Italy which it was Austria's policy to maintain. When Italians discussed science together, even in Naples and in Venice, where Bourbon and Hapsburg ruled, there was a consciousness of coming unity; much more therefore when

Italians pictured in the future railways connecting Piedmont with Venice or Brindisi.

When minds are full of excitement very little things contribute to cause the explosion. Very early in January 1848, whilst Parisians were excited about their political banquets, yet before the Republicans of Paris actually rose, occurred the "tobacco riots" in Milan. The Austrian government had a monopoly of tobacco, and good patriots suddenly agreed to abstain ostentatiously from smoking in the streets. Of course the Austrian officers and soldiers smoked with equal ostentation until the patriots resented it. There were riots, and Radetzky, the veteran general commanding in Italy, having created trouble so as to have the excuse for punishing it, let loose his soldiers in the streets. Yet a serious rising was delayed, for the Milanese required first to be assured that Charles Albert, the "Wobbling King," *Re Tentenna*, would come across the frontier with a trained army to their aid. They were waiting for his promise, while he was waiting for the city to rise in earnest. In February the French Republic was an actual fact. In March the people of Vienna rose in the streets, and Metternich fled to Saxony. Then Milan rose on March 18. Even 29,000 troops were unable to storm the multitude of barricades in the streets, and after five days Radetzky withdrew to the fortresses of the Quadrilateral, Peschiera and Mantua on the Mincio holding the narrow neck of plain between Lake Garda and the Po, and Verona and Legnago on the Adige in second line. Charles Albert's army crossed the Ticino on March 25, late but not too late; perhaps by a resolute movement he might have carried Mantua, whilst the capital of Austria was in the hands of the mob and therefore Radetzky could expect no reinforcements. Even as small an army as 23,000 men

could have done much as a nucleus to the numerous bodies
of armed volunteers now pouring in, many of them old
Italian soldiers who had been drilled in the Austrian
service; Wellington's experience is quite enough to show
how a small resolute force can prevail against numbers—
Radetzky had some 60,000 men in his four fortresses—
when guerilla bands distract attention.    But the king
seemed unable to strike hard and quickly.

Almost simultaneously Venice rose.    The mob released
from prison Daniel Manin, an arch-conspirator and a Jew
by birth, who took the lead relying on the number of
Italians in the Austrian garrison and in the fleet.    He
surprised the arsenal of Venice, and finally proclaimed the
Republic of Saint Mark.    City after city both in Lombardy
and in Venetia, and after them Parma, Modena, Bologna,
and other papal cities, followed suit; everywhere a proportion of the soldiers of Italian blood joined them, and
volunteers hurried towards the Mincio.    Even the Pope
and the King of Naples were forced by public opinion to
send contingents up north.    Garibaldi appeared with some
devoted friends from South America, where he had had
much experience in guerilla tactics in Brazil and Uruguay,
and these were ideal leaders of volunteers to worry and
threaten the Austrian lines of communication.    United Italy
certainly had numbers on her side.    But would she remain
united?    There was a fatal rift.    Charles Albert and the
Republicans were opposed to each other, and co-operation
was impossible as long as it remained uncertain what would
be the state of Italy after the defeat of the Austrians.
The Republicans accused the king of bad faith in admitting
the incorporation of Parma and Modena into his dominions;
Lombardy was already incorporated, but the king was
accused of slackness in arming the Lombards.    Neither

the Romans nor the Neapolitans were ready for union
with the distant north; Pius, much opposed to the
ascendancy of Savoy and Piedmont, ordered his general
not to fight; Ferdinand withdrew his contingent, and
in Naples overpowered by force and dissolved the Constitution which he had had to grant.

Thus it is probably beside the question to argue whether
Charles Albert was or was not incompetent as a general,

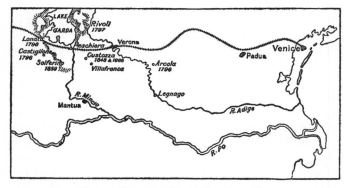

Map to show details of the Campaigns
of 1848 and 1859.

for the elements of weakness were fatally present. Though
the Austrian Court was in despair and even offered to
consent to the annexation of Lombardy to Piedmont, the
deciding voice was that of Radetzky, and he actually
received reinforcements and at last was in a position to
take the offensive. He reconquered Venetia up to the
lagoon which protected Venice herself; then he threw
himself upon Charles Albert's army which was divided by

the river Mincio, won a victory at Custozza on July 25, and threw him back on Milan. Charles Albert refused, amid the howls of the disappointed citizens, to defend Milan, and fled to Piedmont. Thus concentration and determination prevailed after divided counsels. There were yet thousands of volunteers in arms, but they had no rallying point, while Radetzky's army was in the flush of victory; he entered Milan, and only the consideration that after all he had barely enough men to hold the country that he had occupied, also knowledge that an advance on Turin would be resented by the new French government— the days of the barricades were now over and Cavaignac was the master of Paris, but Louis Napoleon was not yet President—prevented him from marching into Piedmont where demoralisation was complete.

Therefore we have now to turn to the other problems which faced the Austrian government. Hungary demands attention first. The Magyars of Hungary, headed by a proud aristocracy which ever opposed the political domination of the German Austrians of Vienna, had been alternately restive and loyal, according as each Emperor had tried to coerce or conciliate them: in the previous century they had been loyal to Maria Theresa and again to Francis II in his wars against Napoleon, but resentful towards Joseph II whose policy of unifying the whole Empire threatened their individual right. They acknowledged only the authority of their own Diet, for theirs was an independent monarchy, and Francis II and Metternich from 1825 were forced to acknowledge it too. But the privileged Hungarian nobles had all the power in the Diet, besides exemption from taxation. Transylvania, with a mixed and patchwork population of Hungarians and Germans and Rumans, had a historic right to have its own Diet, and here

noble Hungarian influence prevailed to the detriment of
the non-Hungarians. In the land of the Drave and Save
the Croatian Slavs, of the same race as the Serbs but Roman
Catholics, resented Magyar supremacy and the compulsory
use of the Magyar language as much as the Magyars
resented Austrian interference; they had their local Diet
at Agram, as well as representation in the Hungarian Diet;
and in their country there was opposition of native Slavs
against Hungarian immigrants and officials.

In the midst of the complex series of troubles various
reforms were being carried out up to 1848. Count Szechenyi,
one of the great Hungarian nobles, led the way in a policy
of material interests; to him was due the construction of
the bridge connecting Buda and Pesth, also the blowing up
of the Iron Gates in the Danube at Orsova: "he was no
revolutionist, nor was he an enemy to Austria." The hero
Kossuth started a journal in 1840 with the aim of uniting
all classes of Hungarians, encouraging expression of
opinions; for only by discussion could the need of recon-
ciling noble and non-noble Hungarians, or Magyars and
non-Magyars, be expressed. Thus new ideas spread in
Hungary, and the Diet in 1843 seriously took in hand the
questions where reform was demanded, equal representation
of towns with nobles in the Diet, equal taxation, trial by
jury, etc., problems which were bound to be important
when the "liberal" ideas of Western Europe were influencing
a feudal aristocracy; in fact democracy as well as nationality was in question. The fiercest controversy raged over
the problem of language; was Magyar to be the official
language both in the Diet and in government employ?
The Croats appealed in favour of Latin, and the question
was not yet settled in 1848, for neither nation would give
way on so vital a point.

In the north Bohemia was an island of Slavs surrounded
by Germans, and indeed inside the island there were both
Germans and Slavs. The Czechs were conscious of their
nationality, and had traditions from their past history and
a love of their old literature.

Therefore when Vienna rose in March 1848, and Milan
immediately after Vienna, the Emperor, Ferdinand IV,
had troubles as well in Hungary and Bohemia. The Vienna
insurrection was the work of both the middle classes and
the mob against despotism and a haughty German aristocracy of a most exclusive type; and the university students
played a conspicuous part. In England, if some proportion
of ardent young men and even dons are violently radical,
or if pro-Boers and even pro-Germans are to be found,
we take it as a temporary craze; otherwise, our universities
may be liberal but never revolutionary. But abroad things
are different. In Vienna in 1848, and in Paris in 1871,
the students were very genuine radicals and revolutionaries, as must happen when aristocrats keep power and
privilege to themselves and the intellectual poor are
slighted. A Teufelsdröckh can so easily become rabid
and dangerous.

The demands in March were for a National Guard and
a Constitution. The Emperor's ministers did not draw up
a satisfactory scheme, and in May there were more riots.
Then the Emperor fled to Innsbruck. A Committee of
Public Safety was appointed to represent students, the
middle class, and workmen, and governed Vienna. Here
the movement was German and democratic. At Prague it
was national and Slav, yet the Slav element was comparatively weak, and there was no sympathy between
Vienna and Prague. In consequence it was possible to use
Austrian soldiers against the Czechs, without any fear that

the Viennese would help them. Windischgrätz, an Austrian aristocrat who was in command in Bohemia, was able to capture Prague June 17.

The Hungarian demand was for absolute self-government, and the Emperor in the early months of 1848 was quite unable to resist it. Moreover the demand was for democratic self-government, extending as far as abolition of serfdom. Kossuth was supreme, not the old native aristocracy, though Prince Batthyany was Prime Minister. For a time the Hungarian government was independent of Austria, having army, finance, and foreign policy under its control. The Viennese democracy, inasmuch as both movements were directed against a hated despotism, was not ill disposed to Hungarian Nationalism. But as the year proceeded new features presented themselves. The Slavs demanded recognition of their peculiar rights, free of Hungarian ascendancy: Kossuth refused to listen, and the Croats were roused against the Hungarians even as the latter against Austria. Already the province or "banat" of Croatia had as governor or "ban" a Slav officer named Jellacic. The Hungarian ministry demanded that Jellacic should be subordinate to them, and even obtained from the Emperor, then residing in humiliation at Innsbruck, an edict to suspend him. But he played his cards very cleverly; he appealed to the Croatian regiments in Italy to remain loyal, and thus made himself necessary to the Austrian cause. By this time the Austrian arms were successful both in Bohemia and in Italy. Jellacic and Batthyany were at daggers drawn, the Slav leader being in favour of a single government at Vienna to control war and finance and foreign policy, and the Magyar still devoted to Hungarian independence which included domination over the Slavs. The Serbs of Hungary were in arms for union with their kindred in Croatia. The Emperor, as was natural, threw in his lot finally with Jellacic.

Once more Vienna broke into revolt when it was seen that the Austrians had made this alliance with the Croats, all the sympathies of the city democracy being with Hungary against the Emperor. Late in October Windischgrätz from Prague marched on Vienna; Kossuth, feeling that the city rising was saving Hungary from Jellacic, prevailed on his associates to depart from their defensive attitude and march to the relief of Vienna; Jellacic marched to support Windischgrätz. The Austrians were successful; while Jellacic held off the Hungarian relieving force, Windischgrätz stormed Vienna and treated it with considerable severity.

It would be wrong to leave this part of the story without reference to another part of the Austrian dominions. The Tyrolese were always devotedly loyal to the Emperor, so that there was no need to play a double game for however short a time to secure their fidelity. As in Napoleon's days when they rebelled against Bavaria under whose rule he put them to weaken Austria, they fought, and fought well, whether in Italy or in Hungary. Had the Croats and the Tyrolese wavered, one does not see how either Windischgrätz or Radetzky could have been victorious.

The restored Emperor did not at once cancel all the reforms that had been granted so far. In November the Reichstag met at Kremsier in Moravia. But a new minister, Prince Schwarzenberg, was meditating a decisive move; he persuaded or ordered Ferdinand to resign, and the crown passed to his nephew Francis Joseph, then aged eighteen, who lived to 1916. The young man was bound by no personal pledge towards Parliament or Hungary. So Schwarzenberg was able to dissolve the one and to decree the abolition of the freedom of the other by the "Unitary Constitutional Edict" in March 1849, by which one Austrian system of government was to be applied to the whole Empire. But Hungary was not yet conquered, and more risings were yet to occur in Italy.

Germany was as deeply affected as Austria. But whereas the movements against Austria were, with the one exception of Vienna, racial, and the Slav support of Austria was racial, in Germany as a whole and in each German state in particular there was no aspiration but for German unity and freedom. The Federation of 1815 was a sham; it was merely a union of sovereigns, who profited thereby to be autocrats in their own states. Since 1815 a really popular and national movement was gathering momentum, and in 1840, when Thiers nearly induced France to defy the will of Europe, this feeling was voiced in the cry that the German Rhine would be defended and "they" should not have it. Now in 1848, after various preliminaries were settled, a real Pan-German Parliament met on May 28 at Frankfort. Dreams seemed to have come true; liberals of all kinds, patriots, poets, professors, doubtless also theorists and faddists, came together to create a Constitution which should govern United Germany for all time.

Yet first Prussia claims attention. In March Berlin rose, and, strange as it may seem to those whose knowledge is only of the 20th century, Berlin forced its Hohenzollern king to grant a free Constitution, and Berlin defied the Prussian army. Some lives were lost in the crowd, the troops were withdrawn in face of popular hatred, and the king did a sort of penance before the corpses. Between the two great kings, Frederick II and William I, the Hohenzollerns were not the strong men that our fancy paints. On the contrary the three Frederick Williams,

descended from Frederick II's younger brother, were mean
and selfish intriguers; one gained a good share of Poland
by allowing Austria alone to fight the French Republic;
a second established a claim to Hanover as the price of
standing by while Napoleon crushed the Austrians and
Russians at Ulm and Austerlitz, did not even rise in a
manly fashion after the Moscow catastrophe, yet claimed
on Napoleon's collapse a large amount of land in Saxony
and Poland and Rhineland; the third was mean in 1848.
Having promised a Constitution, he plunged into a war
against Denmark to recover Holstein and Schleswig for
Germany,—the first cry of Pan-Germanism in 1848 was to
"liberate" these duchies,—and then he drew back when
Russia and England remonstrated and the Danish fleet
was too strong for him.    When the Prussian troops returned
from Schleswig he turned them against Berlin; this was
at the end of the year, when both Prague and Vienna had
been regained by the Emperor of Austria, and monarchy
was recovering generally from the shocks of the early spring.
The Assembly which met at Berlin was dissolved.   A new
royal Edict announced a new Constitution; it was on the
time-honoured principle of the Hohenzollerns that Prussia
might do nothing for herself, but was to receive everything,
whether a form of government or material prosperity, from
a benevolent despotism supported by the aristocrat-
officered army.

Such was the character of the King of Prussia.   The
German Assembly met at Frankfort on May 18, amidst
much excitement and high hopes, and the newly granted
Prussian Assembly met at Berlin about the same time.
From the very beginning it was seen that the question of
the relations between Austria and Prussia on the one side
and the Pan-Germanic body on the other was difficult

M.                                                    7

# HOUSE OF LORRAINE-HAPSBURG

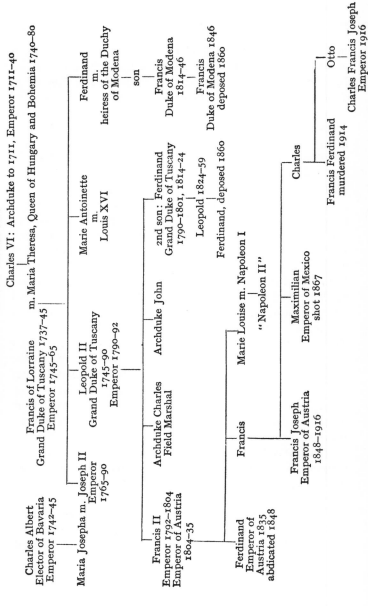

beyond solution. First the Archduke John, an uncle of the Emperor of Austria, was created Administrator; as this office carried with it control of the armed forces of Germany, including the army of Prussia as one of the members, it was clear that either the Administrator would have no real authority, or Prussia would be offended. Another point at issue was whether the Austrian Empire as such should be considered a member or only the purely German part of Austria. When towards the end of the year Schwarzenberg, confident that the Italian and Hungarian dangers were over-passed, brought out his Unitary Edict, centralising the whole of the Austrian Empire at Vienna, he clearly showed that he did not mean Austria to be a mere part of Germany as represented at Frankfort. Who then was to be the head of Germany? The four independent kingdoms of Bavaria, Saxony, Hanover, and Wurtemberg stood by Austria. The minor German states seemed to have no choice but to offer the headship to Prussia. Frederick William promptly refused the offer; it was against Hohenzollern principle to accept as a popular gift what the dynasty might create for itself; he was not strong enough to assert himself by arms, even if he had the courage, against both Austria and the four minor kingdoms: if the Empire came to him at all as a gift, it must be offered by the sovereigns and not the peoples of Germany, after Prussia had done something conspicuous to earn it. If these ideas were not consciously present to the Prussian King, at least we can see from our knowledge of 1871 that such conditions alone would make the much-desired German Empire a possibility.

After a year of futile talk and disappointed hopes, the Prussian refusal coming in April 1849, the Frankfort Assembly published its projected Constitution of Germany.

Twenty-eight minor governments accepted it.   Austria and
Prussia would have nothing to do with it.   The unfortunate
Assembly could not even suppress a feeble rising in Baden,
for the Archduke John refused to accept its orders.   Some
of the deputies departed in despair; some of them sat for
a short time at Stuttgart; and there was an end to a democratic attempt at Confederation.

There remained in 1849 the final suppression of Italy
and Hungary.   Charles Albert had only obtained from
Radetzky a truce which came to an end in the March of
that year.   The Austrians were now quite strong enough to
refuse terms.   Nothing short of a complete restoration of
their power in Lombardy and Venetia would satisfy them.
Charles Albert had not the smallest chance of success if
he took up arms again; Naples and Sicily were crushed;
Rome was in open insurrection against the Pope and had
gallantly declared a Republic, but with no prospect of
success; the Tuscans had declared a Republic; Venice
was still holding out, but was strictly blockaded.   But
Charles Albert was cut to the heart by the hatred which
he had incurred the year before by giving up the struggle
too soon.   He and the army of Piedmont could at least,
though without allies, strike one more blow to show their
true manliness.   He made the same mistakes as before,
spread out his army behind the river Ticino, and allowed
Radetzky to concentrate and break across the undefended
river, and the result was the battle of Novara March 23.
Then in the midst of the rout of his troops he abdicated,
presented his son Victor Emmanuel to his generals, and fled,
without returning to Turin, to self-imposed exile and death
in Portugal.   Radetzky had Piedmont at his mercy, yet
did nothing more than quarter his troops on the country
for a time and impose a heavy fine.   Young as he was

Victor Emmanuel refused the friendship of Austria, which indeed would have lowered him to the position of a puppet like the Duke of Modena or of Parma; he refused to destroy the Constitution of his kingdom and reign as a despot at Austria's bidding. The only thing which was in his favour was Austria's fear to drive him to extremities, for then France and Great Britain could not have failed to interfere.

As to the two Republics, Tuscany was overrun at once by the Austrians and the Grand Duke restored, but Rome put up an unexpected resistance. The government had Mazzini himself at its head. Garibaldi came with his volunteers from north Italy, and a few of his old South American comrades, forming the Legion of the Red Shirts. An energetic young Lombard, named Manara, led a legion of desperate refugees from Lombardy. Students and artists of various nationalities, citizens of Rome, and even some papal guards, were ready to man the walls. After all the enemy was, not Radetzky nor any other Austrian general, but an army sent in defence of the Church by the French Republic and its President Louis Napoleon. The forces of reaction were so strong in France against anything which savoured of Red Republicanism or Socialism, and Louis Napoleon was so keen to appeal to the respectable element to prove that he was a good Roman Catholic, and to prevent Austria from getting all the glory and corresponding influence in Italy, that a French army appeared off Civita Vecchia in April under General Oudinot. Rome was surrounded by the walls of the Emperor Aurelian, built in A.D. 275; but the high ground on the right bank of the Tiber had not been enclosed in ancient Rome at all; here was the medieval city of the Popes and its wall was medieval. It was against this higher ground that Oudinot advanced; for if once he gained possession of it, the old city of the left

bank lying low would be at the mercy of his artillery.
But he had only 7000 French and no heavy guns, and he
was quite unable to carry the papal wall.    Garibaldi
made a sortie amongst the villas and gardens outside, and
drove the French off with considerable loss on April 30.
During the whole of May Monsieur de Lesseps was negotiating with the Roman Republic, whilst Louis Napoleon
was waiting to see how the elections would turn out in
France; as soon as ever he saw that a Roman Catholic
majority was assured in the new Chamber, Louis Napoleon
repudiated Lesseps and reinforced Oudinot.    Attempts at
revolution in Paris and Lyons failed completely.    So the
attack upon Rome could proceed safely.    On July 3
Oudinot stormed the breaches of the same wall where he
had previously failed, in the face of desperate but unskilled
valour.

Garibaldi took a pathetic farewell of his comrades in
Rome, and fled while there was yet time to the mountains.
Hunted in every direction by Spaniards and Papalists
from the south, and Austrians from the north, he reached,
after hairbreadth escapes, the little State of San Marino
and afterwards Piedmont.    His wife Anita, a South
American Spaniard, died of exhaustion after having
accompanied him everywhere.    The value of the last
desperate attempt of Charles Albert and of Garibaldi's
hopeless defence of Rome is that the Italians and all the
Liberals of Europe and America saw the devotion and self-
sacrifice of both, and forgot the failure.    Young Italy had
something to which to look back, for an apparently mad
devotion to a cause may lead to future success by means
of the memories that are evoked.    In England, at least,
there was strong excitement and much sympathy.    Our
government as represented by Palmerston did little beyond

negotiating between Austria and Piedmont; there was no thought of making a strong stand on behalf of a distressed nation, but, though mere sympathy may seem to be very cheap, it was at least something that Italy knew that she had aroused a kindly feeling. On the other hand France seemed to have betrayed a sister Latin nation. Yet Pius IX, when restored to Rome, had no wish to take French advice, and refused to grant a Constitution. Under the influence of Cardinal Antonelli he returned as an autocrat with the fixed opinion that the maintenance of the temporal power of the Papacy over Rome and the Marches and Legations could only be ensured by despotism. The French, therefore, had the satisfaction of having forestalled the Austrians, but had not influenced the Papacy towards mild methods.

In August Venice capitulated, though Manin escaped to Piedmont. At the other end of Italy Ferdinand not only crushed liberty at Naples and gave asylum to Pius during his exile; he also reconquered Sicily after a cruel bombardment of Palermo, from which he received the name "Bomba," swept away self-government, and made for himself a reputation for vindictiveness surpassing that of any of the Bourbons. Some time later Gladstone was allowed to see some of the prisons of Naples, and startled Europe out of its smug complacency by his tale of horrors; even those who thought that every despotism was justified, as long as it prevented revolution, were shocked by his revelation of Bourbon brutality.

This year also witnessed a collapse of the Hungarian movement; yet the Hungarians offered a resistance which roused almost as much sympathy in Liberal countries as the efforts of Garibaldi himself. In January, indeed, the Austrians seemed to be in a winning position; the loyalty of the Croats, the consequent entry into Vienna, and the policy of Schwarzenberg in procuring the abdication of the Emperor, followed by the issue of the Unitary Edict, seemed to promise immediate success. Windischgrätz occupied Pesth. But then there was a wonderful change of fortune. An untried general chosen by Kossuth, by name Görgei, was marvellously successful; and even when Görgei was rashly superseded by a Polish refugee, Dembinski, the tide was still in Hungary's favour. In April the Austrians were even forced to retire from Pesth. A Declaration of Hungarian Independence was proclaimed, though the original demands of 1848 had only extended to self-government separate from Austria under the personal rule of the Emperor as King of Hungary. But in July the Tsar of Russia came to Austria's aid. This was decisive; the Hungarians were crushed on each side, and finally Görgei capitulated unconditionally to the Russians. The brutalities of the Austrian revenge were a by-word throughout Europe, more particularly those of General Haynau, who had already earned an evil reputation in Italy. Even Batthyany the Constitutionalist, who had never gone so far as Kossuth, was executed. Kossuth himself escaped into Turkey; he afterwards visited England and was fêted here.

The Austrian Empire was now distinctly strong, even though it was galling to Austrian pride that the final victory was only achieved by the help of Russia. Within Germany proper also, the Austrian position was distinctly strong. The great majority of the small states, some twenty-eight of them, sided with Prussia and formed a new Confederation, but the four minor kingdoms Bavaria, Saxony, Hanover, Wurtemberg, with the Hesses and Baden, stood by Austria. There was a rising in Hesse Cassel, and Prussian troops were sent to suppress it, so that for a moment there was actual danger of a war between Prussia and Austria. This was avoided by the mediation of the Tsar, who in a meeting at Warsaw in 1850, decided in Austria's favour; indeed Austria was in the position of being his protégé, and he had particularly disliked the Prussian interference in Schleswig Holstein. Finally the Treaty of Olmütz in Bohemia was arranged, by which the Prussians withdrew from both Hesse Cassel and Schleswig Holstein, and agreed to recognise the Federal Diet as set up in 1815. Therefore for the time being Prussia took quite a second place. Another ten years were to go by before a new king would enter upon the path of enterprise and take up again the question of Prussian supremacy in Germany. During these ten years Prussia slept.

Young Germany had so far failed as much as Young Italy. The moral of the failure in each country was the same, namely, that divided interests lead to certain failure. But Germany had no glorious memories of 1848–49 to counterbalance failure as had Italy.

*Note.* The King of Hanover at this date was Ernest Augustus, Duke of Cumberland, son of George III and next in age to William IV. The Salic Law prevented Victoria from succeeding to a German throne, and thus in 1837 the dynastic union of Great Britain and Hanover came to an end. It was his son, George V, who lost Hanover in 1866.

# CHAPTER V

## NAPOLEON III's FIRST DECADE

The Constitution of the Second Republic was drawn up November 12, 1848. Louis Napoleon, elected President December 20, took an oath to remain faithful to the Republic and defend the Constitution. In 1849 he sent his expedition against the Roman Republic, and yet Article No. 5 in the Constitution said, "the French Republic will never use its forces against the liberty of any people." But the elections in June to the Legislative Assembly were entirely anti-Republican; they were conducted by the "Party of Order," managed by the so-called "Committee of the Rue de Poitiers," being a mixture of Legitimists, Orleanists, Bonapartists, and Roman Catholics in general; about 500 members represented the "Party of Order," and there were 250 Republicans. When Ledru-Rollin protested against the Italian policy, he was outvoted in the Chamber; and when he tried to appeal to the men in the streets, many of his brother members were arrested, and he escaped to England. Both the Chamber and the Army having thus declared themselves in favour of the Roman Catholic policy, there was passed in 1850 an Education Law, by which the University of France and the schools were put almost entirely under the control of the Church. Next the Assembly, following the lead of Thiers,

passed an Electoral Law to enforce a three years' residence
and a contribution in direct taxation as the qualifications
for a vote; here it put itself in opposition to the President,
who was in his turn quite clever enough to avail himself
of such a blunder, and to pose before the French people
as the champion of Universal Suffrage. In fact the
Assembly was mostly Legitimist and Orleanist, and he
was determined to crush not only the Republic, but also
Monarchists of both kinds.

In 1850 and 1851 his policy was to secure the army, and
it was no light task to bring even the army round to
Bonapartism. At a grand review the cavalry saluted him
as Emperor, but the infantry marched past him in silence;
in revenge he got rid of various superior officers, even
those who had in the previous year suppressed the rising
of Ledru-Rollin. Throughout the year 1851, in proportion
as he was gaining over gradually the army, he was more
and more opposed to the Assembly. The celebrated *coup
d'état* was carried out in the night of December 1–2. Officers
such as Cavaignac and Changarnier, and politicians such as
Thiers, were arrested. In the morning Paris found the
walls placarded with the President's " Appeal to the People,"
by which he announced that a *plébiscite* would be held at
once by universal suffrage; he would claim for himself the
Presidency for ten years, in defiance of the Constitution of
1848, with a ministry dependent solely on him; a Legislative Chamber should be elected by universal suffrage,
with a second Chamber or Senate nominated by himself.
December 3 and 4 were days of barricades, not only in the
quarter of Saint Antoine, but also farther west in the wider
and more respectable streets. The soldiers destroyed the
barricades without much trouble and fired almost indis-
criminately in the streets. Military law was declared all

over France. It is said that there were 100,000 arrests, and certainly several thousands were exiled or deported. Yet the promised *plébiscite* of December 14 was taken, and 7½ millions of votes approved of the *coup d'état* against 650,000. Just one year later, on Austerlitz day, December 2, 1852, he threw off the mask and took the title of Napoleon III; a second *plébiscite* approved of this by 7,800,000 votes against 253,000.

Napoleon III was now seriously in the saddle, how would he govern his mount? It is certainly not too much to say that for a score of years his will seemed to dominate Europe; for ten of these he really was a power which counted actively, and for a second ten his influence was mainly negative or destructive, yet was the deciding factor. Or to put it in other words, for ten years his sword settled the affairs of nations, and then for another ten his backwardness and failure to seize his opportunities allowed Prussia, or one ought more properly to say Bismarck, to advance from success to success. At first he was trusted, or if people did not trust him they believed in his star; he was almost thought to be, as he himself posed to be, the Man of Destiny. Then he was less trusted, even suspected, yet thought to be still safe and powerful, so that the fearful suddenness of the collapse in 1870, which was a matter of a bare four weeks, was a startling surprise. Then arose against him a howl of detestation. Yet it is very difficult for us even now to judge him. He violated his oath in suppressing the Republic, yet the almost overwhelming voice of France approved of him. One can only suppose that the general horror which the Reign of Terror of 1793 and 1794 made to sink deeply into the hearts of all lovers of law and order was still powerful sixty years later, that the fiasco of the National Workshops and the

four days of the Barricades of June 1848 raised fears lest
there would be a second Reign of Terror, and that a new
Bonaparte was justified, even as his uncle before him in
1795, in having recourse to "a whiff of grape-shot."
Granted that his *coup d'état* was a crime, he had a chance
to show that he could govern France and influence Europe,
if he should use his power wisely and show sympathy in
those directions where it would be reciprocated. Many an
empire has been founded by sheer brutal conquest and
questionable methods, yet the conquerors, by wishing to
govern justly and sympathetically, have justified themselves in the eyes of history. The doctrine of the *fait
accompli* is indeed dangerous. Queen Victoria was no bad
judge of character; she reserved her judgement after the
*coup d'état*, and by no means approved of Palmerston's cool
offhand pronouncement that Napoleon was justified and
could hardly have done anything different, but very soon
she was almost fascinated by him and accepted the deed as
done. The howl of execration was not heard till after
Sedan. It is very easy now after half a century to
argue that a Republic can be both permanent and truly
patriotic, but the great majority then, especially French
peasants, feared that it would be unstable. One name
however always comes into our minds; Victor Hugo
from the very first dubbed him Napoleon the Little, the
false-swearer and tyrant; he wrote the *History of a Crime*
and lived in exile for conscience sake. Thiers indeed never
served under him, but continued to write his uncle's life
and indirectly approved of, because he popularised,
Bonapartism.

His real fault was that he was an ordinary and even a
weak man, called by force of circumstances and the accident
of being his uncle's nephew into a position which he could

not adequately fill. The Napoleon Legend pushed him to the front, and when he was there he could not justify himself. Unworthy people got his ear and then betrayed his confidence. He had no power to go below the surface and find out when things were going wrong.

His chief confidants were his half-brother Comte Morny and the Comte de Persigny, and it can hardly be said that they had a good influence over him, besides that they were men of very ordinary capacity put in power by the Imperial pleasure. In 1853 he married Eugénie de Montijo, a beautiful young Spanish noblewoman, who was a devoted Roman Catholic, and is always thought to have been under the control of the Jesuits.

From the beginning the Imperial government, nominally liberal and based upon universal suffrage, was upheld by various tricks which tended to absolutism. The Emperor could raise money beyond what was voted by the Chamber, and could commence public works on his own authority. He could appoint the mayors of towns and villages, propose and recommend official candidates at parliamentary elections, and demand an oath of fidelity—he himself having broken his oath of 1848—from deputies and civil servants, and even from the university professors. So great was the official influence over elections, because not only were the Emperor's nominees recommended, but also the mayors, who were the Emperor's choice, had entire control of the voting papers, that in the Chamber there was a very small and weak Opposition; in fact there were at first merely five deputies for Paris, one for Lyons, and one for Bordeaux, who formed any opposition at all. These men were elected in 1857, and one of them, Emile Ollivier, in course of time, rallied to the Emperor. In 1863 the Opposition increased in numbers to thirty-five, whether Republicans or

Royalists; amongst them were Thiers, elected for Paris as an Orleanist, and Jules Favre as a Republican. Their chief protest was against governmental control of elections which made universal suffrage a farce. Opposition in the newspapers was controlled by a censorship, and by special tribunals which had the right to suppress a newspaper after a second offence. But one right of free speech the Emperor was quite unable to control; any lawyer who defended an accused pressman was practically beyond the Emperor's vengeance, and it was in the law-courts that the Opposition was adequately voiced.

It was on the side of material prosperity that the Empire did most to justify itself to the people. The luxury and extravagance of the Court, largely copied by the richer classes in spite of the severe aloofness of the Legitimists, were good for trade. Paris was largely rebuilt, with wide streets and boulevards, great open spaces and "quais," under the control of Baron Haussmann. There was a Universal Exhibition in 1855 and another in 1867. A Treaty of Free Trade was negotiated with Great Britain through the services of Cobden himself, which indeed did not introduce an absolute free trade, but which regulated the tariff on British products and in return lowered the tariff on French wines and corn. The railway systems were widely extended during the reign. The Suez Canal scheme was carried through. Whilst France seemed to be the centre of commerce and wealth in Europe, as well as of fashion and show, the peasant proprietors, strengthened by the institution of banks and agricultural societies, were still the real backbone of the nation, and the peasants supported him. Consequently it was a long time before Napoleon III was "found out." In fact, if his foreign policy had been more sane and steady, if he had not rushed from one scheme to another to show his military glory as a true Napoleon, and then failed to carry each scheme to a really satisfactory finish, he might have founded a dynasty. The corruption of his rule was such that he himself was not aware how badly organised was the army on which his safety depended. Yet, only a very short time before that fatal four weeks which wrecked his power, when by its last *plébiscite* the French nation gave him an enormous number of votes, our *Punch* issued a cartoon which depicted him as making his throne safe for "Napoleon IV." So little did the public opinion of Europe suspect that eighteen years of corruption had undermined his throne.

"*L'Empire c'est la Paix*" were Napoleon's words in a speech at Bordeaux, whilst he was only yet Prince-President. Whether he was deceiving himself or not when he spoke, it would be impossible to say. He plunged into a series of wars, because he could not control his destiny. He was a Napoleon, and therefore he had to follow after glory; the army had made him, and he now had to satisfy the army. Nobody could at first say in which direction he would turn his arms, and indeed he might have provoked a quarrel with Great Britain to avenge the memory of Waterloo. But chance threw in his way the opportunity to take advantage of the Eastern Question, and he was drawn into a war to avenge his uncle's retreat from Moscow, dragging in his wake Great Britain as his ally. The more that one looks into the causes of the Crimean War, the more one thinks that both Nicholas and Napoleon were whirled into war as if by fate, while Great Britain was pushed in by the two strong men who knew their own minds, Palmerston and Stratford de Redcliffe, the rest of our statesmen and our country at large being indifferent at first and then excited into enthusiasm for war. France, carried away by *une idée*, and willing enough to rush into war, had reached a period in her history when *la revanche* took the place of *les idées révolutionnaires* which had launched the first Republic on a career of conquest.

It was quite easy for any Tsar to meditate a new attack upon Turkey by straining the terms of the treaties of Kainardji and Adrianople[1]. He had only to claim a sort of general championship of all the Christian subjects of the Sultan, and thus would have an excuse to satisfy the traditional policy of Russia to expand towards the sea. The particular occasion was a dispute as to the rights of the Greek or the Roman Catholic monks at Jerusalem to have the keys of the Holy Places; Nicholas supported the first; Napoleon, already offended because Nicholas did not acknowledge him as a "brother" sovereign, saw his chance in supporting the second. The Sultan gave way to France. Then Nicholas meditated an attack upon Turkey, "the sick man" of Europe, and suggested to Lord Aberdeen, our prime minister, that Russia and Great Britain should unite to partition the country. He liked our country and people; he remembered how his brother Alexander, our warmest ally against the great Napoleon, had been welcomed in London in 1814. So he thought it natural that he should make the other Balkan provinces as independent as Rumania was already, even occupy Constantinople for a time, and give the British a free hand as regards Egypt and Crete. What he failed to understand was that the British were no longer as well disposed towards Russia as in 1814, regarded him as a cruel despot, and remembered the Holy Alliance and the merciless suppression of the Poles and the Hungarians. Wellington's policy of keeping the Russians away from the Eastern Mediterranean was now

[1] See pages 39 and 57.

supported by two energetic men, Palmerston who was most influential in Aberdeen's ministry[1], and Lord Stratford de Redcliffe[2] our ambassador to Turkey. The cry was to uphold the integrity of the Turkish Empire, and this just suited Napoleon III. Thus, in place of joining an old ally against an old enemy, the British government drifted into alliance with Napoleon, who on his side was ready to avenge Moscow rather than Waterloo. It was at least to the good that Britain and France could be allies. Otherwise our statesmen were committed to an impossible task, namely to bolster up an oriental government, which never could, and never wished to, reform itself. Of course it is difficult to criticise our statesmen of 1853–54 without thought of 1876–78 or 1912–13, and we must remember that Gladstone in 1876, even in his fiercest speech against the Turks, said definitely that he believed the Crimean War to have been really necessary, and that he accepted fully his responsibility for his share in it. Having so many Mohammedan subjects in India our statesmen could not refuse to help the Turks simply as being Mohammedans. Thus to-day it is not for their religion, but for their failure to reform after all the help given to them by the western nations, that they have lost the sympathy and support of the West. Lastly, British enthusiasm for war is curiously spasmodic. In 1853–54 public feeling seemed to be set on war as if we had had enough of peace since Waterloo, as if we were ashamed of being a nation of shop-keepers devoted only to free trade and manufacture,

---

[1] Palmerston, who had gained a reputation for being too head-strong as Foreign Secretary, was Home Secretary in 1854.

[2] Sir Stratford Canning, cousin of the late premier George Canning, known in Turkey as "the Great Eltchi," and recently made a peer.

and required a little excitement and glory. The tone of
our country is seen when men talked of 1851, "The Great
Exhibition year," as the beginning of a new era of peace
and trade, and yet at a moment's notice the lust of war
flamed out.

Thus, when in 1853 Nicholas demanded not only the
Holy Places for the Greek clergy, but also his right to
protect all the Christians of Turkey, the Sultan, relying
on Lord Stratford, refused. Russian armies appeared on
the Danube. British and French fleets appeared off the
Dardanelles, and then passed through the straits; but
they were not promptly sent forwards, and the Russians
destroyed the Turkish squadron at Sinope, a port on the
south shore of the Black Sea. War was inevitable, and
the general impression left on our minds is that none of
the powers engaged expected war, or thought that the
others meant war, and so they all drifted into war. In
1854 the Russians besieged Silistria on the Bulgarian bank
of the Danube, and the French and British armies arrived
at Varna on the Bulgarian coast. Now the Emperor of
Austria played his part; if the Tsar could have calcu-
lated on the help of any monarch at this date, surely the
Emperor of Austria was that monarch, for the Russians
had helped him to crush Hungary. But he demanded the
evacuation of Rumania, and Nicholas had to submit. Henceforward Austria was always Russia's opponent in Balkan
problems.

The Allied armies still lay at Varna, and what more
could they do? To call them home, now that the Russians
had left Rumania, seemed to be a feeble ending after much
excitement, and Nicholas might begin the war again at
any moment. So the demand was made that he should
give up his right to protect the Christians. He refused.

Thereupon both armies were ordered to the Crimea to destroy
Sebastopol, the one great arsenal and place-of-arms on the
Black Sea.  It was now late in the year, cholera was raging
at Varna and would accompany the troops, the climate of
the Crimea was unknown, stores for a long siege were not
ready.  Thus it is difficult to acquit the governments of a
blind eagerness to prolong the war to satisfy the excitement
at home, France being critical about the new Napoleon,
who had·yet to prove himself a great ruler, Britain bent
on proving herself not wholly given to trade and manufacture.  The armies landed to face the unknown, each
about 30,000 strong.  Marshal St Arnaud commanded the
French, but he was at death's door; Lord Raglan, aged 66,
who had seen no service since Waterloo, commanded the
British; our allies had mostly had much experience in
Algeria, but only a few of our officers and men had been
in India, and all our traditions were of the Peninsular War
forty years earlier.  One has to emphasise this point, for the
military administration was rusty, and the economy of a
nation devoted to trade as a sacred duty until the blaze of
excitement came had prevented efficiency.  It must be
noticed here that this is the first war when all the infantry
had muzzle-loading rifles; in our ranks it was quite a new
weapon, except for a few special regiments, for Wellington
had resolutely refused to discard the old musket, and he
had only recently died.

Advancing southwards along the coast the Allies found
the Russians drawn up on the far bank above the river
Alma.  The British, September 20, made a straight frontal
attack on the left; the French on the right by the sea had
a steeper bank to climb, and were just threatening to
outflank the Russians when they retreated.  But the
beaten enemy refused to let themselves be locked up in

Sebastopol and retired inland, leaving in the place, under the command of Todleben, a garrison and the sailors of the fleet and a small army of trained workmen. Ships were sunk to block the mouth of the harbour, and Todleben worked hard to throw up fortifications. He said himself that the Allies could have rushed the northern defences at once. But they swept round, and occupied an upland in front of the south side of the harbour, the British on the right with their base at Balaclava, a small and distant harbour, the French on the left resting on Kamiesh Bay close to them. While they waited for their siege guns, Todleben dug and built. Meanwhile St Arnaud died, and Canrobert took his place.

Siege in the ordinary sense of the term there was none. The Russians always held the north side of the harbour, and there was free access across by a bridge; reinforcements and supplies could enter Sebastopol during all the eleven months. The Allies, having received their guns, simply bombarded and prepared to assault. As fast as they destroyed the works by day Todleben rebuilt by night, and the wooden warships, trying to force the harbour mouth, were powerless against the land forts above it. Then on October 25 the outside Russian army crossed the river Tchernaya and tried to capture Balaclava, that is to say tried to cut off the British from their base; they were repulsed, but held a strong position on our rear. On November 5 an attack from Sebastopol and the outside army fell on the British extreme right on the upland at Inkerman, and was repulsed with greater difficulty. Before the bombardment could be renewed came a storm of rain, which converted the upland into a sea of mud. Siege works were out of the question when stores and food could hardly be moved. The horrors of the winter, semi-starvation,

disease, lack of clothing and drugs, loss of stores in bad
weather at sea, frost and snow in the trenches varied by
mud after a thaw, utter inability to help the sick and
wounded, congestion at Balaclava when the stores did
arrive but could not be distributed, the awful story is only
too well known.    Miss Nightingale arrived in November at
the hospital at Scutari, on the Asiatic shore opposite to
Constantinople, but it was some time before her influence
was felt.    In January 1855, Lord Aberdeen resigned, and
Palmerston formed a new and more energetic ministry.    In
March died Tsar Nicholas I, and Alexander II succeeded.

Things were very much better for the Allies in the
spring.    The French, who had suffered less, were strongly
reinforced till they had in May about 100,000 effectives;
the British after all their losses, having sunk as low as
12,000, numbered 30,000;    about 40,000 Turks arrived
whose services were considered to be worthless, and 15,000
"Sardinians," for Victor Emmanuel, who had no quarrel with
Russia, wanted to put both France and England under an
obligation to the House of Savoy.    Consequently there
were enough French and Italians to occupy the ground
between Balaclava and the Tchernaya, and the Russians
retired beyond the river.    On the upland the British were
too few to carry on the whole of the right attack, where
Todleben had erected several new forts, notably the
Malakoff;    so the French took over the extreme right as
well as the left, while our men had only the right centre.
Now Napoleon interfered much with the generals, this
being the first war when field armies were tied to head-
quarters at home by the telegraph, and his idea was to
give up the siege and attack the Russian outside army.
Lord Raglan was clearly right in insisting that the Allies
were committed to the siege, and that the Malakoff was the

key of the defence. Canrobert, distracted between them,
asked to be superseded, and General Pélissier came to take
command, a man of energy and fire, able to carry out his
own ideas in spite of Napoleon.   So the siege was pressed,
but expeditions were also sent to the isthmus to cut off the

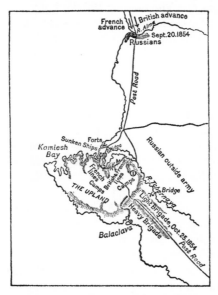

Map to illustrate the Crimean War.

M   Malakoff, stormed Sept. 8, 1855.
R   Redan.
Ⓘ   Battle of Inkerman, Nov. 5, 1854.
✕   Battle, August 16, 1855.
╫╫╫╫ Railway, 1855.

ever inflowing stream of Russian reinforcements and supplies.   The bombardment was far more severe than before
and the siege guns heavier.   Some of Todleben's forts were
carried by the French.   But a great combined attack on

Waterloo day failed, and then Raglan died worn out[1].   In
August the Russian army crossed the Tchernaya to relieve
the tension of the siege, but the French and Italians easily
repulsed them with great loss.   After a fiercer bombardment, Todleben being wounded, the final assault was made
on September 8.   The mighty Malakoff, occupying entirely
an isolated hill, seemed to be impregnable, but the French
had sapped to within a dozen yards, and its weakness was
that it was enclosed all round, so that, when they rushed
it under General MacMahon, they were covered against fire
from the rear.   The British carried the central fort, the
Redan, but it was open to the rear and the Russian fire
drove them out again.   General Simpson, Raglan's successor, has always been unfavourably criticised, and the
honour of the day belonged to Pélissier.   On the other hand
the very powerful British artillery had greatly contributed
by its cross fire to the fall of the Malakoff.

Next day it was found that Sebastopol had been
deserted in the night.   The Allies spent another winter in
the Crimea and there was no repetition of horrors.   The
British were over 50,000 strong and in good condition, and
a German legion of 10,000 was in our pay, the last of those
mercenary corps so common in the 18th century.   But
Napoleon had the deciding word, as he had constantly kept
up his army to some 120,000 men and they had won
Sebastopol.   He seemed to think that enough had been
done for glory.   The Russian army still held the Crimea
and was not attacked, though Russia was for the time
exhausted and nearly bankrupt.   Peace was made with

[1] He had shown little skill or alertness in battle, but much quiet
persistence in the winter months of the siege; and much tact towards
the French.   Had he died earlier, probably Napoleon would have
had his way and given up the siege.

Alexander II by the *Treaty of Paris* in March 1856; the navigation of the Black Sea and the Danube was to be free, and no warships might be kept and no military-maritime arsenals maintained on the coast by Tsar or Sultan.

Turkey received a new lease of life if only the Sultan had been clever enough to take advantage of it, for the offensive power of Russia was crippled for the time being. But Rumania was acknowledged as completely free, even as Serbia practically was already. The British government wished to keep Moldavia and Wallachia separate, Napoleon preferred the union of the two Provinces, thinking to see in the United Rumania an additional barrier against Russia. But the Rumanians settled the question for themselves, when they chose the same man to be "Hospodar" of each province for life, though each still had a separate government. In 1862 the Union was effected, and in 1866 Prince Charles of Hohenzollern, a distant connection of the King of Prussia and a Roman Catholic, was recognised as Hereditary Prince; in 1881 he became King.

Sea Power, and Sea Power alone, had enabled the Allies to conquer the Russians. All the French and British stores and reinforcements had come easily by water, and, assured of their naval base, the armies were not straitened in any way when once the horrors of the first winter had been overcome. On the other side all the Russian reserves had been forced to tramp on foot mighty distances; it was not only the terrific losses that the Russians suffered in battle when they fought in heavy unwieldy masses, or in the siege when they were crowded under the fire of the Allied heavy artillery in anticipation of a bayonet attack at any moment, which left Russia exhausted at the end of the war, but also the tremendous severity of the marches from inland to the Crimea, during which unknown numbers died; in fact this was the last war in which the transport upon one side at least was entirely of the old-fashioned type, before the advent of railways.  Yet the Sea Power of the Allies was useful only so far as it controlled the lines of communication; as an offensive power the navy of neither Britain nor France contributed at all to the fall of Sebastopol.  The wooden ships could not carry guns powerful enough to destroy land forts.  Floating batteries were designed during the war to attack the Russian defences at Kimburn in 1855; they were plated with 4-inch armour and carried 50-pounder guns.  After the war it was the French Admiralty, not our own, that first experimented in constructing an ironclad sea-going battleship.  It was only natural that the country, which had so long enjoyed a sea power which rested on wooden ships, should be slow to experiment in a new direction; but in the sixties our Admiralty was doing something slowly but surely.  Meanwhile the first war in which ironclads were actually used was the American Slave War.

At the same time, as the Crimean War saw the last of the old "wooden walls," so too the nature of land fighting was changed.  The rifle, even if awkwardly loaded at the muzzle, was destined to revolutionise strategy.  The siege of Sebastopol foreshadowed the coming era of trench warfare; and, if this be thought to be a far-fetched argument because the great campaigns of 1866 and 1870 were fought out by marching and not by entrenched armies, we have the entrenchments of 1877 in justification.  "The more powerful the weapon of the infantry, the greater the power of the defence," is the lesson of 1854–55, especially when we reflect that there was really no siege at all but only a frontal attack upon a fortified position, where the enemies' lines of communication were uninterrupted.  Moreover the interest for us to-day is that the permanent fortifications of Sebastopol were not so important as those devised by Todleben after the "siege" had begun.

Both Napoleon and the French nation were pleased with themselves. The bulk of the work had been done by their army; theirs was the honour of the capture of the Malakoff and the victory of the Tchernaya; if Pélissier's resolution refused to abandon the siege against his Emperor's will, yet even so the reflected glory was the Emperor's. When the Concert of Europe met to settle the terms of peace, Paris was chosen, not London. Whilst it was sitting the Prince Imperial was born, and thus succession was so far safe. Napoleon III was not yet found out as the potentate who would embark on a scheme and abandon it at once; but his uncle would not have been satisfied to make peace so quickly, and the British were disappointed that he was unwilling to continue the war to exhaust Russia still further by a campaign in 1856; so that as we look back we can hardly say that the war really revenged Moscow or showed him as a worthy Napoleon.

On the other hand our nation is much too ready to depreciate the services of our soldiers. Many people still believe that we did nothing more than "muddle through somehow," a phrase that no self-respecting statesman should ever use. The truth is that a nation devoted to trade as the one serious pursuit of life, having just recently held a Great Exhibition as a memorial of the arts of peace, and looking forward to an era of manufacturing prosperity based upon free trade, as if all the world would henceforth send to us raw materials and corn duty-free, whilst we manufactured for the world, was suddenly dragged into a war and roused again to the idea of glory, and then was bitterly disappointed that the fighting machine was too

small and too rusty. Hardly any one paused to reflect
that the nation itself was responsible if our army was not
immediately successful, if we had scanty reserves when once
the really good trained men of the first line were exhausted,
or if the officers, who had never been allowed to practise
manoeuvres on an adequate scale during peace time, were
not able to reduce Sebastopol at once. Public opinion
seemed to take delight in criticising Raglan and Simpson
as if they were solely to blame, just as if in 1793 the fault
belonged to the Duke of York alone, and not to Mr Pitt
who had cut down and starved the army in the years
between the War of American Independence and the
French Revolutionary War. Even modern historians seem
to think it sufficient to jeer at the generals and not at the
false economies. Yet of course there is a reason why one
section of Englishmen at least have always feared to
maintain an army, namely the suspicion that it is maintained by the aristocracy to give them a weapon against
reform. "Yet barracks there must be," wrote Cobbett in
1821, "or Gatton and Old Sarum must fall, and the
fall of these would break poor Mr Canning's heart."
Therefore when Dr Russell of *The Times* poured out his
criticisms, he was not very happy in attributing blame.
Unfortunately it is only too notorious that after every
war, when the newspapers have satisfied themselves by
criticising the generals and officers, on the assumption that
their own reporters could have done very much better,
there has never been a strong move to strengthen adequately
the much-criticised army; the one party seems to have
always thought that officers ought not to be paid a living
wage, so that only aristocrats and rich men could hold
commissions; and the other party has always starved the
army in order that it may continue to make economies,

and has seemed to look upon soldiers simply as hirelings kept ready to suppress rioters and strikers.

In the next few years after the Crimean War, the French and British were not very good friends. In fact at one time there was even some danger that there might be war. Even a personal interview between Napoleon and Victoria did not do much good, in spite of the strong friendship that had somewhat quickly sprung up. This is the period when the volunteers were raised in England, and there was a certain complacent feeling that mere volunteers without serious training would be as good as regular soldiers. Of course in 1857 our government was quite unable to take a strong position in Europe because of the Indian Mutiny which was almost directly caused by the Crimean War; for even the excitement about the greased cartridges would hardly have been sufficient to cause it, had not the leaders thought that our army had been defeated in Russia, and that the time was ripe for a mutiny, so that the excitement of the sepoys could be utilised.

As to the more serious question of the wrongness of war between France and Russia and Great Britain or any two of them, it is impossible now to lay down the law. We can see now that the profit was to Germany alone. Yet sixty years ago no human mind could foresee the wonderful development of Germany, much less the alliance of Prussia with Austria. When we look back to the wars of the great Napoleon, we see how Russia wavered between fear of France and respect for France. There is no such thing as either a natural alliance or natural enmity. In spite of the overtures of Tsar Nicholas I and his admiration for England, it could hardly be expected that Palmerston could entertain friendship for the power which represented

absolute despotism, kept alive the policy of Metternich,
crushed Poland and Hungary, and sent exiles to Siberia.
But one good result of the war was that British and French
could be allies and prove the wrongness of their natural
enmity, even though there was a momentary scare due to
the triumphant boasting of the one nation and the resentment of the other.    In 1859-60 the French and British
did co-operate once more in an attack upon China, but the
feeling of suspicion grew up in the next ten years.    Napoleon
was thought to be insincere and frivolous.    The present
generation of British seem to have forgotten what tremendous influence was exercised at that date by Thomas
Carlyle, the admirer of German philosophy and solid sense
as opposed to French lightness, so that for the time it
seemed as if the natural enmity would be revived.

In 1858 occurred Orsini's famous attempt to murder
Napoleon on his way to the opera at Paris.    Orsini was
a Roman who had had his share in the defence of Rome in
1849, and hated Napoleon as the conqueror of the Roman
Republic.    But Napoleon was even then meditating a new
war against Austria on behalf of Italian Independence, and
though Orsini and a fellow conspirator were executed, the
speech of their advocate Jules Favre, an oration in favour
of Italian patriotism, was authorised to be printed in the
*Moniteur*.

The bringing of Napoleon into Italian politics was due
to the minister of Victor Emmanuel, Camillo Benso, Count
Cavour.    The Kingdom of Sardinia had embarked on a
strongly anti-clerical policy as a step towards proving the
right of Victor Emmanuel to be the leader of Italian
liberalism in opposition to Rome, as his father had, as it
were, consecrated him to be.    The clerical courts were suppressed and their rights transferred to the ordinary civil

courts. Religious houses were suppressed, and when the
Senate, frightened by papal anger, would have thrown out
this law, Cavour resigned; it was impossible to create any
other ministry, he was recalled and the Senate gave way.
A policy of material prosperity was seen in the construction
of railways and canals, the press was practically free and
old Republicans and Revolutionists were conciliated, so
that even Daniel Manin wrote publicly to Victor Emmanuel
"Make Italy and I am with you." The most notable
stroke was Cavour's alliance with France and Great Britain,
which resulted in the dispatch of the expeditionary force
to the Crimea, putting the two countries under an obligation; from this it resulted that Sardinia had the right to
be represented at the Congress of Paris as an acknowledged
member of the Concert of Europe; it was Cavour himself
who attended that Congress. He found Great Britain
sympathetic but not ready to take up arms so soon after
the Indian Mutiny; our country was not ready for anything
of the nature of knight errantry, and Palmerston was under
a cloud for a time in 1858 because he had introduced a
bill to punish conspiracy hatched in England, which bill
it was thought was dictated by Napoleon, because Orsini
had received asylum over here. Also from February 1858
to June 1859 Lord Derby's Conservative ministry was in
power. Palmerston, therefore, not being in a position to
help Italy even by moral influence, Cavour had no one but
Napoleon to whom to appeal. In July 1858 he was invited
to meet Napoleon at Plombières, when an Austrian war was
decided. Evidently Cavour flattered Napoleon into imagin-
ing himself the patron of Italy; Lombardy, Venetia, and
the Papal Legations were to be added to Piedmont, a central
Italian kingdom was hinted at, but there was no question
yet of an absolutely United Italy. Of course Napoleon

was too shrewd to be a mere knight errant; he wanted all
the glory of fighting for an idea, that is to say chivalry
and the help of the weak, but he demanded his price.
Nobody knows what really was settled at Plombières on
that point, but one supposes that the bargain was then
made that his price was the cession of Savoy and Nice
to France. Prince Napoleon[1], the Emperor's cousin, was
to marry Clothilde, Victor Emmanuel's fifteen-years-old
daughter.

During the latter months of 1858 the press of Piedmont
was full of talk about war. Volunteers were being enrolled,
Lombards were coming in from across the border, and
Garibaldi was making ready to lead them. Victor
Emmanuel's regular army was obviously making preparations and war was in the air. On January 1, 1859
Napoleon spoke coldly to the Austrian ambassador at
Paris, regretting that "our relations with your government
are not so good as in the past." It was obvious therefore
that the Austrians had timely warning, and indeed they
were hurrying up army corps from the more distant parts
of the Empire. It might be thought therefore that a strong
demonstration in arms would have overawed Victor
Emmanuel's government before the French armies had
time to cross the Alps or Apennines. Probably however
it was the attitude of Russia that made for delay; ever
since Francis Joseph had showed his ingratitude to Russia
at the outbreak of the Crimean War, the relations between
the two countries had been badly strained. Yet even so,

---

[1] Son of Jerome King of Westphalia, Napoleon I's youngest
brother. He was heir to Napoleon III before the Prince Imperial's
birth. He was very unpopular and a poor soldier, and was nicknamed "Plon plon." But he was a very good friend of Italy, and
often kept his cousin up to the mark as Italy's protector.

when an Austrian ultimatum, demanding the disbandment of the Piedmontese forces and volunteers, was sent in to Victor Emmanuel, and was rejected by Cavour in a spirit of defiance on April 27, the Commander-in-chief, Marshal Giulay, was unaccountably slow. Negotiations indeed were going on, and both England and Prussia were trying to mediate up to the last moment, suggesting a Congress of the five Great Powers, to which a representative of Sardinia should be admitted for a general disarmament to be discussed; yet to trust to such a Congress was childish.

On May 1 the main Austrian army about 100,000 strong was massed on the river Ticino and began to cross. Canrobert's army corps was only then crossing the Mont Cenis pass, and he did not reach Turin until May 2; Niel's corps came eight days later; four other corps came rather slowly by water to Genoa and crossed the Alps and concentrated around Alessandria on the plain to the south of the upper Po by about May 10. Yet Giulay wasted all this time in moving a very few miles west of the Ticino, though he had Turin for a time at his mercy. By the time that the French were concentrated he had lost the initiative[1]. There were now rather over 100,000 French ready for battle, the Piedmontese numbered from 50 to 60,000, and the problem for the Austrians was to guess where the main blow would fall. The strategy of Napoleon I in 1796 was to strike rapidly south of the Po where a spur of the Apennines left a narrow pass, and cross east of Pavia, thus

[1] Readiness to take the initiative is so clearly the right thing, as long as it is not confused with rashness, that it is wonderful to see how often the lessons of history are wasted. Radetzky twice concentrated and attacked successfully, in 1848 and 1849, yet Giulay failed to imitate him now, and Benedek failed in 1866. Napoleon failed badly in 1870, and the Turks in 1877. But it must be a readiness based on preparation.

turning the line of the Ticino and taking Milan in the rear;
whoever now planned Napoleon III's campaign certainly
knew how to frighten Giulay that the same would happen.
He concentrated to his left towards Pavia, and one
French army corps feinted in that direction to keep up the
illusion; then corps after corps pressed northwards from
Alessandria to cross the Po at Casale, whilst the Piedmontese pressed eastwards towards the Ticino and covered
the French advance.    MacMahon's corps, pushing furthest
to the north and then eastwards, crossed the Ticino high
up, on June 2.    By this time Giulay had withdrawn the
whole of his army behind the Ticino and some of it behind
the canal in the rear.    In fact the French army had carried
out a long flanking march straight across the enemy's
front, a most dangerous move, but one which when successful gives to the army which carries it out a winning position.
Napoleon I himself very rarely tried such a move, for he
almost always aimed at distracting the enemy on his
wings, and then breaking his centre.    The risk once taken,
the general who carries it out, if confident of the fighting
superiority of his army, can push on to battle with security.
On June 4 MacMahon stormed the village of Magenta and
by nightfall threatened the Austrian right rear, whilst the
Austrian right centre had been driven in and was in danger;
at the same time those French who were still south of the
Po pushed on down the river.    Outflanked on one wing
and threatened on the other, whilst higher up in the
mountains Garibaldi's volunteers were carrying everything
before them, and neutralising at least a whole Austrian
army corps, Giulay had no choice but to abandon Milan
and fall back.    Napoleon and Victor Emmanuel entered the
Lombard capital amongst scenes of tremendous enthusiasm
on June 7.

Of course the Austrian rallying-point was the Quadri-lateral. Strongly reinforced and commanded now by Francis Joseph in person, some 160,000 men held the line of the Mincio from Mantua to the Alps, but they recrossed to the westwards and held a position on the rising ground to the south-west of Lake Garda, which dominates the flat ground further south. The village of Solferino was the key of the position. Here Napoleon I had fought to beat off the Austrians who were trying to save Mantua from him in 1796. On June 24 the Piedmontese and four French corps, about 135,000 in all in line, assaulted and by nightfall had carried a position to turn the Austrian left. It was a fierce and not very scientific fight on a front of several miles. The Austrians retreated behind the Mincio in the midst of a terrific thunder-storm.

Then occurred the great surprise of the campaign. Just at the critical moment, when his uncle would have made a dash, regardless of his own losses, to throw his enemy into confusion and to isolate Mantua, Napoleon hesitated, then on July 11 he had an interview with Francis Joseph at Villafranca, on the Austrian side of the Mincio, close to the field of Custozza of bad omen.

An armistice was concluded between the two Emperors; Victor Emmanuel, they agreed, was to have Lombardy, and there was to be a vague sort of Italian Confederation to include both Austrian Venetia and the Pope. It was an almost farcical conclusion to Napoleon's grandiose schemes. There had been a bare two months' campaign after all his parade of taking arms in the cause of freedom and knight errantry. Partly no doubt he was frightened of the attitude of Prussia, who had begun to mobilise upon the Rhine; partly he was frightened of the spirit of enthusiasm and even of revolutionary fervour, which had

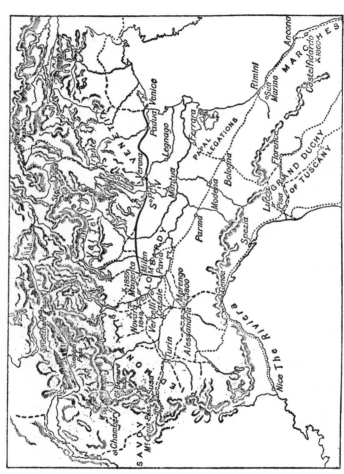

Map of North Italy to illustrate the Campaigns of 1848 and 1859; see p. 90.

———— railways laid down before 1848.
– – – railways laid down between 1848 and 1859.
········ railways laid down between 1859 and 1870.

Mont Cenis tunnel opened 1870.
St Gotthard tunnel opened 1882.
Simplon tunnel opened 1906.

been let loose by the Austrian defeats, and perhaps he felt that he had promised too much at the Plombières interview; a good Catholic could not afford to strengthen too much the Italian kingdom which was so anti-papal in character. He retired himself towards France the very next day, passing through Milan and Turin, where he saw nothing but cold looks. Within a month the French army quitted Italy. In November a formal peace was made between Victor Emmanuel and Francis Joseph, by which the cession of Lombardy was confirmed.

But the spirit of Italy was not going to be content with so tame a result. It was altogether a different spirit from that which had been evoked in 1848; failure then had been due to the rivalry between the republicans and the adherents of the House of Savoy; now there was no party but that of Savoy, for Victor Emmanuel had justified himself. The Austrian garrisons being withdrawn from Tuscany, Parma, Modena and the Papal Legations, because their services were required in the Quadrilateral, the entire population of these countries called out for annexation to Piedmont. Cavour suggested a *plébiscite*. Obviously annexation was not in Napoleon's programme, yet a *plébiscite* was his favourite method of obtaining a vote of confidence from the French nation, and he could hardly object to Cavour's policy, which took a leaf out of his own book. The voting was practically unanimous, and Victor Emmanuel accepted the decision. Tuscany was incorporated as an entire province; Parma and Modena and the Legations were grouped together as the province of Emilia, so called because the old Roman road, the Via Aemilia, ran through the country from the Adriatic in a north-westerly direction, passing through Bologna, Modena, Parma, and striking the Po at Piacenza. It was a decision fraught with danger of

offending both Napoleon and Francis Joseph. In all Europe
Victor Emmanuel had but one friend, namely Great Britain,
whose sympathies were warmly aroused, and where
Palmerston had returned to office in the very month when
Magenta and Solferino were fought. Palmerston and Lord
John Russell, who was his Foreign Secretary, were indeed
pledged to non-intervention; but to them this word was
double-edged, it implied not only that Great Britain wished
to keep out of foreign entanglements, but also that we
wanted fair play for Victor Emmanuel without the intervention of either France or Austria. However much
Napoleon himself or his officers might jeer at the military
weakness of our country, as exemplified according to their
ideas in the Crimean War, and however much he might
try to frighten our statesmen by making them think that
his next move would be against us—it was in 1859 that
the volunteer movement, started the previous year after
the Orsini plot, was widely extended as an answer to
French boastings—he knew perfectly well that he could
not dispense with our good-will. Francis Joseph dared not
move for fear of bringing Napoleon's armies back again,
and was not sure of Russia. Consequently the annexation
was a *fait accompli*.

Now the price had to be paid, and it was impossible for
Cavour to refuse it. A *plébiscite* was taken in Savoy and
the territory of Nice, for what was good for one district
was good for another. The Savoyards had really little in
common with the Piedmontese; they had previously been
incorporated with France for twenty-two years, they were
considerably attached to the Roman Church, so now they
voted in favour of transference to France. Though the
red cross of Savoy on a white shield still holds its place
in the middle of the national Italian flag, the tricolour of

red, white and green, the home of Italy's royal family has
now been French for some seventy years, and one never
hears that any Savoyard has regretted it.   Similarly the
people of Nice had no sentimental tie binding them irre-
vocably to Italy, except that their town was Garibaldi's
birthplace.   Modern Nice has been entirely rebuilt and has
been the resort of the devotees of fashion, so that it too has
not regretted the change.   Victor Emmanuel forced himself
to accept the one sacrifice, Garibaldi bitterly resented the
other.   On April 2, 1860, Parliament met at Turin, to which
came deputies from Lombardy and Tuscany and Emilia,
and the surrender of Savoy and Nice was accepted.

Ferdinand II of Naples, King Bomba, died in 1859.
Francis II succeeded, and refused to grant a Constitution
to either Naples or Sicily, though advised to do so by
Napoleon.   An insurrection broke out in Sicily early in
1860.   Garibaldi had done useful work in the campaign of
1859, though of course the stress of the fighting had fallen
chiefly upon the regular armies of Napoleon and Victor
Emmanuel.   Now was the chance for the hero and his
volunteers.   He collected at Genoa his celebrated Thousand
Red Shirts; he was planning what the adherents of
despotism would call a filibustering raid, but, after his
tremendous efforts in Rome in 1849, nothing seemed to be
impossible to such a man, and he knew how to get the utmost
results out of the devoted men ready to accompany him.
His Thousand were badly armed and two steamers were
sufficient to take them across from Genoa to Sicily.   Cavour
played a double game ready to disown or to profit by the
movement.   Persano, the Piedmontese admiral, was under
orders to stop Garibaldi if he put into a Sardinian port,
yet he let him pass and may be said to have shepherded
him.   The Thousand landed on the south-west coast of

Sicily, then, marching across the island towards Palermo, they charged and routed a Neapolitan force on the hills of Calatafimi.    Then they advanced on Palermo itself.    Some of the best regiments of the garrison being absent chasing Sicilian rebels, Garibaldi stormed his way in through the streets of the city; then when the returning Neapolitan regiments might have overwhelmed him yet, the King sent orders from Naples that the troops were to evacuate Palermo and retire to Messina May 30.    Garibaldi took the title of Dictator in the name of Victor Emmanuel.

King Francis, it is thought, should have taken the stronger course, defied Victor Emmanuel and Garibaldi alike, and appealed to Austria.    Actually he did the worst thing possible; he granted a Constitution and formed a ministry of Liberals, wishing to conciliate both France and Great Britain.    It is clear that Napoleon strongly disliked the union of South Italy to the already overgrown kingdom, as it seemed to him, of North Italy, and to pose as a Constitutionalist was to make a bid for French help.    But twice already had a King of Naples granted a Constitution when under the influence of fear, and twice had it been set aside when the cause for fear had departed.    There was no security that Francis would be more inclined to keep his word than his father or grandfather had been.    His one chance was to make proper use of his regular army, 100,000 strong in all and containing some good Swiss mercenary regiments.    Palermo had been lost ingloriously, but the Neapolitan force in Sicily was yet strong and, when concentrated on the straits, could easily prevent Garibaldi from reaching Messina and thence crossing to the mainland. But the Liberal policy was to stand on the defensive, a most fatal choice.    Garibaldi pushed eastwards and overcame a small force at Milazzo on July 20.    Meanwhile there were 15,000 men in Messina, only twenty miles distant, and Neapolitan warships were in the neighbourhood. Yet on July 28 a treaty was made between the Bourbon commander at Messina and one of Garibaldi's officers to stop hostilities.

All this summer reinforcements were being collected for Garibaldi in north Italy, partly by his own friends, partly by Cavour secretly. There were a few Hungarians amongst them, and one of his most useful officers was the Hungarian Türr; there were a few French and even English, but the great majority were Italians of the north, specially of Lombardy, which was in the throes of enthusiasm for his cause ever since the annexation to Piedmont a year before. The men were being shipped across in detachments to Sicily, and were much better equipped for battle than the original Thousand. Sicilians, excited enough in the liberation of their own country, were not keen to enlist under Garibaldi for an attack on Naples. The chief danger however was in the anxiety of Mazzini himself and Garibaldi's adherents in Piedmont to divert these reinforcements into an attack upon Rome. Garibaldi looked upon a conquest of Naples as merely a step to the ultimate conquest of Rome; this of course would have simply meant that Napoleon would openly interfere. Cavour therefore had a most anxious time. He allowed Persano to cover the passage of the reinforcements to Sicily, but spoke of preventing Garibaldi from crossing to the mainland; in the meanwhile he did his best to provoke a revolution in Naples in favour of Victor Emmanuel and annexation to North Italy. When this was found to be impossible, he laid his plans to encourage Garibaldi to cross whilst he mobilised the regular army, so as to get as much profit out of the Garibaldian revolution as possible, and then he would seize the country for Victor Emmanuel. For this purpose Persano was officially ordered to stop Garibaldi, but a secret letter from Victor Emmanuel himself authorised him to give his help. At the same time Sir James Lacaita, a Neapolitan exile and a naturalised Englishman, obtained a personal interview with Lord John Russell in London, to persuade him to abstain from making an agreement with the French to send the united fleets of England and France to the Straits of Messina. The action of Lord John was decisive. There was no *entente* between these two countries; Napoleon was not prepared to stop Garibaldi by himself, and confined himself to non-intervention as long as Rome itself was not threatened.

There was still the difficulty that the straits had to be crossed in the face of the Neapolitan navy. Garibaldi's main force was on the beach near Messina. On the night of August 18–19 some 3000 Garibaldians slipped across from Taormina to the tip of the toe of Italy where they were not expected. There were thousands of Neapolitan troops along the coast, but they were scattered in detachments. Reggio was surrendered. When the warships sailed southwards too late to stop Garibaldi or to save Reggio, another detachment crossed from Charybdis to Scylla in row-boats. One by one the disconnected fragments of the Neapolitan army retreated or surrendered, and Garibaldi's policy of disbanding the men so that they might go to their own homes had a great effect in encouraging others to surrender. Now he posted ahead on the great high-road towards Naples. Would Francis come out to offer pitched battle with the remainder of his regular army which still numbered close on 50,000 men ? Certainly he could have driven back the Garibaldians, as they came up detachment behind detachment in rear of their leader.

But on September 6 he departed from Naples to retire
to Capua, leaving a considerable proportion of troops to
garrison the castles of Naples.  Persano was already in the
bay with the navy of North Italy, and had been intriguing
with all his might to undermine the allegiance of the
Neapolitan sailors.  Thus Francis and his queen quitted
Naples alone in one small ship, and almost all his navy went
over to Persano.  On September 7 Garibaldi made his entry
into Naples.  His nearest brigade under the Hungarian Türr
was still two days' march behind him; the guns of the
castles of Naples were trained on his carriages as he came
into the city by way of the quays ; but he risked all to save
Naples from anarchy and possible mob-rule.  Then as his
army came straggling in from the south he rested them,
and finally pushed on against Capua.

The next move was Cavour's.  His difficulties were
always the same.  He must offend neither France nor
Austria; he must secure Garibaldi's conquests for Victor
Emmanuel, without either driving the Revolutionists or
Republicans to extremities, or tempting the Moderates to
repent of deserting Francis; above all he must stop
Garibaldi from attacking Rome.  Between the Kingdom of
North Italy and Naples still lay a compact block of papal
territory from sea to sea.  As yet only the Legations had
been taken over by Victor Emmanuel; there still remained
the Marches between the central Apennines and the
Adriatic, as well as the Patrimony, and across this papal
ground Cavour had to strike to join hands with Garibaldi.
Fortune favoured him, if indeed the ever-present jealousy
between France and Austria can be put down to fortune.
Napoleon's troops garrisoned Rome; Austrian troops,
though they were actually in the Pope's service, garrisoned
Ancona and the Marches; therefore Cavour might be able

to invade the Marches without offending Napoleon, and
indeed might even hope to have his protection so far as to
set him off against Francis Joseph, in case the latter threatened to send an Austrian army across the Mincio.  Moreover
Napoleon was a man of moods; he had his pro-Italian
moments, when he remembered his youthful enthusiasms,
and, although he posed as the good Roman Catholic and
defender of the Pope to conciliate the orthodox and respectable French, he knew perfectly well that the real French
Legitimists either detested him or at best only tolerated him.
A wave of Catholic feeling was sweeping through Europe.
Enthusiasts were enlisted for the cause of the Faith,
Germans, Irish, Belgians, Austrians, and French Legitimists,
forming an army of "Crusaders."  He knew that such men
were against him.  Their feelings were anti-Bonapartist,
and they were commanded by Lamoricière, once republican,
now Legitimist, but always anti-Bonapartist. Cavour might
fight against such extremists without offending Napoleon.
A decision had to be made quickly.  Prince Napoleon
counselled action and did his best to influence his imperial
cousin.  Cavour sent his confidential agents, the statesman
Farini and the general Cialdini, to a secret interview with
the Emperor at Chambéry in Savoy on August 28.  "Be
quick" was his advice.  Cavour was quick; September 7
he sent a demand to the Pope that the foreign mercenaries
must be disbanded ; September 11 some 33,000 regular
troops entered the Marches, and Persano's fleet was ordered
round to the Adriatic.

The bold plan indeed succeeded.  Whilst the remainder
of the army of North Italy waited in Lombardy in fear that
the Austrians would make this a *casus belli*—a fear which
was not realised—the invaders in two columns swept
southwards.  General Cialdini intercepted Lamoricière at

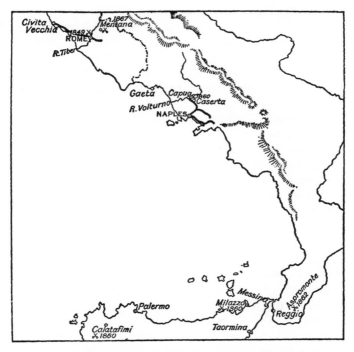

Map of South Italy and Sicily to illustrate Garibaldi's
Campaigns.

——— railway in 1860.

Castelfidardo on his way to Ancona, and overpowered him
on September 18 by superior numbers; on September 29,
Persano co-operating in a strong bombardment, he forced
Ancona to surrender.  Inland the other column, under
General Fanti, received the submission of city after city,
whose inhabitants had even to be restrained by the Piedmontese from taking vengeance on the Papalist garrisons.
The quickness that Napoleon had advised took the various
detachments by surprise, and whether Italians or foreigners
the Papalists were routed before they could be concentrated.

Meanwhile Garibaldi was facing the Neapolitan army
before Capua.  He was no longer enjoying a triumphal
procession, for the best and most determined of the Bourbon
troops were now in line under the eyes of their king, and
the peasants of this country were not revolutionists.  He
had to fight now; the magic of his name and the sympathy
of Constitutionalists and Liberals, which had done so much
for him up to his entry into Naples, would no longer make
his enemies to melt away before him.  Some 50,000
Neapolitans were in arms, based on Capua and Gaeta.
Garibaldi had up with him about 20,000 men, his old
volunteers and new levies, who had come straggling into
Naples in rear of him and were now concentrated around
Caserta and Old Capua; there was a Bourbon palace and
park at Caserta, connected with Naples by a short line of
railway, for even Bourbon despots were not backward in
benefiting by modern science for their convenience and
pleasure.  On October 1 the Neapolitans crossed the river
Volturno to assail Garibaldi's position, while a separate
corps made a wide detour to take him in the rear ; from
his head-quarters at Caserta he was able to put in his last
reserves to beat off the frontal attack ; the detached corps

split into two bodies in the mountains and lost touch, thus
spoiling what would have been a dangerous move. But
now Victor Emmanuel's army was approaching, and it was
a regular army with heavy guns and baggage for a pro-
longed campaign. Though repulsed by Garibaldi, the
Neapolitans were still strong enough to hold the line of
the Volturno against him, and fully strong enough to prevent
him from making that dash on Rome which was so dear
to his heart ; but their rear and left were threatened by
Victor Emmanuel.

The danger now was not that the Bourbon army might
yet upset anticipations by some great victory, but rather
that Victor Emmanuel and his soldiers might fall out with
Garibaldi and his volunteers. Enthusiasm had done all
that it could do. It was now the time for organisation
and discipline. That bitterness should be aroused was
only natural, for the enthusiast cannot but be heartsore
when the fruit of his labour is plucked by another, and
the volunteer is ever ready to take offence at the professional pride and coldness of the trained regular. On
October 26 Garibaldi, having ridden out the previous day,
met his King. "Saluto il primo Re d' Italia." His
patriotism stood the test; melancholy rather than bitter,
he understood that he had to go to the rear, and he went.
His bitterness was for Cavour, whom he violently attacked
later for having, by the cession of Nice, rendered him
homeless; yet in truth he was hardly fair, for the price of
Napoleon's aid in 1859 had to be paid, and it was Cavour's
cleverness that made Napoleon benevolently neutral throughout 1860.

The events of 1860 may indeed be described by an
application of the words used by Hallam concerning our
own Revolution in 1688: "it united the independent

character of a national act with the regularity and the
coercion of anarchy which belong to a military invasion."
The North Italian army, like William III's army, prevented
anarchy and put the finishing touch to the collapse of the
Bourbon régime.    After a day's bombardment Capua fell
on November 2, and with it 10,000 Neapolitans surrendered.
Another 17,000 fled over the frontier into the Papal States.
The remainder fell back, fighting well, into Gaeta, and did
not surrender till the February of 1861.

On November 7 Victor Emmanuel made his state entry
into Naples with Garibaldi in the same carriage.    Already
the *plébiscite*, which the Italians were by this time
accustomed to expect, had been taken in the Kingdom of
Naples, in Sicily, and in the Marches; and the customary
"yes" had been given by enormous, though it may be
intimidated, majorities.    On November 8 was signed "the
act of annexation."    Garibaldi retired at once to his
cottage on Caprera[1].    The new government had much work
before it, the reign of law and order to introduce, and
brigandage to suppress, for Sicilians in particular like no
law at all, and all along the southern Apennines there were
thousands of disbanded soldiers and of sham volunteers,
ex-servants of the Bourbon and mere lovers of mischief,
who put on red shirts as an excuse to gratify their instincts.
The strongest admirer of Garibaldi[2] admits that the suddenness of his conquests upset calculations, that as "Dictator"
he was not wise in his choice of men, that many professed
to be liberationists who were only selfish and covetous, all
of which simply means that anarchy had to be coerced and

---

[1] A little island off the north coast of Sardinia, which Garibaldi
had bought.

[2] Mr G. M. Trevelyan, Macaulay's grand-nephew.    His references
to our English Revolution of 1688 are most apt.

Victor Emmanuel's government alone could do this. The same writer suggests that the officers of the regular army influenced the King, who otherwise could have done much by tact and courtesy to make up to Garibaldi for the sad necessity of getting him for a time out of the way. Gratitude is impossible in history if it implies that the real advantage of a country must be disregarded for its sake, but it may be possible to be tactful whilst showing ingratitude. As to whether North Italy would have had a happier history between 1860 and 1914 if Naples and Sicily had not been annexed, it would be rash for an outsider to lay down the law. Certainly the complaint of Piedmont and Lombardy in recent years has been that they, the richer and industrial provinces, have been too heavily taxed in order to support the clever lawyers and professional politicians of Naples and Sicily, who outvote them in Parliament and secure all the best places for themselves. But in 1860 they could not be deaf to the call of the south, for history has certainly made up its mind that the Bourbon government was too utterly brutal and uncivilised to be endured.

Mr Trevelyan also points out to us very strongly how Lord John Russell deserves a greater credit for resolution and practical assistance to the Italians than he has usually received. Palmerston left to himself would have carried out very literally the doctrine of non-intervention, that is to say, would have stood aside whatever the Emperor of Austria might have decided to do. Lord John very definitely put it before the autocrats of the three Great Powers, when they met at Warsaw, that they too should observe the policy of non-intervention, that "the Italians are the best judges of their own interests." He adds that when a few years later Lord John was staying at San Remo, he found portraits in the house of four great men, Mazzini, Cavour, Garibaldi, and himself. The Italians evidently did not think that the Foreign Secretary of Great Britain had given them only a cheap sympathy, but had, to use a homely phrase, kept the ring to see that Italy had fair play. Odo Russell, the ambassador of Great Britain at the papal court, who was afterwards better known as Lord Ampthill, wrote to his uncle December 1860, that this was "a great and real national movement, which will at last be crowned with perfect success, notwithstanding the legion of enemies Italy still counts in Europe." Lord John also wrote at an earlier day, "I wish to put in a caveat against the indiscriminate use of the words revolution and revolutionary. A revolution may be the greatest of calamities; it may be the highest of blessings." He pointed to the revolutions in England and in France respectively, to show that it is not necessary to imagine that a revolution "from government maintained by torture to a free regular government" is *per se* wicked. *Punch's* comment was "Well said, Johnny Russell." Garibaldi himself, saying goodbye to the British admiral before he departed for Caprera, thanked him, England, Her Majesty's Government, and above all Lord John, for their sympathies for Italy. Perhaps, also, even Napoleon deserves some little credit, however much he wavered and threatened; at least he confined himself to a defence of Rome and the Patrimony, being rather anxious not to offend public opinion in France than ill-disposed towards Victor Emmanuel.

The Parliament which met at Turin in March 1861 represented an Italy of 22,000,000 inhabitants. By its vote Victor Emmanuel definitely took the title of King of Italy; in 1860 he had struck coins as "Re Eletto." Cavour openly said that he looked upon Rome as the natural capital of Italy, yet for the time he was unwilling to take the risk of defying Napoleon. Next June he died. In 1862 Garibaldi was once more on the war-path. Starting in Sicily he proclaimed a new crusade for the possession of Rome. It may be that Napoleon, freely abused by the papal party for his consent to the dismemberment of the Legations and the Marches, wavered for a moment as if he would no longer defend Rome. But when Garibaldi crossed the straits he was confronted by royal Italian troops; he refused to let his men fire upon them, but was himself wounded and taken prisoner. He was imprisoned for a short time at Spezia and once more allowed to retire to Caprera. Later, Napoleon withdrew his troops from Rome on the understanding that no further attempt would be made. Garibaldi did however make one more effort in 1867, and again Napoleon sent a French army which routed his volunteers at Mentana near Rome; on this occasion General Failly bitterly offended Italians by his scornful jeers, when he remarked on the superiority of the breech-loading chassepots.

It may seem strange that the Great Power which ultimately consummated the Union of Italy was Prussia. In that decade Prussia was winning her way to the supremacy as against both Austria and France, so that Italy could not but profit thereby. The humiliation of Austria in 1866 gave Venetia to Victor Emmanuel; the humiliation of France in 1870 caused the French troops to be finally withdrawn, and Victor Emmanuel's men marched into Rome September 20, 1870. Therefore the balance of power compelled Italy to be the ally of Prussia. She was forced into the Triple Alliance at a time when her relations with France were much strained, and when Germany required the assistance of the Italian navy in the Mediterranean;

German aggressiveness and German peaceful invasion of
Italy by merchants and manufacturers, seizing a large part
of Italian trade and arousing Italian hatred of the ill-
mannered Tedeschi, prevented Victor Emmanuel III from
supporting William in 1914. The charge of ingratitude
was hurled against Italy as a matter of course, although
Bismarck himself had once openly said that gratitude counts
for nothing in politics, and the whole course of Prussian
history proves it.

A portion of the United States.

# CHAPTER VI

## NAPOLEON III's SECOND DECADE

Napoleon was still the chief figure of Europe throughout the sixties. Europe indeed was accustomed to his waverings and trusted him very little. Palmerston, in particular, up to his death in 1865, would in all probability have taken a course quite different from that which he actually took, if he had been quite sure of the hearty co-operation of France on the question of either Poland or Schleswig Holstein; also, had the Entente Cordiale endured, it is just possible that a Franco-British interference would have profoundly influenced the Civil War in the United States. After Palmerston's death, neither Disraeli nor Gladstone had any wish to interfere in European politics, and Napoleon had to pursue a course alone, or when British influence was exerted at all it was exerted against him. In these years it was partly what he did, and partly what he was suspected of wishing to do, that left him without an ally in Europe. If we are to particularise any one scheme which damaged him more than any other, it is his Mexican policy.

In 1860 Great Britain was still engaged in a Chinese War, which had indeed broken out in 1857, but had not been pressed to a conclusion because of the Sepoy Mutiny. The French and British were united to punish China for the proclamation of a Chinese official, by which he offered rewards for the heads of Europeans. In 1859 the allied squadrons were repulsed from the Taku forts at the mouth of the Peiho river; in 1860 a second expedition captured the forts, and proceeded to attack Pekin, where the summer palace was taken and looted. For many years to come the behaviour of the Chinese towards Europeans was much better. In this year Napoleon sent an expedition to Syria, where in the district of Mount Lebanon Christian Maronites were persecuted, and many of them massacred by Mohammedans; when order was restored there was no excuse to keep French soldiers there any longer, and they were withdrawn.

In 1861 the most important question in Europe was the emancipation of the serfs in Russia by the Imperial Ukase of February 1861, which is the chief title to honour of the Tsar Alexander II. On the Imperial domains, serfs were not only freed but were made absolute proprietors of their plots of land. On other estates a part of the land remained to the noble owners, part was given to the peasants on certain terms, indemnity being gradually paid to the nobles on money advanced by Imperial banks. Emancipation in itself does not of course mean absolute prosperity; Russian peasants might be free, but free to starve; the money-lender, we have been told, has been the great curse of the small holders in such a country, who are dependent upon the produce of their small farms, who are cut off from their neighbours by enormous stretches of flat and therefore depressing plains, and have not everywhere a ready market; moreover a system was established by which lands were re-divided every year amongst the inhabitants of each village, so that permanent improvement of the farms was almost impossible. Yet troubles could not but happen when the serfdom of many centuries was abolished.

The general tendency of succeeding years was to remedy mistakes, and at least personal freedom was assured by Alexander's great act, by which he was hailed as "Liberator." He proceeded to put local government into the hands of Zemstvos, councils elected by the inhabitants of each district. He introduced jury trial. But he considered that Russia was not then ripe for parliamentary government. The growth of anarchy and especially the rise of the Nihilists at the end of his reign culminated in the murder of the "Liberator" by a bomb in 1881.

In 1863 there was a new Polish rising, which took the form of isolated attacks upon Russian garrisons, and bitter guerilla warfare raged. The insurgents never occupied Warsaw and set up no national government. Even a liberal Emperor was forced to suppress the Poles with severity. He made a distinction between nobles and peasants, the bitterest enemies of Russia being the nobles who a century earlier had been absolute masters of the land, and whose pride resented their treatment by Russians as an inferior class. Lands of rebel nobles were made over to the peasants who betrayed or attacked them. Of course the military superiority of the Russians was soon seen, and the rebellion collapsed. Local government and local customs were abolished and the country was henceforth governed directly from Petrograd. The natural protectors of Poland would have been France and Britain if they had been united; but they were by no means united at this date, and whatever remonstrances they made to the Tsar only served to irritate him. In the meanwhile the new King of Prussia, William I, prevented Polish refugees from crossing into his country; it was clearly to his advantage to put Russia under an obligation to him, in view of the struggle which he foresaw was coming.

Meanwhile events of enormous importance were taking place across the Atlantic, and had their cause in the development of the United States. We have to go back to the 18th century to understand them. The critical year is 1763, when by the Treaty of Paris at the close of the Seven Years' War the French lost all their territory east of the Mississippi, leaving an immense field for Anglo-Saxon expansion. The remnant of Louisiana west of the river was handed over to Spain, who in turn handed over Florida to the British. The War of Independence left the United States free to expand and settle questions as to boundaries with both France and Spain. In 1800 by a secret treaty Spain transferred Louisiana once more to France; in 1803 Napoleon I sold it to the United States for 15 million dollars; in 1812 it was included in the Union as a State. Shortly afterwards Mississippi and Alabama became States. Not only now was the control of the cotton crop almost entirely, and the control of the tobacco crop very largely, in American hands, which meant that the slave question would soon become more acute, but also men of Latin blood were in the Union with Anglo-Saxons[1]. The dominant race would soon be stretching forward along the curve of the gulf further west. In the meantime the "building up of the Middle West" was proceeding very rapidly. Kentucky entered into the Union in 1792, Tennessee in 1796, Ohio in 1803, Indiana 1816, Illinois 1818, and Missouri 1821; the chief factor here was the inability of the Eastern States to compete with Great Britain in manufacture, so that

---

[1] Both "Anglo-Saxon" and "Latin" are unsatisfactory terms, but have come to be accepted. "Anglo-Saxon" covers the lands occupied by and the civilisation represented by both the British and the Americans of the United States. "Latin" covers the Spanish and Portuguese lands of Central and Southern America.

emigrants from the Old World and from the original States alike flocked towards the great river. The problem of the future was that of slavery, and mere temporary compromises could not last. In 1821 there were twelve slave-owning and twelve free States, but the last formed, Missouri, which was carved out of the indefinitely wide Louisiana purchase and at the date of the purchase was practically vacant, was admitted as a slave State. Would then other western lands be free soil or slave soil as the newer waves of emigrants crossed the Mississippi, the future Kansas or Arkansas for instance?

The Monroe doctrine was laid before Congress by President Monroe in December 1823; he had negotiated the Louisiana purchase twenty years earlier. The main points were these: "With the existing colonies or dependencies of any European power we have not interfered, and shall not interfere. But with the governments who have declared their independence and maintained it"—*i.e.* Spain's revolted colonies—"we could not view any interposition by any European Power.... Our policy in regard to Europe is to consider the government *de facto* as the legitimate government for us." The doctrine is quite simple and straightforward. But it says nothing of what would happen if one of the governments concerned, Mexico for instance, were to repudiate its debts to Europeans, or offer violence to the persons of Europeans. Would then an European Power have the right to demand redress by force, or would the United States demand it for that Power, acting as schoolmaster to punish, as well as to defend, the schoolboy Latin state? Surely there would be a moral obligation on the United States to compel the Latins to act with some regard to the decencies of civilisation, if they should consider European compulsion to be an unfriendly act. No civilised

country should allow pandemonium to flourish next door.
Then comes in the question of profit. No civilised community can afford to play the schoolmaster for the benefit
of others alone without profit to itself. Now the newly
freed Latin republics, like schoolboys of whom too much
has been expected, disappointed their early admirers.
They were too democratic in form, and the party in power
used democratic privileges for personal gain; hence arose
civil wars, dictatorships, revolts, etc. Mexico chiefly
concerns us, being nearest to the United States, having
a population in which the proportion of Indian blood to
Spanish blood is very high—this is the real crux of the
position in every Latin-American state, but in none is the
Indian proportion so high as in Mexico—and even to-day
showing a disposition for uncivilised method and a disregard
for paying just debts.

The old Spanish province of Texas was governed
separately from Mexico. In 1824 it formed part of the
new state of Mexico, and had its grievance in that it
depended on slavery and Mexico abolished slavery in
1829. It welcomed emigrants from the United States, for it
was a land of rich possibilities, and Mexico excluded them.
It rebelled in 1836, and successfully asserted its independence, being acknowledged by the United States and France
and England. Annexation to the United States was inevitable. But delay was caused as annexation brought up the
question of slavery. The Republican party, known as
such in 1856 but previously styled Whigs, was based on
the rights of the Union as the *res publica* to legislate for
the whole community over the heads of the individual
States; the Democratic party insisted on the right of
each State to regulate its own concerns and especially
its own property, and slaves were included in property.

Compromise after compromise was made, but the question always cropped up again. In 1821 it was settled that Missouri should be a slave-owning State, but that its southern boundary 36° 30′ should be henceforward the limit. Now Texas was slave-owning, and was admitted into the Union in 1845 on the condition that 36° 30′ should remain. War with Mexico resulted. The Americans can certainly boast that their campaign was well planned, and well executed, especially when the smallness of their regular army is taken into consideration. Whilst a small force held the frontier of Texas, the main attack under General Winfield Scott landed from the Gulf and captured Vera Cruz, March 1847; in May Puebla was taken, and in September the city of Mexico; when it is added that Mexico is 260 miles from Vera Cruz, that the enemy had vast numbers of guerillas as well as a regular army of between 20,000 and 30,000 men, whilst the number of the Americans who finally stormed the capital did not amount to 7000, the skill of Scott and his officers may be faintly appreciated; yet in the United States the profession of regular soldiering has always been despised. Meanwhile other troops occupied New Mexico and California. In 1848 by treaty New Mexico and Upper California were ceded, a vast amount of territory which was afterwards apportioned into States as it was gradually peopled by immigrants. In 1850 Mr Henry Clay arranged a compromise as regards slavery, but the history of the next ten years is one long tale of bitter squabbling on the interpretation of the compromise. Soon the nature of the controversy changed. As far back as 1831 the *Liberator* had been founded by William Lloyd Garrison, demanding total abolition, and in 1833 was established the American Anti-Slavery Society; this being the year in which the

British Parliament finally carried abolition throughout our own Empire. In 1848 gold was discovered in California, and the gold rush began, which, rather than the fact of conquest from Mexico, led to the rapid peopling of the new country, with the ultimate result that the importance of the old Eastern States was balanced by a new Far West.

In 1859 John Brown made his celebrated raid across the river Potomac into Virginia to raise a slave insurrection, after which he was hanged by the authorities of Virginia. The election of Abraham Lincoln to be President, November 1860, was the final signal for war. Even now the issue at stake was not slavery itself, hardly even the right of slave-owners to carry their slaves with them when they migrated. It was a question, as Burke so strongly insisted, when the troubles were brewing which caused the War of Independence in 1775, of "Temper and Character." The slave owners were aroused to passion by the extravagant attacks upon them and accusations of horrible cruelty, such as were read in *Uncle Tom's Cabin*, published in 1852. Time had greatly modified the iniquity of the system ; the slaves, it was passionately asserted, were happy and merry, well fed and well cared for, as the devotion of thousands of them to their masters when once the war began certainly seems to prove. It was the jealousy of the free States, the Puritan N.E., where manufacture and trade had no need of the negro, which was the cause of the exaggerated outcry against the planters, who could not raise their tobacco, their cotton, and sugar, without black labour; and yet the slave-owning south had been the home of the aristocracy as represented by Washington himself, Lee, Hamilton, and Monroe, the greatest leaders, without whom there would have been no United States. But a new type of politician was arising, who had none of the old high ideals, to whom politics

were merely a game, and abolition an insincere cry.   On
the other hand, the character of Abraham Lincoln is a
sufficient answer to the insinuation of mere jealousy and
insincerity.    The new Republicanism was not represented
only by Puritan Massachusetts and trading New York;
the newer farming States, Ohio, Indiana, Illinois, Michigan,
Iowa, Wisconsin, produced a new type of men, who were
even then laying the foundations of the mighty industries,
corn-growing and stock-breeding, which are the foundations
of modern America; such men based their life on free
labour, and had no respect for the past services and historic
traditions of Virginia.   Yet again we have to make a strong
distinction between two classes of Virginians; the old
planters of the hot lowlands, the traditional aristocracy as
represented by the great hero of the coming war, General
Robert E. Lee, "Marse Robert " as he was affectionately
called ; and the small free farmers of the Shenandoah Valley
and the western Blue Mountains, who had either no or few
slaves, men reared in a bracing climate, and descended from
old Irish or Scottish families from Ulster, whose sturdy
sense of independence resented dictation from New York,
as represented by that ideal hero of the Havelock and
Gordon type, Thomas "Stonewall" Jackson. To both classes
the Secession was a movement dictated by devotion to the
ideas of State liberty under the terms of the Declaration of
Independence.

In March 1861 was constituted the government of the
Confederate States[1]. At first only the seven Cotton and

[1] In contrast to "Confederates" the Northerners, holding for the
Union, are termed "Federals." Nicknames were "Rebs" and
"Yanks." Their uniforms were grey and blue. The Southerners
sang "Look away down South to Dixie" (see the Mason-Dixon line
in the map, p. 148); the Northerners sang "John Brown's body."

Gulf States were represented; Virginia, N. Carolina,
Tennessee, and Arkansas, joined in when Lincoln called for
the service of militia and volunteers.    Jefferson Davis was
their first and only President.    Fighting first began in
S. Carolina, where the Confederates attacked Fort Sumter
and captured it on April 13.    The area of the war was
very great, practically the great square of the south-
eastern States, between the coast and the Mississippi, of
which the diagonal, from New Orleans to the northern point
of Virginia at Harper's Ferry, is close on 1000 miles.    The
vastness of the struggle may also be estimated by the
official figures available for the North alone; in 1861 Lincoln
raised an army of 150,000 men and a navy of 25,000;
in January 1863 he had 900,000 under arms, and in May
1865 he had 1,500,000; the total raised was about 2,700,000.
At the end of the war there were 671 ships, with 4717 guns
and 51,500 seamen.    There was a considerable number of
competent officers trained at West Point and some of them
had served in the Mexican War, but not nearly enough to
train the vast numbers of raw recruits, who had very
little sense of discipline, and who were inclined towards
both desertion and malingering to a degree which one
suspects from the various hints was far more common than
official accounts allow.    The habitual American contempt
for the military profession was bitterly punished by the
awful loss of life amongst the hastily raised and poorly
officered armies of the first few years.    Where, therefore,
but little military skill and organisation were forthcoming,
everything depended on devotion to the cause.    The dash
and impetuosity of the devoted Virginians, cleverly
directed by the skill of the few great soldiers such as Lee
and Jackson, at first carried the day; then gradually the
tenacity of the North, the readiness of the prairie farmers

to enlist in great numbers, the organising power of Lincoln's officials, and Grant's discipline and steadiness, prevailed in the long run, and numbers plus devotion and skill wore down devotion and skill alone.

Two sources of strength the North always had, command of the sea and manufacturing superiority. The U.S. navy was manned from the north-east and was solid for the Union; throughout the four years it blockaded the Confederate ports, stopped the export of cotton and tobacco and the import of munitions from Europe, and directly contributed to the first and definite Northern success, namely the conquest of the line of the Mississippi. Meanwhile all the coal and iron of the United States at that date was in the North. Rifles, heavy artillery, munitions, ironclads, could be turned out in a steady and unending stream. Here again we see that the problem of success for the South depended upon time; if their armies in Virginia could at once win such victories as would force peace, then their poverty in ships and material would matter little; but when the Northern superiority in these, as well as in numbers, was fully developed, there could be but one end. It was owing to this that the attitude of Britain and France was so important. If the two *entente* Powers combined to help the Confederates, they would supply just the things that were needed, munitions and manufactured goods, release the bales of cotton and tobacco, and, if not overpower, at least contest the Northern control of the sea. Public opinion here was mostly in favour of the South. This was but natural, for the United States had won independence by fighting for self-government, the right to settle both taxation and trade for their own benefit, and not for that of the mother country; even so the South had seceded to control their own domestic

concerns as against a dictatorial Union. Also there was
a prevalent feeling that the Southerners were a more gallant
and more gentlemanly race[1], less given to jeering at the
Britishers or "tail-twisting," less loud and self-assertive.
There can be little doubt that a feeling of this kind existed,
and that the Northerners resented it very bitterly. On the
other hand they did not take enough into account that
very many British, even if a minority, still sympathised
with them on the main question of slavery. On one occasion a Northern warship took two Southern ambassadors
off a British ship and held them as prisoners. A loud cry
was raised, and Palmerston took steps which threatened
war; the ambassadors came from a *de facto* independent
government, and the Monroe doctrine recognised *de facto*
governments, so that the arguments of the Americans were
turned against themselves. Lincoln gave way, somewhat
grudgingly, and released them; the Northern press asserted
that he did so for justice' sake, and not because "John
Bull" blustered. Another cause of bitterness was that
ships were built in England, the *Alabama* in particular,
which were armed and converted into privateers, and did
much damage to Northern commerce. Smuggling of arms
and munitions from the West Indies into the blockaded
Southern ports was common, but the capture of smugglers
and confiscation of contraband rested with the Northern
cruisers, and could not give rise to international incidents.
Very luckily war did not result from bad temper on each
side. Yet the bitter taste remained for many years.
One doubts if Napoleon ever seriously thought of entering
into the war; he took advantage to enter upon his Mexican

[1] This comes out strongly in Disraeli's *Lothair*, where one of his
characters speaks of a Virginian as a gentleman fit to associate even
with a duke.

scheme, which will be discussed later on; yet, if he had foreseen the end, it would have been better by far for him to have first fought and weakened the North, rather than to have sent his troops to Mexico under cover of the Civil War, only to withdraw them when the North was triumphant.

The Potomac, which divides Maryland from Virginia, was also the eastern dividing line between the North and the South. Washington, the capital of the Union, lying in the "district" of Columbia which is a piece of Maryland cut off, is on the Potomac at a distance of just 100 miles from Richmond, the Confederate capital. Such armies as could be immediately equipped met in a preliminary campaign in 1861 at Bull Run in Virginia, 45 miles from Washington. As in the preliminary battle at Edgehill in our own Civil War, not much science was shown, except by Jackson, whose Virginian brigade "stood like a stone wall." Early in 1862 a much wider campaign was planned; McClellan developed a main attack, by means of the superior sea power of the North, upon the promontories which jut out into Chesapeake Bay between the estuaries of the Potomac, York, and James rivers; a subsidiary attack was directed up the Shenandoah Valley, from which a powerful flank attack could be made upon Richmond on the other side. McClellan was a good organiser of partially trained troops, and by no means a bad strategist; he pushed upstream to within a few miles of Richmond, where Lee stood at bay. But on the other side Jackson cleared the valley by rapid marches which disconcerted the larger but ill-combined forces opposed to him, then came down to form up on Lee's left flank. Lee and Jackson united pushed McClellan down the peninsula in a six days' fight, June 26 to July 1, themselves losing heavily but forcing the evacuation of the peninsula. A second invasion of Virginia in force, this time by an advance straight down the centre of the State, was foiled in a still more remarkable manner; Jackson made a wonderful flank march, seized the Northerners' base and all their supplies, compelled Pope to retreat, and with Lee's main army advancing won a great victory at the second battle of Bull Run, August 29 and 30. Now came a Confederate counter-attack into Maryland, which resulted in Lee's repulse by McClellan's reorganised and numerically superior army at Antietam, September 17. A third invasion of central Virginia, under Burnside, was repulsed at Fredericksburg on December 13; a fourth, under Hooker, was badly defeated in the district of the "Wilderness" at Chancellorsville, May 2 and 3, 1863, when Jackson made another wonderful flank march to the Northerners' rear, but he was killed at the critical moment. In all these battles the same features are seen; both Presidents interfered too much with the plans of their generals, but Lincoln was the worse offender[1] as he rang the changes and tried one general after another; Lee's strategy was much superior, but the Confederates were always out-numbered, lost heavily in both attack and counter-attack, were too weak in artillery, and never had a sufficient reserve to follow up a success, so that no crushing victory, no Jena or Sedan, resulted. The dash of the Virginians, Carolinans, Texans, and others, was undoubted; their moral was undoubted; Jackson's demands on his men were nobly answered; but the finishing touch was just not added.

Now President Davis was at fault in attempting to raise too many armies to hold too many lines, and did not give a wide general power to Lee to superintend the whole war. The Confederate strength was "nibbled away" for lack of concentration. Too far advanced a position was held in

---

[1] In a recent book General Colin Ballard asserts that Lincoln was the best strategist of the war.

Kentucky and Tennessee to contest the lines of the various tributaries of the Mississippi. The Northerners had a strong force of gunboats to support them, and chiefly by its help and their superior numbers they had several successes, winning the line of the Tennessee river and of the middle Mississippi in the course of 1862. One of their subordinate generals, Ulysses Grant, was now marked out as their coming man.

But the greatest of the Northern successes were at sea, on the one side in the mouth of the Mississippi, on the other in Chesapeake Bay. Not only the entire United States navy was available, but their manufacturing resources and skill turned out gunboats and monitors and battleships to give them an overwhelming superiority. Admiral Farragut, with some wooden ships, gunboats, and a powerful flotilla of schooners each carrying a 13-inch mortar, forced the defences of the Mississippi; he overpowered the river forts and a Confederate squadron, which included some hastily devised ironclad rams, and then he had New Orleans at his mercy. The great city, 110 miles from the river's mouth, the workshop and rallying point of the Confederates in the West, was occupied on May 1, 1862. Then Baton Rouge fell, and only Vicksburg remained to separate Farragut from the victorious Grant upstream. On the other side some naval developments were carried out which had profound influence on the ship-building of the world. The Confederates had the hulk of a United States frigate which they cut down nearly to the water-line; on it they placed a wooden casemate strengthened by 4-inch plates of iron, and they named her the *Merrimac*; and she rammed one Northern warship, and forced on shore and sank another, March 8, 1862. That same night arrived from New York the *Monitor*, 172 feet long, 1000 tons displacement, 10½ feet draught, carrying two 11-inch muzzle-loading guns in a solid iron turret; she had been designed by Ericsson, a Swede of New York  Her weak points were that she could not live in a rough sea—ultimately she sank when water poured in at a leak where the turret revolved—and that her guns confined in the turret were too short, and therefore too weak to stand a heavy charge of powder.    But for the time she neutralised the *Merrimac*, though unable to sink her.    In course of time Ericsson turned out a whole fleet of improved monitors for coast action, known as the "mosquito fleet," and these bombarded unsuccessfully the forts of Charleston in 1863.    The actual services of the monitors in this war, though considerable, were after all not so important as the tremendous impetus which they gave to the new construction in Britain and France.

In 1863, after his great success at Chancellorsville in May, though terribly crippled by the loss of Jackson, Lee invaded Maryland for the second time and penetrated into Pennsylvania.    There he was repulsed at the very critical battle of Gettysburg, July 1–3.    It was his last offensive operation.    If he had succeeded it is difficult to see what permanent gain he would have secured; he was too weak to occupy any part of the North, and he could but have put off the evil day for a little time by forcing the withdrawal of Northern troops from elsewhere.    He would not have saved the line of the Mississippi, for on the very next day, July 4, Grant received the surrender of Vicksburg.    The complete success of the Federals in the West was now so complete that, holding the Mississippi, they could press in on the Confederates in Tennessee and so link up their attacks.    Some very fierce fighting in eastern Tennessee was to a certain extent in the Confederates' favour, but it

brought Grant and Sherman across from the Mississippi,
and then the third decisive victory of the year was won by
Northerners at Chattanooga.

The year 1864 saw new arrangements. Grant was made
General-in-chief and took over the direction of the main
army in Virginia; he gained no success over Lee, but
reduced him to the defensive. In the meanwhile Sherman
took command in Tennessee, and thence invaded Georgia,
first occupying Atlanta and then pushing through to the
sea at Savannah. Part of Sherman's army, left behind
in Tennessee under Thomas, won a crushing victory at
Nashville. Thus when 1865 opened the end was almost
reached. Sherman swept northwards through the Carolinas
towards Lee's rear, Charleston being occupied in February.
Lee, surrounded on all sides, abandoned Richmond, and
capitulated with his last force of only 28,000 men at
Appomattox Court House on April 9. In the last two years
since the double disasters at Gettysburg and Vicksburg
the resistance of the Confederates was being gradually
and relentlessly worn down. Their coasts blockaded, their
supplies running short, their recruiting ground across the
Mississippi cut off, their lands systematically ravaged, they
could only fight at bay. Yet up to the very last Lee held
the capital.

The story returns to Mexico. Since the war of 1847–48
the state of this country seemed to go from bad to worse.
The American army was withdrawn, but the Mexicans
could not govern themselves. Towards the end of the
fifties the parties were clerical and anti-clerical, headed
respectively by Miramon and Juarez. In 1861 Juarez, an
Indian, won the day; he attacked the religious houses, and
drove many Catholics into exile, who naturally appealed
for aid to Napoleon and were patronised by his Spanish

wife Eugénie; money debts incurred by Miramon were, of course, repudiated, and unluckily one of the chief creditors was Morny himself. It can be easily imagined that Napoleon was ready enough to interfere, persuaded by Eugénie of the sacredness of a crusade to repatriate distressed Catholics, and egged on by Morny, who wanted to get his money back. Various European merchants suffered by the troubles in Mexico, so that the British and Spanish governments were ready to contribute to a joint expedition in the winter 1861–62; the United States were too distracted to prevent such interference, and in any case the Monroe doctrine implies that the United States should keep Latin America in the path of civilisation, failing which European nations have a clear right to act. A joint British, French, and Spanish fleet appeared off Vera Cruz. Juarez gave such satisfaction as pacified the British and Spanish, but refused to pay Miramon's debts for the benefit of Morny and other Frenchmen. So a French expeditionary force was landed.

In 1863 the French captured Puebla and Mexico, but Juarez continued to carry on guerilla tactics. An Assembly of the clerical party offered the crown to Maximilian, brother of Francis Joseph, and therefore a Hapsburg and akin to the old dynasty of Spain. Persuaded by Napoleon and promised a regular French army for at least five years, Maximilian accepted and was crowned as Emperor of Mexico. He was a mild and cultured man. He had been the only Hapsburg that the Italians of Lombardy had not bitterly hated. He had an idea that a policy of material progress would reconcile the Mexicans to civilisation and the restoration of Catholics, when they saw the advantage of railways and had a gay court in their capital. On the contrary, Juarez waged his guerilla warfare to the knife;

the Americans in 1847-48, on capturing Mexico, demanded
the cession of land, Texas and California, and then departed;
the French seemed to have come to stay. Juarez was
wearing them out; Bazaine, the French general, who had
risen from the ranks, had no tact and retaliated by executing
prisoners, and he was credited with a wish to become
himself Emperor. Napoleon was probably in any case tired
of his adventure, especially as it locked up thousands of
French soldiers, who would be much more valuable to him
in Europe in those critical days. At any rate when the
United States government, their war finished, ordered him
to withdraw his men, he had no choice but to obey. For
the only time in their history they were in a position to
enforce their demands; if need were, Grant could have
marched many hundred thousands of war-hardened Federals
over the frontier, and Farragut could have concentrated a
large fleet against Vera Cruz. Thus, profoundly humiliated,
the French evacuated Mexico in 1867. Maximilian was at
once caught and shot by Juarez. Napoleon's crusade ended
in utter failure. Yet, had the North come out less powerful
from the Civil War, had a better man than Bazaine been in
command and a less grasping man than Morny possessed
Napoleon's ear, the adventure might have been as glorious
as was hoped. We must never forget that history judges
Napoleon and Bazaine by the awful catastrophe of 1870,
and therefore cannot but judge unfairly. Mexico, restored
to civilisation at last by the strong dictator Diaz, has in our
own days fallen off from the ways of decency and is the
scene once more of absurd faction fights, which the United
States have not had the courage to stop as their duty to
civilisation demands. So one regrets that the French did
not remain, but with more noble ambition.

The after-results of the American war affected England

also.  A distinctly hostile feeling lasted for many years, being partly due to sharp criticisms of Yankee methods and manners in our press.  A definite demand was made for compensation for the ravages of the *Alabama* and other privateers on Federal commerce.  These ships were built in English yards, and being warned of their destination our government could have stopped them from leaving our coasts; yet when vast quantities of munitions were made in the States and sold to us in 1914–17, how can a modern American justify to-day the outcry then raised against us?  At last Gladstone accepted arbitration, and an International Court sitting at Geneva awarded over three million pounds as damages to the States.

It may be thought that too much stress has been laid on Napoleon's difficulties as caused by his Mexican schemes. Certainly when he first interfered in 1862 he could not anticipate how weak he would be in 1866–67, how Juarez would not be suppressed, and how strong Prussia would become.  The military resources of France ought, one would have said, to have been adequate for the dispatch of an expeditionary corps and yet to allow him to pose as the arbiter of Europe.  But we have to remember that the French army was, like our own, a professional army of no great size as compared with the modern "nation in arms," indeed it was by far less strong relatively to ours than the conscript army of July 1914.  We know from our own experience how small a fraction of a professional army remains for an emergency in Europe, when its chief duty in peace is to provide drafts to maintain the corps scattered throughout the empire.  Thus crippled, Napoleon was confronted by question after question at home, whether forced on him by events beyond his control as the Poland and Schleswig Holstein questions and the great German crisis

in 1866, or due to his own ambition and increasing need to
assert himself, as the questions of the Rhine frontier and
Luxemburg and Belgium. He could not count on Great
Britain as a certain ally, for the conclusion of the Crimean
War and the boastings which disturbed us in 1858–59
showed that he might even turn against us. The whole
history of Italy showed that nobody could calculate what
step he would take next. And in the meanwhile Prussia
was growing ever stronger and stronger; if we say that
Napoleon's policy dominated the decade, this must be
taken in a negative sense, for it was precisely what he did
not do that was so important, whereas the doing was
Prussia's, or rather Bismarck's.

The events of 1848–49 left Prussia humiliated. It was
the work of Bismarck to create for her a new moral
ascendancy, but the circumstances were by no means
favourable. In 1857 Frederick William IV was out of his
mind, so that his brother William was Prince Regent; in
1861 he died; William I succeeded; and both as Prince
Regent, and as King at first, he had much trouble. Liberalism was very strong, and he formed a ministry of Liberals
with the Prince of Hohenzollern-Sigmaringen, his distant
cousin and head of the Roman Catholic branch of the
family, as President. Would Prussia therefore enter on a
"new era" of parliamentary government and become a
constitutional nation? The army question was of absorbing
interest; by her army alone could Prussia ever hope to
rise superior to the Federal Diet; foreign policy and control
of the army belonged to the Crown, and the Chamber could
do no more than vote supplies; would the Liberals, as in
past English history, gain through parliamentary control
of the purse such a position as to make Crown and ministers
responsible to them, and thus have their say on foreign

policy and army questions? William I was not going to
be a mere limited monarch. In 1859 he called Albert von
Roon to be War Minister to draw up a scheme of army
reform, which was based on an increase of the number of
recruits, a service of three years instead of two with the
colours, and a reorganisation of the reserve of landwehr.
For a few years the Chamber refused to vote the money,
yet Roon persisted. In 1862 matters were at such a crisis
that William had even some idea of abdication. Then, on
Roon's advice, he called Bismarck to be Minister-President.

In 1863 there was a Polish rising against Russia[1]. It
had been threatened for some little time, being due at
bottom to the new excitement in Russia over the emancipation of the serfs, but the immediate cause was that the
Tsar seized the disaffected for service in the army as conscripts; he "made the conscription of January 1863 an
engine for seizing upon his supposed enemies." Moreover
there was a complication because in Poland noble and serf
were, as ever in their past history, most hostile to each
other. This rising was one of townsmen and nobles. It was
entirely of a guerilla type. Earl Russell—for Lord John
accepted a title and went up to the Peers in 1861—saw
that here was a question of nationality and constitutional
liberty, as in Italy. But he only offered advice to the
Tsar; he counselled an amnesty to the Poles, liberty under
a constitution such as Alexander I had intended in 1815,
freedom of religion, the use of the Polish language, etc.
At the same time he saw the terrible difficulty. "The
aristocracy of Poland were distrusted: wide in their
projects, narrow in their notions of government....The
democracy of Poland were hostile to the aristocracy: wild
in their desires, bloody in their means." He could hold

[1] See p. 151.

out no hope of British practical help, and he failed, therefore, to help by sympathy; Poland was rather like the
disunited and unready Italy of 1848–49, not like the determined Italy of 1859–60, which he helped so powerfully by
"keeping the ring." Napoleon suggested the landing of
a force from the Western Powers on the Baltic coast.
Palmerston and Russell could not agree. If Napoleon had
been really in earnest in his Russian policy, he would not
have been so ready to make peace in 1856; now forcible
co-operation with him was unwise, for he might leave us
in the lurch once more in 1863 as in 1856. Nothing seemed
possible but words, and Alexander II was not to be moved
by words and an appeal to what his uncle meant to do.
Napoleon thought that the British ministers had deserted
him in refusing to use force.

On the other hand William I and Bismarck helped him
very practically; some Prussian troops were mobilised, and
a convention was made by which Prussians and Russians
might cross the frontier in pursuit of rebels. Prussia had
no sympathy for Polish nationalists, for liberty at Warsaw
would suggest a revolt for liberty at Posen. Bismarck was,
at the very outset of his political career, determined to
have Russia as his friend in the background, as his ally
if the need should arise. But first the Prussian Liberals
had to be brought round. However strange the idea may
seem to us, there was then a strong feeling among the
Liberals of the "new era," both Prussian and German, in
favour of Polish nationality, and in the Chamber it took
the form of protest against the military convention.
Bismarck taunted the Liberals with words which one might
imagine were really addressed by some high-spirited Conservative in England hurling reproaches at Gladstone.
"Enthusiasm for foreign nationalities was a political

disease unfortunately limited to Germany....No English
House of Commons would have acted as they did." His
idea was that Prussia must Prussianise her part of Poland,
and let Russia Russianise her part. The great error of
Austria was acceptance of Russian aid against Hungary in
1849, followed by gross ingratitude in 1854. Such a mistake
he would never make. Of course the upshot was a thorough
Russian conquest of Poland.

Meanwhile the domestic crisis in Prussia continued.
Roon was increasing the army, and the Chamber was
refusing the money. Bismarck was bent on subduing the
Chamber, for only by the army could Prussia make herself
the head of Germany. Responsibility of ministers to
Parliament rather than to Crown was at the root of the
Liberal movement, but that meant sympathy for Poland
as well as for Holstein, and Bismarck's policy was that
Poland was to be held down, and that Holstein was to be
annexed to Prussia and not to Germany. His attitude in
the Chamber was strange in the eyes of Englishmen
accustomed to our ideals of ministerial responsibility. He
attended meetings and spoke in debates, not as a member,
but as an official; therefore he insisted on saying what he
had to say regardless of the President, who tried to rule
him out of order. We are accustomed to think of him as
Prussianising Germany, but here we see him Prussianising,
or we might say re-Prussianising, Prussia herself into a
spirit of meekness that would please old Frederick the
Great, and combating the new nonsensical Liberalism.
Of course the annexation of Rhineland and part of Saxony
in 1814 meant that a great many non-Prussians had to be
brought into line.

From the Polish and domestic questions he had to
plunge into the Danish question. It had come up in 1848,

but was now once more prominent because of the succession
to the Danish crown. Frederick VII was the last of the
direct line. There were two collateral branches, those of
Glücksburg and Augustenburg, and the trouble was that
the Salic Law was not in force in Denmark, but was in force
in Schleswig Holstein. A Congress in London in 1853, to
which Austria and Prussia were parties, but not the Federal
Diet of Germany, settled the succession on Christian of
Glücksburg. To this the public opinion of Germany was
hostile, especially as the avowed policy of Denmark was to
make at least Schleswig an integral part of Denmark, while
Germans wanted at least Holstein for the Federation. Now
Bismarck's sympathies were at first for Denmark, for, if
Prussia had the right to her share of Poland, Denmark had
the right to the Duchies; his whole policy was anti-Federal,
and he had not yet seen his way to seize the Duchies for
Prussia. In November 1863 Frederick died. Christian
succeeded to the Danish throne, and signed the act for the
incorporation of Schleswig. The Federal Diet promptly
decreed a Federal occupation of Holstein, to be carried out
by Hanoverian and Saxon troops. But then the eldest
son of the Augustenburg candidate put forward his claim,
regardless of the London Congress. Of course the sequel
showed that he was simply used for the time, and then
thrown aside when to support his candidature was unnecessary, and a modern official apology that the war
against Denmark was undertaken in fairness to his claim
is preposterous; a German cry as an excuse for German
interference was all that was wanted. Bismarck's position
was different. He made his *casus belli* the November
incorporation of Schleswig as an infringement of the
London settlement, and, as Austria and Prussia were
parties to that settlement, they and not the Federal Diet

had the right to act. The wonderful thing is that he persuaded the jealous and suspicious Austrians to act with
him. The hostility of the Prussian Chamber he thwarted
by a prorogation. Of course the Prussian and Austrian
armies swept through the country at will, and the Hanoverians and Saxons looked on.

What then could the British do? One argument has
to be put aside at once; the recent marriage of the Prince
of Wales to Alexandra of Denmark was no reason for war.
The co-operation of Napoleon was not to be expected, as
he was still sore because Russell had not supported his policy
towards Poland. His only suggestion was that a *plébiscite*
should be taken in the Duchies, as if it were a question of
nationality to be solved, as in Savoy; neither Austria nor
Prussia could allow policy to be settled by a national
*plébiscite*, else what would become of Poland or Venetia?
A month's armistice was arranged. The neutral Powers
were summoned by Russell to a Conference in London in
April 1864. Russell thought that in 1863 "Denmark was
not a little wrong," but the joint invasion had put Austria
and Prussia in the wrong. His own suggestion at the
Conference was that Christian should give up Holstein and
the German part of Schleswig, and this, coupled with his
previous language on several occasions, was interpreted by
Denmark as a promise of real help. But, as the most
bitter of his opponents put it[1], he was too fond of "might"
or "may" or "probably," words which did not deceive the
Prussians, but were interpreted by the Danes as stated.
His own defence, made some years later, was that a section
of our press, *The Times* in particular, used very strong

[1] Lord Robert Cecil, the future Marquis of Salisbury and Prime
Minister. The Conservative official leaders, Lord Derby and
Disraeli, of course denounced the Liberal ministers very strongly.

language which influenced the Danes beyond the reasonable interpretation of official utterances of ministers. Palmerston, however, was more explicit than Russell; even if taken out of their context such words as "it would not be Denmark alone with which they would have to contend" were unmistakable, and the context cannot be doubted. Thus, apart from the heated language of newspapers or the weird excitement of those who imagined that the marriage implied political alliance, there was justification for Danish expectations. But on the other side Queen Victoria's influence was in favour of Germany; our military power was insufficient if not supported by the French; a large body of public opinion here, the opinion of thoughtful and serious men, was influenced by the strong pro-German writings of Carlyle, whose "spiritual home" was certainly Germany, who admired the profundities of German philosophy, and saw in the steady honest home-loving German character the exact opposite of the frivolity and insincerity of the French, and whose heroes in history were the men of action and strength rather than words; also our leading school of historians of that period looked upon Germans as our "natural" allies and were looking back, beyond the Crimean *entente*, to the days of our hereditary feud with France[1]. Thus we come back to the central fact, the lack

---

[1] Freeman's *Norman Conquest*, Vol. I, came out in 1867. The book treats of the war between Saxon and Norman as if part of a long natural struggle between England and France. Yet Freeman hated the use of the word, as applied to frontiers, etc., for instance to the Rhine as France's "natural" boundary. Carlyle wrote later, November 18, 1870, in praise of Bismarck, "That pathetic Niobe of Denmark, reft violently of her children (which were stolen children, and were dreadfully ill-nursed by Niobe-Denmark), is also nearly gone, and will go altogether as soon as knowledge of the matter is had."

of trust in Napoleon. His negative influence, the fear of what he might do, or of what he might leave unfinished when once he had begun to do it, governed the situation.

It is perfectly maddening to reflect that neither political party made the smallest effort to improve our military resources. The Conservatives might accuse Russell of alternate bluster and surrender, but they put forward no programme of army reform, whether from fear of radical resentment or from motives of economy does not appear. This fact takes away from the sting of their attacks upon him. For several years yet to come the question was not tackled boldly. Any one can see that the impotence of Britain at each stage of Prussia's advance was due to the size of our army. But it was still the period of commercialism, and a strict neutral non-intervention suited this idea. The navy indeed was treated better, and even Cobden believed in a standard of three keels to two as against the French. The need of ironclad ships and heavy guns[1] was so clear after the experience of the Crimean and American wars that no political party dared to economise. All nations started on a level when wooden ships were being scrapped, and rival designs of sea-going ironclads— for the American monitors could only be used in-shore— were being worked out in both England and France.

Consequently the Prussians and Austrians, the month of armistice over, renewed the war. Both Schleswig and

[1] The sixties were the period of experiment in iron, the seventies of development; and it was some considerable time before our navy, which at the start was barely equal, won once more a position of superiority over the French navy. Steel armour, steel wire-wound guns of heavy calibre, water-tube boilers, turbine engines, oil fuel, and all the modern ideas, date from about 1895, when the Majestics were being built, down to the Dreadnought and super-Dreadnought periods of this century.

Holstein were taken, Christian submitting to the Treaty of
Vienna, October 1864, and yielding the Duchies to the
sovereigns of Austria and Prussia. Even then it was foreseen that the possession of Kiel, and the possibility of the
construction of a canal across Holstein, implied a new
factor in history, namely the birth of a German navy.
But was it to be a German navy or a Prussian? Of course
the claims of the Prince of Augustenburg to this territory
were never seriously entertained. He had played his part
for the benefit of Prussia, and of course was thrown aside
at once, so that to excuse the war as undertaken in the
just cause of an aggrieved and wrongfully dispossessed
claimant is so palpably false as to be farcical. Bismarck
demanded that if he was made Duke he was to introduce
into the Duchies Prussian law, conscription, postal and
railway systems, even an oath of military allegiance to the
King of Prussia. He was ready even for war immediately
against Austria and the Federal Diet, for he had but used
Austria to cover his own direct designs upon the Duchies.
However, there was still a party in Prussia unwilling to go
to such extremes, and Bismarck was not yet strong enough.
The Hanoverian and Saxon troops were withdrawn from
Holstein, the former willingly, the latter unwillingly, and
only after a vote had been given in the Federal Diet by a
narrow majority. The Holsteiners themselves were actually
ready to fight, and so was the King of Saxony, in defence
of an ideal German policy. But the Emperor of Austria
was not ready; he had been used as a catspaw in the matter
of the joint invasion, and was now used again as a catspaw
to persuade the Diet to withdraw the Saxons; then he
agreed to the Treaty of Gastein, August 1865, by which,
pending an ultimate settlement, his government was to
administer Holstein and the Prussians Schleswig; a third

Duchy, Lauenburg, was to go to Prussia definitely. It
was cleverly done, for the Holsteiners, who whole-heartedly
supported the Prince of Augustenburg, were put under
Austria as a sop to their feelings. Meanwhile Bismarck
was already sounding the ministers of Victor Emmanuel as
to a possible alliance between Prussia and Italy against
Austria.

Two duties were now laid upon Bismarck; to create
finally in Prussia a strong public opinion that would be
proof against the insidious liberalism which he had com-
bated previously, against the tenderness towards the idea
of national aspirations whether of Holstein or of Poland,
and against the dislike of increasing the Prussian army;
and to blind Napoleon to his further designs. His first
object was being attained by the very nature of his success.
There was opposition from the Crown Prince, who was
always the supporter of the Augustenburg claimant, who
was then popular, and against whom it was not yet reckoned
as a crime that he was married to Queen Victoria's eldest
daughter, our Princess Royal, or that his ideas of parliamentary government were in some degree of an English
type. The Crown Prince's ideal of German unity was
rather Federal than Prussian, but he was a soldier more than
a politician. The general tendency of liberalism against
methods of ruthlessness Bismarck fought in the Chamber
and in the press. Napoleon it was not difficult to deceive.
Bismarck had only to copy the method by which Frederick
William had been hoodwinked by Napoleon I in 1805;
provided that Prussia would remain neutral while he
crushed the Austrians and held off the Russians, he would
allow some compensation, Hanover perhaps; the Austrians
and Russians once crushed at Ulm and Austerlitz, he
threw away the mask, scoffed at the idea of Prussia annexing

Hanover, goaded Frederick William into war, and annihilated his army at Jena. How Napoleon III could allow himself to be similarly hoodwinked, when he knew how his uncle had treated Prussia, is simply beyond comprehension. He was taken in by Bismarck's bonhomie and apparent guilelessness. He believed in the sincerity of Bismarck's offer of compensation, if he should stand by neutral while Austria was being overwhelmed. Just as he settled matters privately at Plombières and Chambéry to help Cavour, so he had interviews with Bismarck at Biarritz. He had received Savoy and Nice, surely he would receive again whatever he bargained for. What was the territory offered? Part of Rhineland, or Luxemburg, or Belgium? We can never know, for Bismarck was not so stupid as to put anything on paper. It was quite enough to promise something, not Prussian territory of course; the controversy of later days makes one think that it was Bavarian Rhineland, part of the old Palatinate, for Bismarck could always deny afterwards that he had offered it, and nothing could be more fatal to Napoleon than for the Bavarians to be offended. Richelieu, Louis XIV, Louis XV, and Napoleon I, all of them had paid court to Bavaria, promised increase of territory to Bavaria at the expense of Austria, promoted the disunion of Germany by alliance with Bavaria—with Saxony also and Wurtemberg and Hesse, if it were possible, but always with Bavaria in the first place. Therefore even to hold out before Napoleon's eyes the bait of the Palatinate was a remarkable bit of cunning, yet it is more remarkable that Napoleon seems to have swallowed it.

The next step was to approach Victor Emmanuel. A Treaty of Alliance was made in April 1866. Naturally the Austrians were aware that some project of this kind was in the air, and as a declaration of war was obviously coming nearer and nearer, the Austrians made an offer to surrender Venetia to Napoleon, for him to hand over to Victor Emmanuel. But the Italian minister, General La Marmora, preferred the Prussian alliance after the treaty had been definitely signed, being, it is thought, one of the few men of that time who foresaw the military superiority of Prussia; Palmerston, for instance, a few years before his death, said that Prussian methods and discipline were inferior to those of the French.

The *casus belli* was the Austrian administration of Holstein followed by Austrian proposals in the Diet. In January 1866 a mass meeting was allowed to be held at Altona, and there were demands for the summoning of the Estates of Holstein. The Austrian officials governed the country as if they were agents for the Prince of Augustenburg, even abstaining from taxing the country, and allowing liberty to the local press, at the very time when General Manteuffel, the Prussian Governor of Schleswig, was violently suppressing public opinion there. Then an Austrian proposal was made in the Federal Diet to take in hand the question of both Duchies and to summon the Holstein Estates. This was Bismarck's opportunity, and he declared the Treaty of Gastein to have been violated thereby, whilst the Prussian army was ordered to march into Holstein. Austria persuaded the Diet to mobilise the armies of the Federal States, which Bismarck considered a declaration of war. All the States who followed Austria in the Diet, even those which tried to be neutral, were denounced and considered as the enemies of Prussia; Hanover, both Hesses, Nassau, and even Frankfort itself, were thus involved, as well as Saxony and Bavaria: only the Mecklenburgs and the quite smaller States were pro-Prussian. There still existed in Prussia a liberal feeling against war, against *bruderkrieg*, against the destruction of Federalism and of German Unity. It was Bismarck's policy to drown this feeling by joy in a great Prussian victory, after which Unity would be possible under Prussian headship.

Time was of the utmost value to Moltke. The Austrians had already mobilised several corps in Bohemia, and it was vital to strike at them immediately before the Bavarians could mobilise. Westwards the Hanoverians had to be contained, for which purpose a Prussian corps was detached, and here the extreme value of Napoleon's blindness can be seen, for even a limited number of French threatening Rhineland would have so distracted the Prussians that the great invasion of Bohemia, on which Moltke's strategy was based, would have been impossible. Even so an enterprising Austrian commander-in-chief might have anticipated him by pouring a force into Silesia. But Benedek, a Hungarian, who held that position, was as fatally slow as Giulay had been in Piedmont in 1859; he allowed Moltke to take the initiative, an enormous advantage when promptness can rely on the moral of the soldiers to carry out the main plan. It is the old story of a daring strategy supported by a steady moral which enables the full advantage to be gained by tactics. This bold strategy consisted of launching two great Prussian armies from two separate bases towards a rendezvous on the actual field of battle. It may be foiled by an enemy who is ready to divine it and sees his opportunity. If it succeeds it gains an overpowering advantage, but it may fail in the execution. Napoleon I, trusting to the marvellous marching power of the French, was thus able to bring off many a brilliant coup. "March separately, and concentrate at the right point" may be said to be a

Napoleonic maxim.   On the other hand, wherever he saw
an enemy trying to outwit him in that way, he was always
quick to take up a central position and annihilate separately
two converging armies.   But Benedek was not a Napoleon ;
not only he delayed to take the offensive, but when on
the defensive failed to strike strongly at either the one
or the other of the converging Prussian armies, so as to
annihilate the one while he held off the other.   It must
be added that the alliance of Victor Emmanuel was of
great advantage, for 100,000 Austrians were required in
Venetia.

The war as against Austria dates from June 12, as against
the other German States from June 15.   The First Prussian
Army and the Army of the Elbe commenced to cross the
frontier into Saxony on the 16th.   The Saxons withdrew
into Bohemia so as to fall in on the Austrian left flank,
and they were thus the only allies ready for battle.   The
Prussian advance into Bohemia across the mountains
commenced on the 23rd.   Prince Frederick Charles, King
William's nephew, known as the Red Prince, was in
command of both armies.   In the meanwhile the Second
Army, under the Crown Prince, was massed in Silesia to
cross the Giant Mountains into eastern Bohemia.   Touch
was maintained between the two princes by telegraph, and
Moltke was in touch with both at Berlin, which he and the
King and Bismarck did not leave till June 30.   The total
of the Prussians and of the joint Austrians and Saxons was
rather over 270,000 men on each side, a strength of eight
army corps.   It was possible for Benedek to invade Silesia
by the south-eastern angle, and thus crush the Crown
Prince as he was beginning to negotiate the mountain
passes.   But he had his head-quarters at Josephstadt, on
the upper Elbe, at a distance of about 15 to 25 miles from

the foot of the passes on the Bohemian side, and about
60 miles from the Saxon frontier.   Common sense dictated
that he should make his main blow in that case at the
Crown Prince's corps as they were debouching into Bohemia
and crush them separately, whilst the Saxons and one of
his own corps watched and delayed the advance of the
Red Prince.   He did exactly the opposite, and massed his
main force against the Red Prince and watched the Crown
Prince.   Now the Red Prince was marching very slowly,
much too slowly to suit Moltke, not much more than an
average of 6 to 7 miles a day;  yet Benedek's slowness
more than compensated for this.   On either side the
Austrians were beginning to be despondent because the new
breech-loading needle-guns[1] of the Prussians, which were
quite a novelty, and were not so highly thought of by
other Powers as to be worthy of being copied, were after
all highly efficient;  they were single-action rifles loaded
with one cartridge at a time and were good for 6 or 7 rounds
a minute, and the Prussians were severely trained to fire
steadily to avoid a waste of ammunition, yet even so their
rate of fire took the Austrians by surprise;  of course
another advantage was that the men could load whilst
lying down.   Thus Benedek, after considerable losses in the
preliminary skirmishes, fell back to a central position on
the heights surrounding the village of Sadowa, a few miles

[1] A German from Nassau told me many years ago that he
remembered seeing, when a boy, a Prussian detachment marching
through his village with handkerchiefs tied over the locks of their
rifles to hide the action.   The Prussians had needle-guns in
Schleswig, so that they were not a novelty in one sense in 1866;
the novelty of this year was their success, which the war of 1864
did not lead critics to expect.   The Austrian muzzle-loader in range
and accuracy was much superior, but was slow and compelled the
men to stand to use their ramrods.

south of Josephstadt, near the Elbe, whilst the road crossed
the river a little to the rear at Königgrätz.

Benedek taught the Prussians one valuable lesson at
least; if his rifles were inferior his artillery was quite
superior to theirs, and he massed his guns very strongly in
the Sadowa position.    On July 3 he accepted battle, having

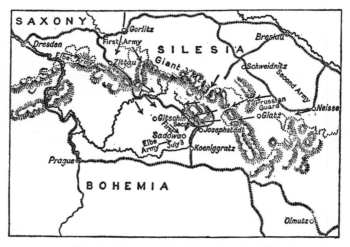

Map to illustrate the Campaign of 1866.

the advantage of numbers as against the Red Prince alone,
of position, and of a superior artillery.    Frederick Charles
attacked and was held off during all the morning; it was
a very strong attack and resulted in correspondingly heavy
losses.    But Moltke, exactly as Wellington had counted on
Blucher, counted on the arrival of the Crown Prince, who
was in touch with the Austrian outposts on the right flank

about mid-day; by 3 o'clock he had four corps well in action. The Austrians began to retreat at 4 o'clock and broke into considerable disorder as they crossed the Elbe, so that retreat became a rout. The Prussians were too exhausted to pursue after nightfall.

Meanwhile the western Prussian army, numbering about 45,000 men, was in central Germany. The Hanoverians, advancing towards Gotha with the object of joining with the Bavarians, encountered the Prussian van at Langen-salza, not very far from Jena, and beat them off on June 27. But the main Prussian army came up and surrounded them, and they surrendered on the 29th. The Bavarians, taking longer to mobilise, did not fight a main action, and the battle of Sadowa had already taken place before they were ready to do any service to their allies.

In Italy the Austrians routed the army of La Marmora on the fatal and historic ground of Custozza on June 24. This was very galling to the national pride of the Italians, especially as shortly afterwards Admiral Persano with a superior and partially ironclad fleet, making a disconnected attack upon an Austrian squadron, was badly repulsed off the island of Lissa, near the Istrian coast. The Italians had, however, at least the satisfaction of having tied a large number of Austrians to Italy. On the other hand their Italian victories took off some of the bitterness which the Austrians must have felt.

The Prussian success, being both rapid and decisive, was due to many causes. Roon had turned out a highly efficient war machine, freely spending money which had not been sanctioned by parliament but which was at once voted after the success. It could be trusted and had a moral high above that of the Austrians, whose Hungarian and Italian regiments were backward and unwilling, though the

Croats and Tyrolese were as ready as in previous wars. Without Roon's services neither Bismarck nor Moltke could have carried on their plans. The Prussians fought with a purpose, and their officers belonged to a military caste, as in Frederick the Great's time, tyrannical enough and even brutal as we know them, but terribly efficient in the face of the enemy; in 1866 Bismarck indeed boasted that there was no plundering and burning, and that they paid when they could for what they took; the coarseness, of which we have had only too clear a proof in the recent war, was probably there, but there was no accusation to be compared, not only with the bitterly true accusations of to-day, but even with what we are told of 1870, for it was in war against the French that the traditional hatred of the Prussians in revenge for what Prussia suffered after 1806 was chiefly manifested. Their own military writers consider that Moltke is not to be compared with Napoleon, but that the efficiency of the regimental and brigade officers atoned in action for whatever the high commands did amiss. The greatest military authority, Clausewitz, had done a great deal to create a good spirit amongst these men, and in particular in his study of the Waterloo campaign he had taught the supreme necessity of marching to the sound of the guns, division supporting division, and corps supporting corps, so as to bring a decisive superiority on one point. Thus even where the strategy was defective —and Napoleon I would have made Moltke rue it both in 1866 and 1870—even when Frederick Charles had had to engage his army in a desperate offensive at a great sacrifice, it was done for a purpose because the Crown Prince was coming; in the meanwhile he was pinning Benedek to a position, and in the end moral and tactical skill triumphed. Railways also had, since the Crimean War, come to play

an important part; two main lines leading from Saxony
into Bohemia, the one by way of Torgau over the Zittau
pass, and the other from Dresden up the Elbe, and the
main line running up Silesia, parallel to the Giant Mountains, enabled Moltke to plant his two armies on either side
of the Austrians, so that he could deliver his two convergent
blows.

The Prussians were already beginning to pursue towards
Vienna, when on July 5, the Austrian government appealed
to Napoleon to mediate, and offered Venetia to him to be
handed over to Victor Emmanuel. Napoleon proposed
arbitration to Bismarck in such a way that it was naturally
assumed that he would join in the war in case of refusal;
he could at least rally the South Germans, amongst whom
the Bavarians at least might be dangerous, though the
Hanoverians had been crushed, whilst there was no knowing
whether the Tsar might be more frightened than friendly
to Prussia. Bismarck answered in a conciliatory tone, but
would not consent to an armistice. He urged Moltke to
push on for Vienna, which is 140 miles from Sadowa, so
that while he negotiated with Napoleon the Austrians
should be reduced to extremities. He played with Benedetti[1] as if he was still ready to allow some compensation
to France in return for neutrality. As a matter of fact
Napoleon withdrew from what was really a very strong
position; he found out that Victor Emmanuel would not
accept Venetia as a gift from France; he only asked
that the Prussians would spare Saxony. Bismarck was
then able to grant an armistice for terms to be discussed at
Nikolsburg on July 22[2]. Three days later the preliminaries

[1] The French ambassador at Berlin.
[2] The Prussian van was then on the historic ground of Wagram-
Aspern, a few miles out from Vienna.

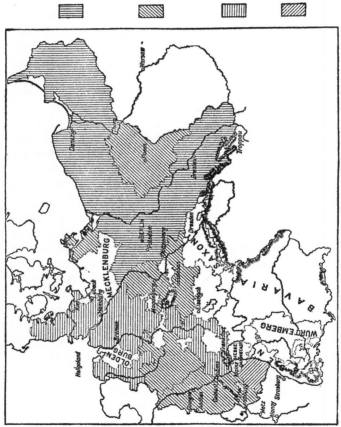

Prussia as under Napoleon I; viz. Brandenburg, E. & W. Prussia, part of Pomerania, and Silesia.

Provinces added in 1814; viz. part of Poland, part of Saxony, Swedish Pomerania, Magdeburg, Westphalia, and archbishoprics of Cologne and Trier.

Provinces added in 1866; viz. Schleswig, Holstein, Hanover, Hesse Cassel, Nassau, Frankfort.

The Bavarian Palatinate.

Map of Germany to show the growth of Prussia in the nineteenth century.

of peace were signed, and the definite Treaty of Prague was accomplished August 23. He was deliberately moderate towards Austria, excluding her entirely from Germany but demanding no cession of territory except Venetia, which thus, after all, became Italian as the gift of Prussia. He spared Saxony, but made that kingdom join in a new North German Confederation with her army at the full disposal of Prussia. The North German Confederation was to include Prussia, Saxony, the Mecklenburgs, Oldenburg, and all the small states north of the Main. But Schleswig Holstein, Hanover, Hesse Cassel, Nassau, and Frankfort, were to be annexed definitely to Prussia, a solid gain of 4,500,000 souls, linking up old Prussia and Brandenburg with Westphalia and Prussian Rhineland as settled in 1814. The next part of the programme was very clever, but Bismarck found considerable difficulty in persuading King William to agree; in fact he had to call in the Crown Prince to persuade his father. He was determined not to push to extremities the four South German states, so as to drive them into Napoleon's arms. For this purpose Bavaria, Wurtemberg, Baden, and Hesse Darmstadt, were to lose no territory; they were simply to agree to a secret treaty with Prussia as allies, putting their armies at the entire disposal of the Prussian king. Such generosity in itself was clever. He made it acceptable by letting the Bavarians know that Napoleon expected to receive the piece of the left bank of the Rhine which belonged to Bavaria. The Napoleonic trickery of 1805 had now come home to roost. But it is only fair to add that the French Emperor this year was desperately ill, and on some occasions was so racked by pain that he could not carry on an important conversation. Great Britain was negligible, being simply wedded to the extreme form of non-intervention.

The Austrian Empire, it may be easily imagined, was profoundly influenced by the result of 1866. Hungary demanded separation and independence, as against subjection to a centralised Austrian government which was established in 1849; as a matter of fact Austrian severity towards Hungary was already being relaxed before 1866, though there was still only one Chamber for the whole Empire. The leader of the movement was Deák, an Hungarian aristocrat and patriot of the pre-1848 school, who believed in reform but not in revolution, and who had in consequence stood aloof when Kossuth brought about war. The constitution of the Dual Monarchy was Deák's work and was brought to accomplishment by Beust in 1867. Francis Joseph was crowned as King of Hungary that year. The Austrian Reichsrath and the Hungarian Diet were separated; but whereas the Reichsrath was practically subordinate to the Emperor, the Diet was controlled by the Hungarian upper classes; hence it followed that the Diet, being able to oppose the Emperor, ultimately controlled his policy. Matters of joint interest concerning foreign policy, the army and navy, finance, customs, etc., were settled in common; local concerns, such as education, belonged to the separate governments. The most serious question was the treatment of the Slavs. Bohemia and Galicia were united to Austria. Croatia and Slavonia, as well as the Rumanians of Transylvania, were united to Hungary; consequently the men whose ancestors boasted that they had saved the Austrian Empire in 1848–49 were now under the heel of their hereditary enemies, the genuine Magyars, who controlled the Diet: the Magyar language was supreme in the army and in schools, and all officials were Magyars. Therefore in gaining Hungarian loyalty Francis Joseph lost Slav loyalty. From his own point of view it was a gain, for Hungary was led astray by anti-Russian feeling in 1914, and, supported by Germany and Hungary, the Austrian contempt for the Slavs was so far successful. The leader of the Hungarians in 1867, after Deák retired, was Count Andrassy, who in 1849 was a rebel and fled into exile to save himself from being hanged; in 1871 he became Austrian Chancellor.

In 1867 the Luxemburg question came forward. Napoleon was becoming desperate, because all France resented the humiliation of the withdrawal from Mexico. Opposition to the Empire was growing bolder and bolder, and something had to be done to justify the name of Napoleon. Benedetti and Bismarck drew up the draft of an agreement after the Bavarian fiasco, or rather Bismarck dictated it to Benedetti; Napoleon was to recognise the North German Confederation, the annexations by Prussia, and the freedom of Prussia to make a union with the South Germans, and in return the King of Prussia was to help him to obtain Luxemburg from the King of the Netherlands or Belgium. The draft was never extended into a definite treaty, for any misunderstanding that there might have been between Prussia and Russia disappeared when Manteuffel went to Petrograd on a special mission; the friendship of Russia secure, Bismarck did not need France. In 1870 Bismarck published the draft of these proposals for the benefit of neutrals. But in 1867 war was on the verge of breaking out on the Luxemburg question. All that Napoleon could obtain was the withdrawal from the Duchy of the garrison which the Prussians had the right to maintain, the neutralisation of the country, and the dismantling of the fortifications. The subsequent history of Luxemburg is simple. Its neutrality was scrupulously observed in 1870. When the King of the Netherlands died in 1890, Wilhelmina could not under the Salic Law succeed to Luxemburg, but a very distant cousin became Grand Duke, though it is somewhat remarkable that his grand-daughter succeeded him in 1905 without comment or reference to the Salic Law; in 1914 of course William II violated the neutrality.   The other project of Napoleon, the acquisition of Belgium, can hardly be taken seriously; that he nibbled at the bait seems clearly established, but one knows of no documentary evidence of details.   Bis-marck was quite capable of playing with him on this subject, if only to make the English angry, and the draft previously written by Benedetti at Bismarck's dictation was published in 1870 to impress Englishmen.

Thoroughly upset by the sight of a triumphant Prussia and by the failure of all his efforts to obtain compensation, Napoleon made overtures to Austria.   There were great difficulties in the way.   France had always been in the past the chief enemy of Austria.   The basis of Napoleon's own foreign policy had been the liberation of North Italy up to the Adriatic, at the expense of Austria.   He had been the rival of Austria as the champion of the Papacy; 1867 was the year of Garibaldi's last raid upon Rome, and he had been suppressed by French troops and Rome was once more garrisoned by French.   But on the other hand it was natural for Austria to be attracted towards a French alliance, as the only chance of recovering a position in Germany, past hostilities forgotten.   The new Chancellor of the Austrian Empire, Count Beust, was the late Prime Minister of Saxony, who hated the Prussian ascendancy and who had been in 1863–64 the strongest adherent of the Federal occupation of Schleswig Holstein, and therefore most indignant at the way in which Prussia had made use of Austria to secure the Duchies, and then had thrown her aside. On the other hand the feeling in Hungary was anti-Russian rather than anti-Prussian; it was no part of Hungarian policy to restore Austrian ascendancy in Germany. It resulted that many letters passed between Napoleon and Francis Joseph, and a sort of vague idea of an alliance existed; an Austrian Archduke went to Paris early in 1870, and a French general to Vienna. Whatever danger there might be to Prussia from a mutual understanding was however countered by Bismarck, who had a far more definite understanding with Russia. Bismarck could do something that Russia had very much at heart; he could consent to stand by and allow Russia to repudiate the Treaty of Paris; this was not too high a price to pay for Russian support to keep Austria quiet when the inevitable Franco-Prussian war should break out.

An Italian alliance was also in Napoleon's mind, and here too the difficulties were considerable. The memory of Mentana, as well as of Napoleon's withdrawal after the Treaty of Villafranca, and his generally half-hearted policy which had contributed to Italian Unity only by holding back the Austrians in 1860, was quite sufficient to make the Italians lukewarm. Victor Emmanuel could make no alliance with France if the Italian Parliament and Italian public opinion were against it, and to the average Italian Napoleon's papal policy was a fatal objection. Yet strangely enough Italian hatred of Austria was beginning to disappear; Count Beust was not responsible for the events of 1848–49 or 1859; the gift of Venetia from the hands of the Prussians was galling, and Prussian taunts of Italian inefficiency and backwardness in 1866 were such that this very gift was a burden for which no gratitude need be shown. There were negotiations between Austria and Italy. Yet nothing definite had been settled by 1870.

Everything seemed to show that when France had to fight she would fight single-handed.

At home Napoleon's policy offended alike the extreme "left" and the extreme "right." Whatever concessions he made did not satisfy the Republicans and angered the extreme Catholics; for instance, a programme of popular elementary education, carried out by the anti-clerical Duruy, was thoroughly secular, yet did little to conciliate the opposition. There was a very small but very resolute body in the Chamber which demanded "necessary liberties," for instance the right of questioning the Imperial ministers, and the withdrawal of official candidates at elections; this group contained both Republicans and Orleanists, such as Thiers. A new group was being formed, the *tiers-parti* under an old opponent of the Empire, Emile Ollivier; they adopted a new party cry, *l'Empire Libéral*, and they professed to be firmly attached to the dynasty which preserved order, but equally attached to liberty. In 1867 Napoleon granted the right of questioning ministers, and promised a greater freedom to the press. But this was the bad year of the withdrawal from Mexico, of Mentana, and of the Luxemburg fiasco. "There is not a single mistake more that can be committed" cried Thiers, who saw all his old ideals disappearing; there was neither liberty nor a sufficiency of glory.

In 1868 the Republicans grew bolder. Victor Hugo, from his home in the Channel Islands, launched at Napoleon *Les Châtiments*. Henri Rochefort brought out *La Lanterne*, which was widely read before it was suppressed. Gambetta, under cover of defending some men who were prosecuted for raising a subscription to restore the tomb of one of the martyrs of December 2, 1851, delivered a tremendous oration against the Empire; of course a lawyer defending a client was inviolable; law-courts in France have often enough been used for political demonstrations. Yet it may be doubted whether the Republicans did more harm or good. At one moment they applauded Prussia, at another denounced Napoleon for being outwitted by Prussia. They opposed the scheme of military reorganisation for fear that Napoleon would use an increased army to revoke the instalment of liberties that he had granted. One sensible project Napoleon set on foot, the reorganisation of the army; there was to be a modified form of conscription, an active army fed by conscripts chosen by lot, with five years in the ranks and four years in the reserve, and the young men who remained after lots were drawn were to be formed into the *garde mobile*. The scheme was excellent in itself, and was very much wanted, for the long-service professional army had practically no reserve, and was quite insufficient to face the great numbers which could be placed in the field by Prussia plus the North German Confederation, not to speak of the allied South Germans. It was not that any French soldiers had even a suspicion that they were inferior to the Prussians; they had their breech-loading chassepot, which was better than the needle-gun in range and lightness, they were proud of their rifled artillery and of their new mitrailleuse or machine-gun, they had good training in Algeria; but they must have been conscious of the drain on men which the Mexican expedition caused. But Napoleon was himself unable to superintend the execution of any scheme; his war minister, General Niel, died, and nobody else seems to have been patriotic enough to take the work in hand; the entourage of the Court cared only for self-advancement; substitutes could be bought, and perhaps the money was paid and the substitute not forthcoming. It is not only the general accusation of

Imperial corruption that makes us think this, but the
terrible unreadiness of 1870 and the lack of men on the
immediate declaration of war, the lack of supplies, and the
lack of organisation. The reserve hardly existed, and the
*garde mobile* had not been properly armed. It is a terrible
indictment. Yet one hardly knows what could be expected
when a very ordinary man held a position which was too
hard for him, simply because he was the heir to his uncle's
reputation, when place-seekers got at his ear, and he was
dinned with talk about the glory of France, but was too
weak in character in any case, and too miserably ill in these
critical years, to carry out any of the necessary details.

In the elections of 1869 the Imperial candidates, now
entitled *les agréables*, in place of the hated *les officiels*,
obtained in all 4,600,000 votes, but the opposition received
3,300,000. Paris elected irreconcileables, Ferry, Simon,
Favre, Gambetta, and Rochefort; Ollivier, accused of
having ratted, was rejected, and had to find a seat for a
provincial department. Napoleon gave way still more; he
gave to the Senate and Chamber the right to initiate laws,
to the Chamber the right to choose its own President.
Late in the year he called upon Ollivier to form a ministry
agreeable to the programme of the *tiers-parti*. A new
Constitution was drawn up and presented by Ollivier in
April 1870; then it was submitted to the French nation
by a *plébiscite*, which gave 7,300,000 votes in support of
the Empire to 1,500,000 against. Apart from official
pressure, it is clear that the French peasants at large and
the bourgeoisie were still solid for the dynasty ; Paris, the
journalists and lawyers, the historians and intellectuals of
all kinds, were the most bitter opponents. Of course the
Liberal Empire never had a chance to show what it was
worth. Eugénie, the Imperialists, the Ultra-Montains,

and the loud-talking and overbearing officers whose influence was undeniably great, were working towards a war in order to revive, after much humiliation at home and abroad, the prestige which was so badly tarnished. When we look at Napoleon's last few years, we can see nothing that he did for the real good of France, except the completion of the Suez Canal scheme; that, indeed, was all French, rendered possible by the subscription of French capital, carried out by French engineers, and pushed through by Napoleon's determination in face of British opposition.

## THE HOHENZOLLERNS

Frederick I: first King of Prussia 1701
|
Frederick William I
|

Frederick II, "The Great"        Augustus
1740–1786                            |
                          Frederick William II, 1786–1797
                               (Treaty of Basle 1795)
                                        |
                          Frederick William III, 1797–1840
                                   (Jena 1806)

Frederick William IV, 1840–61        William I
                              Regent 1857, King 1861
                          First German Emperor 1871–1888
                                        |
Victoria, Princess Royal of Great Britain m. Frederick III
                                    |        1888
                          William II, 1888–1918

# CHAPTER VII

## THE FRANCO-GERMAN WAR

The grand finale to twenty-three years of storm and stress was now approaching, after which Europe was fated to have forty-three years of peace, until the new Germany brought on the recent titanic struggle. That France and Prussia would try to come to a conclusion was inevitable, for temper and character must find some vent. The immediate cause was trivial.

The history of Spain in the 19th century is quite uninteresting, as any long tale of faction and civil strife must be. In 1869, after a successful rising had exiled Queen Isabella, a provisional government offered the crown of Spain to the eldest son of the Prince of Hohenzollern-Sigmaringen, whom we last mentioned as Prince-Minister of Prussia; he was a Roman Catholic, and very distantly connected with the reigning Hohenzollerns; his second son was already Prince of Rumania. Both father and son were unwilling to accept the offer, nor was the King of Prussia ready to consent. But Bismarck manœuvred in favour of the idea. The offer was finally accepted in June 1870, but as the Spanish Cortes were not sitting it was being kept quiet for the time, for Bismarck wished the announcement to appear with the full consent of the Spaniards. But the news leaked out. All France was in uproar, for Napoleon had not been consulted and, although the prince was not actually a Prussian, his father's services in the Prussian ministry and the extreme improbability of his acceptance without the consent of the King and Bismarck pointed to a deep design to plant a partisan of Prussia on France's flank. It was not a question of offering a new crown to a harmless German from a petty state such as Saxe Coburg.

The candidature was withdrawn, and the Prussian official assurance was that the whole affair was a private arrangement between the Spanish ministers and the prince and his father. Benedetti was then instructed to demand that the offer would never again be considered. The French press and public opinion were wildly excited, so that Napoleon's ministers had no choice but to try to obtain some guarantee after so much secrecy which was construed to be an insult to France. Bismarck was away from Berlin, and King William was taking the waters at Ems. Benedetti went to interview the King, who quite informally, on two occasions, once on a public promenade and once at the railway station as he was returning to Berlin, but also quite courteously, informed him that the withdrawal was sufficient and no guarantee could be given. A telegram was sent on July 13 from Ems to Bismarck who was now at Berlin. He was at dinner with Roon and Moltke, and, assured by them that the army was quite ready for war, he prepared for publication part of the telegram. As altered, the "Ems telegram" was not in itself provocative of war, though Bismarck himself in his old age boasted that by doctoring it he brought on the war; but many old men like to exaggerate the importance of their former actions. Indeed he omitted one phrase, namely that the King refused Benedetti's request " somewhat

sternly." But the German papers of July 14, possibly at
a hint from Bismarck, were highly provocative, and the
French papers—it was the national fête day in France—
were insulting. On the one side Benedetti was represented
as intruding on the King's privacy, on the other it was
asserted that the King had deliberately turned his back
on Benedetti. Each nation, most unfortunately press-
ridden, was spoiling for war. The French Chamber on
July 15 voted supplies for war, and the King returning
to Berlin by train found excited crowds at the stations
clamouring for war, though he gave no orders for mobilisation until the vote at Paris was known. That Bismarck
was intriguing and Moltke was hoping for war is certain.
But to point to any one incident or any one person's action
as the immediate cause would be wrong. "The story is
one of national jealousy carefully fanned for four years by
newspaper editors....Bismarck's clever shifts to bring about
a rupture in 1870 would have failed had not the atmosphere
both at Paris and Berlin been charged with electricity[1]."
He at once published Benedetti's paper of 1866, with its
suggestions that France should be allowed with Prussia's
sanction and help to annex Belgium or Luxemburg.

Moltke's general plan of campaign had been drawn up
already. As in 1866, he would take the offensive; it might
be costly in lives, but if successful would be overwhelming.
Two things had to be considered; firstly, would Austria
join in as France's ally, or were the preliminary overtures,
which Napoleon had made with Italy as well as Austria,
vague and unlikely to be realised? Secondly, would the
South German states put their armies entirely at Prussia's
disposal? As regards the first point, it was unnecessary
to disarrange the plan of offence, for the whole half-million

[1] Holland Rose, *The Development of the European Nations*, p. 49.

first line of the army could not be carried to the Rhine at
once; three army corps at least had to be mobilised in the
eastern parts of Prussia, and before the railways were clear
enough for their transport it would be known whether they
could be safely launched against France, or would be
required against Austria; very soon it was seen that as
Austria was not mobilising they were not wanted in the
east, but in the meanwhile there they were in case they
should be wanted.  There can be little doubt that the
attitude of Russia, to which country Bismarck had always
respectfully paid court, kept Austria quiet.  On the second
point the fatal error of Napoleon when he tried to get the
left bank of the Rhine at Bavaria's expense threw her
into the arms of Prussia; two Bavarian army corps were
mobilised as part of the Crown Prince's army, and their
conduct in the war was such that never has there been
any doubt that she would ever fight again as France's ally;
Napoleon himself had thrown away any chance of his
gaining the ally who had been so useful to Louis XIV or
to his uncle.  Similarly the divisions of Wurtemberg,
Baden, and Hesse Darmstadt, were available.  Saxony
was already in the North German Confederation and
provided one army corps, but the Saxons were not at all
anxious to fight against France.

Fourteen corps being mobilised[1], they were concentrated

[1] A Prussian regiment was on mobilisation at once doubled in
strength from its peace footing by the inclusion of reserves, i.e., the
men who had comparatively recently been discharged from the
colours and who were still obliged to do a short annual training.
The landwehr men were ex-reservists, mostly young married men
in civil life, who were called up to the lines of communication or to
the firing line as they were wanted.  It was the devotion of the
landwehr men to the fatherland that so struck Archibald Forbes,
and he often refers to it.

by rail at three points from which they were to converge
on the frontier of Alsace and Lorraine. For a fortnight
Germany west of the Rhine was practically defenceless,
and Napoleon I would certainly have made the first dash
to enter upon German soil and strike between any two of
these armies before they converged; Moltke, it is clear,
counted deliberately upon Napoleon III not being ready,
for his spies must have made him aware of the French lack
of organisation. The three points were in the neighbourhood
of Coblenz, Mainz, and Landau. The First Army, two
corps of Rhinelanders under General Steinmetz, based on
Coblenz, was to be ready in case Napoleon should violate
the neutrality of Belgium; when it was seen that he would
not, it was to march southwards to join in on the right
flank of the Second Army. Prince Frederick Charles
commanded the Second Army, composed of the Prussian
Guard and four other corps and the Saxons, based on Mainz,
and facing south-westwards to meet the line of Steinmetz's
advance. The Third Army, under the Crown Prince, was
on the Rhine, in the north of Baden and round Landau
in the Palatinate, composed of two Prussian, two Bavarian,
and a mixed corps; his destination was the northern
frontier of Alsace.

On the other side the mobilisation of the French
depended entirely upon one main line of rail running due
east from Paris by way of Chalons, to Nancy, thence to
the frontier at Weissenburg to meet the German railway
from Landau; a branch from Nancy ran to Metz, continuing
thence on the one side to Luxemburg and to Belgium, on the
other to the frontier at Saarbruck and onwards to Mainz;
branch lines also ran from Chalons and Nancy towards
Belfort in the extreme south of Alsace at the gap between
the Vosges Mountains and the Jura, thence northwards

up the middle of Alsace to Strasburg, meeting the main
line at Weissenburg. Thus the rendezvous of the main
French army around Metz and Nancy was certain, while
a second army would be based on Strasburg. Napoleon
was himself in command at Metz with four corps, roughly
120,000 men; MacMahon, of Malakoff and Magenta fame,
had about 50,000 men in north Alsace; the Imperial
Guard was in the rear at Nancy; a corps, based on the
strong fortress of Bitsch, connected Napoleon and MacMahon;
and another was based on Belfort far to the south; reserves
were being concentrated in a great camp near Chalons.
It is superfluous to insist further on the unreadiness and
lack of details of equipment among the French, or on the
inability of Napoleon, still ill and in pain, to handle the
force. The main point is that they were spread out behind
the frontier irregularly, the larger army bunched between
Metz and Saarbruck, the other between Strasburg and
Weissenburg, with a corps between them which failed to
keep touch with either, and reduced by want of a common
plan to wait to receive on the defensive the blows which
it remained for the enemy to deliver. The lines of the
German railways running towards Saarbruck and Weissenburg indicated where would be the converging points of
Steinmetz and the Red Prince, and of the Crown Prince,
respectively. It must not be supposed that all the German
arrangements worked with absolute perfection, for both
the battles of August 6 were brought on prematurely;
Steinmetz pushed on too fast and his left incommoded the
Red Prince's right; a day's delay would have concentrated
a greater number of men on each of the French advanced
points, and thus would have prevented heavy losses. But
the general plan was understood and was carried out, and
German corps commanders knew that they must support

each other, whenever they heard the sound of guns, without hesitation or jealousy. Within three weeks the Germans were mobilised, concentrated, and advanced up to and over the frontier; about 160,000 came at once into action, 200,000 were immediately behind them, and another 100,000 were not far off as they were not required against the Austrians.

On August 2 the advanced brigade of Steinmetz was at Saarbruck on German soil; General Frossard's leading division engaged it and drove it back, and the Prince Imperial received his "baptism of fire." As Steinmetz brought up his full army, Frossard fell back into France and took up a strong position at the two villages of Forbach and Spicheren, with all the advantages of steep slopes and woods and garden enclosures in his favour. On August 6, a subordinate general, thinking Frossard to be in full retreat with only a rearguard at Spicheren, attacked; other divisions of Steinmetz's army advanced to the sound of the guns, and Alvensleben's corps of Frederick Charles's command struck in on their left. The French easily repulsed the first attacks, but late in the day the Germans overlapped both flanks and hauled guns up to high ground so as to dominate the position. Then Frossard drew off in the night, leaving behind him indeed a great store of supplies and munitions, yet maintaining tolerable order. *Tout peut se rétablir* ran Napoleon's bulletin, and this was true; for the whole of the German Second Army was not yet deployed, and Frossard was able to rally on the two French corps behind him, which had remained inactive all day though well within the sound of his guns. The French fought very gallantly, and their moral was not badly shaken.

On the other side the fighting began within the French

frontier at Weissenburg, where on August 4 one Bavarian
and two Prussian corps of the Third Army surrounded and
overpowered a single unsupported division of MacMahon's
army. By August 6 he concentrated his whole available
force at the villages of Woerth, Froeschweiler, and Elsass-
hausen, about 50,000 strong, and he too had the great
advantage of slopes and woods and enclosures. The French
fought with great spirit and delivered counter-attacks, but
the Crown Prince, when once committed prematurely to
battle by his corps leaders, brought up more and more
Germans till he had about 80,000 in all. The position was
surrounded in broad daylight, and in spite of devoted
charges of cavalry to certain death to cover the retreat
the French broke. There was a bad rout. Some rallied
and fell back to Strasburg, the rest fled across the Vosges
without any order. German critics accuse the Crown
Prince of losing touch with the fugitives; but it would
seem that the tremendous success of the battle, brought
on a day too soon, but accepted when once he was committed,
was almost too sudden. He preferred to close up his rear
for an orderly advance. Meanwhile the French corps,
under Failly, lay at Bitsch half-way between Woerth and
Spicheren, and assisted at neither battle; it was left in
the air, and now fell back on Nancy on the way to Chalons.
The distance from Woerth to Spicheren is 40 miles.

The general plan of the renewed German advance was
dictated by the plain facts that MacMahon's army no longer
existed, and that all the other French corps were concentrating on Metz. Napoleon handed over the supreme
command to Bazaine, and himself went to Chalons, where
MacMahon met him to organise a new army out of the
reserves and fugitives. Bazaine had now five corps,
perhaps 170,000 front-line men, as the Guard and other

units came up, and his purpose was to retreat on Verdun to make his stand on the Meuse. But confusion still reigned, and on August 14 the retreat was only beginning; Bazaine's apology for his delay was that his stores and transport were insufficient. By this time the Germans were advancing in strength, with at least two new corps coming up which had been in neither the First nor the Second Army on the 6th. The First Army was approaching the eastern face of Metz; its duty was to hinder the French retreat, and one of the generals on his own initiative attacked at Colombey for this purpose; Steinmetz pressed in to support him, and Bazaine, though beating off the attack with considerable loss to the Germans, was delayed for a day. Meanwhile the Second Army was advancing on a broad front to the south so as to circle round and pin Bazaine to Metz; any such encircling movement requires time, hence the value of the action at Colombey which seemed to be a French victory. The Third Army was advancing on either side of the main railway from the northern shoulder of the Vosges towards Nancy; it occupied Lunéville and found no enemy to dispute the plateau, the Grand Couronné de Nancy, where in 1914 General Castelnau stopped the German advance. Part of this army the Crown Prince detached to lay siege to Strasburg.

On August 16 Bazaine had no more troops to the east of Metz, and his retreat on Verdun was really beginning. But by the morning of that day Alvensleben's corps of the Second Army, swinging round from west to north, was threatening the main road. He immediately went into action near Vionville against Frossard's corps, but he had practically the whole French army against him. Bazaine was so taken by surprise that he seems to have thought that he had more than one corps to face, for he could easily have swept it aside. Alvensleben held on, while another corps, swinging round in the same way, but further to the west, and therefore having to describe a wider concentric circle, came in on his left, while another was coming up in his right rear. The result was that, as Bazaine did not put in his whole army for fear of losing touch with Metz in his rear, towards the end of the day nearly equal forces were engaged. Even so, slow as was the development of the French counter-attack, the Germans were for a time in a position of great danger. Three times in the day masses of cavalry had to be sent to charge guns and infantry to gain some little delay, which they succeeded in doing, especially on the extreme west of the field near the village of Mars-la-Tour. But they held their ground and stopped the retreat of the French by the high road.

On the 17th, Bazaine fell back to a new position nearer to Metz. His left rested on the outworks of the great fortress near Gravelotte, and his main line ran northwards and slightly westwards along the slope of a valley, his centre at Amanvillers and his right at Saint Privat, a front of some seven miles, while behind him ran the Metz-Belgium railway. It was quite a strong position, admitting of a good defence, and entrenched, but everything depended on the possibility of maintaining a hold upon Saint Privat; four corps were in line and the Guard in reserve. Moltke took advantage of the day, while Bazaine was consolidating and entrenching his line, to complete the encircling movement. Steinmetz coming round on the inner curve nearest to Metz, faced Gravelotte; Frederick Charles continued the line opposite to Amanvillers and Saint Privat, the Prussian Guard on his left, the corps that had been most engaged on the 16th in reserve, and the Saxons on the outside curve coming up to a position beyond Saint Privat. The French had their faces, and the Prussians their backs, to Paris.

During the whole day of the 18th the Germans were attacking very fiercely. Steinmetz carried Gravelotte, but trying to push on across the wooded valley got his army crowded in a position where it lost very heavily. Frederick Charles could make no impression upon the two villages to his front. But Bazaine made no strong counter-attack; it is thought that if he had put in the Guard, he could have routed Steinmetz and won a position to the south of the Germans which would have placed them in a very awkward position; or again, if he had sent the Guard to Saint Privat, he could have turned the German left; he did neither. Consequently towards nightfall the Saxons arrived, stormed Saint Privat, where apparently the French had shot away almost all their ammunition, and completely turned their right; the chassepot was yet a new weapon, and the French at the period of the previous heavy charges shot very rapidly, and it is said with insufficient aim. The Germans confessed to a loss of 20,000, but they had won their object; even the headstrong attacks of Steinmetz, for which he was deprived of his command, had at least pinned Bazaine's left flank to his position and prevented him from reinforcing the right flank at Saint Privat. So Bazaine retreated to Metz. He had still 200,000, fortress troops included, for active resistance, but by accepting defeat and allowing himself to be locked up in Metz, he put himself out of a position to influence the campaign worthy of his numbers. Moltke promptly commenced the siege with the First Army, and three corps of the Second, together with reserves, about 200,000 men. The rest of the Second Army, including the Prussian Guard and the Saxons, were formed into a new command, called the Army of the Meuse, under the Crown Prince of Saxony, and sent to support the Crown Prince of Prussia's advance on Chalons.

Meanwhile MacMahon was forming a new army at Chalons. He had the remnants of his own men from Woerth, Failly's corps which had retreated from Bitsch without fighting, another from Belfort which had been too far distant to be in action, and a reserve corps, a total of well over 120,000 men. He had before him the alternatives of defending the line of the Marne, or of falling back on Paris, for it was too late for him to advance to make a stand upon the Meuse between the fortresses of Verdun and Toul. The third and worst thing that he could do was to try to march round to the north and east to cut his way through to Bazaine; it has been condemned by all writers, especially as Bazaine could hold out for a long time, but political considerations prevailed. Napoleon was with MacMahon. He dared not return to Paris, where the excitement against him was growing in intensity, and he felt that almost any move, however bad, was preferable to having to face the mob of Paris. So on August 21 Mac-Mahon started from the Chalons camp to make that most dangerous of all moves, a flank march across the enemy's front. The Crown Prince of Prussia was moving on a wide front of about 25 miles on either side of the railway; Nancy had fallen, and Toul was blocked. On the 25th he had some information of what MacMahon was doing, but it seemed too good to be true. On the 26th, the news being confirmed, the whole of the German force, both the Third and the Fourth Army, swerved northwards on a new line down the valleys of the Aisne and the Meuse; by the 29th the leading corps were well upon MacMahon's flank, pressing him off his direct line towards Metz, and inflicting on him

such severe blows on the 30th and 31st that the French
were driven, in an almost demoralised condition, northwards
to Sedan in the Meuse valley.   By the 31st some portion
of the Germans had crossed the Meuse; on September 1st
several corps crossed above and below Sedan[1], and fought
their way to the right and left along the hills curving above
the town.   MacMahon might yet have broken away still
further northwards, saving his army as an army in spite
of all his losses, but he was wounded by a splinter from
a shell.   Both he and Napoleon meant the command to
devolve on Ducrot.   But General de Wimpfen had just
arrived hot-foot from Algeria, and passing through Paris
had been given a special commission by the ministry in case
anything should happen to MacMahon; producing this he
overbore even the Emperor's wishes.   Ducrot's orders to
retreat to the north-west were countermanded, and Wimpfen
made his main effort to break out eastwards towards Metz.
The change of plan meant delay, and this was invaluable
to the Germans, who now had time to press along the hills
so as to form full circle and join hands.   The French efforts,
including a fierce charge of all the available cavalry which,
as at Woerth, led to certain death, were all useless.   Panic

[1] It was at Bazeilles near Sedan that some villagers fired into
the rear of a Bavarian detachment, and the village was deliberately
set on fire so that men and women alike were burnt alive.   It almost
seems as if the memory of such revenge were kept alive on purpose,
in order that brutality might make impossible any return of friendship
for France but bind Bavaria for ever to Prussia.   Some of the foulest
deeds of 1914 are on the clearest evidence attributed to Bavarians.
On the other hand the Saxons both in 1870 and 1914 began the war
with no bitterness against France, and their memory of 1870 is an
entirely honourable one of their great charge at Saint Privat without
any taint of brutality, and we know that they have been very decent
towards our own men in the trenches.

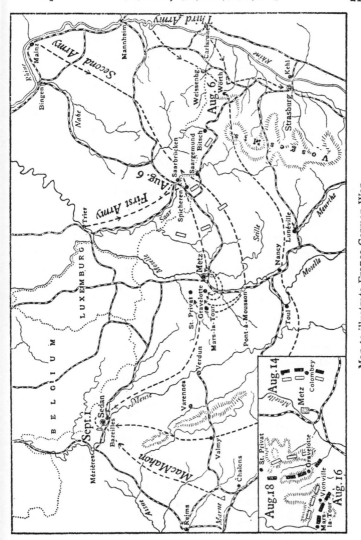

Map to illustrate Franco-German War.

- - - → General line of German advance.    ☐ French Troops.    ▬ German Troops.

was setting in; the streets of Sedan were congested, and German shells were falling there fast; so in the afternoon Napoleon himself ordered the white flag to be run up.

Unconditional surrender, softened only by an offer to accept the parole of officers, was Moltke's sentence. All attempts to get better terms, such as would save the French the bitterness of extreme humiliation and leave some little sense of gratitude, were unavailing. Gratitude does not exist in history. It is best to weaken an enemy to exhaustion so that he may be unable to think of revenge. Thus argued Bismarck, leaving to Moltke the last word. He refused to let Napoleon meet William face to face lest the King should become soft. On September 2 unconditional surrender was accepted, and 83,000 French were made prisoners, making with those already captured a total of over 100,000, including the Emperor and wounded Marshal. The horrors of the last day of the fighting, of the suspense during the discussion of terms, of the herding and starvation of the prisoners for a short time before they could be got away, and of the miserable march to Germany, are beyond imagination.

Eugénie fled from Paris helped by her American doctor; we must leave to her a share of blame for her husband's collapse, for she always urged him on to high enterprise without any consideration as to whether he had the resources to carry it out. The Third Republic was proclaimed in Paris on September 4, and was demanded at Bordeaux and Lyons before news arrived of what Paris had done. Thiers was called to the head, and with him were Favre and Grévy; he was a reputed Orleanist, but for the time there was no thought of any form of government but a Republic. The First Republic had beaten back the Prussians from Valmy in 1792. Now that the French

nation had established "it," they would rise as a nation
in defence of "it," avenge Sedan, save Metz, and restore
the honour that the Emperor had damaged.   But the cases
were not similar; the men of 1792 were mostly the old
trained soldiers that royal France gave to the new Republic,
though their enthusiasm was republican; the enemy in
1792 was the unenthusiastic army of the Prussian monarchy,
rusted for want of use, and lit by no flame of devotion for
the fatherland.   Now the French republican levies were
untrained, however keen would be their devotion, and the
Germans were burning with new enthusiasm for fatherland
and for the watch over the Rhine, highly trained men,
confident of victory, a nation in arms.   Belief in a cause
wins only if it has resources and a power to act.   The
French nation from September 4 onwards was magnificent;
it held out for five months after Napoleon had been ruined
within one; its devotion was such that from 1871 to 1914
it had always a memory of noble efforts to counterbalance
humiliation.   But it had not the resources to hold back the
flood of German invasion as Joffre held it back in September
1914, for Joffre's reserves were not raw or untrained.

The first thought was whether there would be any
fighting at all.   The Emperor began it, would the Republic
continue it?   The Prussian leaders required some security,
Alsace and Lorraine, or at least some part, for otherwise
the Republic might enjoy a breathing space and then,
being ready, think of revenge.   Favre made his famous
answer, "Not an inch of our soil nor a stone of our fortresses."
The war, therefore, went on.

The Germans, held stationary for a time whilst they
gathered in their prisoners and rearranged their plans,
proceeded at last towards Paris.   They had no formed
army before them.   General Trochu commanded a com-

posite mass of a few regulars, a good many sailors who manned the forts, and a large number of national guards and mobile guards; the two latter bodies were armed citizens and country militia respectively, and at either extreme we may place the rabid Parisian democrats, already communists at heart, and the pious Catholic monarchy-loving Bretons. It was a difficult garrison for Trochu to control, and very uneven in quality. The mass of armed men, hardly to be called soldiers, outnumbered the approaching Germans. But it would have been madness to take the open field, and Trochu was certainly wise to allow Paris to be surrounded. The task before the Germans was difficult enough, even when the weakness of the French is considered. The army besieging Metz and the army closing round Paris had to be fed, and a great part of the food had to be brought from Germany, for the area of fighting in France was soon exhausted, both by the French who swept supplies into Paris, and by the Germans who requisitioned, so that war could not entirely support war; one writer, indeed, implies that on one occasion provision trains destined for the besiegers of Paris were diverted to the besiegers of Metz, and that the former were in consequence nearly forced to retreat. Moreover the long line of railway, Nancy—Toul—Chalons—Paris, by which munitions and supplies had to be forwarded, had to be watched, principally by reserves of landwehr; Frenchmen were forced to work on the line, and had to be guarded; it was difficult to prevent destruction of the rails and bridges at each point. Here we have the question of the *francs-tireurs*; men not in uniform, merely decorated with armlets or *brassards*, which they could wear as soldiers, and slip off when they wanted to pass off as civilians, gave the German line infinite trouble by sniping. If the Republican government at Tours could raise and concentrate on the Loire a considerable relieving force, and another in the north, and if Trochu could time his sorties to co-operate, while yet the Germans had trouble with *francs-tireurs* on the line of communication, then the siege of Paris might turn to the advantage of the besieged. Everything seemed to depend on the quality of the new armies and on time. The French really seemed to have a chance, and thus we admire the way in which they tried to seize it. Communications between Paris and outside relief were carried on by means of balloons and pigeons. Léon Gambetta, the ardent anti-imperial lawyer, escaped to Tours in a balloon, and was the soul of the great effort; he was a thorn in the side of Thiers, who dubbed him a *fou furieux*, but he went near to success. Aurelle de Paladines was Gambetta's general chosen to lead the army of the Loire to the relief of Paris.

To help the Germans, a severe bombardment forced the surrender of Strasburg, September 27. Toul fell September 23. Bitsch far away in the north of Alsace was merely blockaded, and did not distract many Germans so as to influence the war. Belfort was later besieged by the army which had taken Strasburg. There were comparatively few Germans to cover, against the relieving forces, the main army blockading Paris. General von der Tann with one Bavarian corps and a Prussian division advanced on and entered Orleans on October 11. Then at the critical moment Bazaine surrendered Metz on October 24. No argument in his defence is worth the least consideration; to say that his commission was from the Emperor, and therefore that he had no duty towards the Republic, is nonsense; a higher loyalty was owed to France. He could have held out longer and detained the Red Prince before Metz, giving invaluable aid to the newly growing

army on the Loire[1]. By surrendering he freed the Red
Prince. Verdun was surrendered, after a bombardment,
on November 5. Aurelle's army of the Loire, 100,000
strong, was not ready to advance till November, when he
drove von der Tann out of Orleans and distinctly defeated
him at Coulmiers on November 9, in the region where the
Maid defeated Talbot and Fastolf in 1429. But it was
only a defeat, and the outnumbered Bavarians drawing
off without more than ordinary loss fell back on Frederick
Charles, who was now free to move after the disposal of
his Metz prisoners. The result was that the so far victorious
French were quite unable to get near enough to Paris to
compel the raising of the siege. Whether they could have
done so, had Bazaine had a little more grit in his character
and a better power of control over his men, must remain
uncertain; Moltke was frightened for a moment, but the
raw French levies, however enthusiastic, were man for man
no match for the Germans; they might have threatened,
or even cut, the main line of communication, and made
Moltke detach a considerable force to rally Tann; then
would have been the moment for Trochu's sortie. But
all guesswork is vain.

[1] On the other hand the evidence of Archibald Forbes is that
Metz was in a disgraceful condition from typhoid fever and general
dirt and demoralisation. Bazaine had no power of leadership,
many of the officers were of the worst type of boasters and haughty
and disobedient, and the men discontented to the verge of mutiny;
the laxity of the Napoleonic rule, promotion by favour, selfishness,
etc., had ruined the spirit that ought to exist between officers and
men. He often speaks of the excessive drinking, especially of
cognac and absinthe, as the curse of France, and plainly thinks that
Bazaine was at the end of his tether. He entered Metz very soon
after the capitulation. The forts round Metz, he says, were
impregnable. The prisoners were 173,000 from the field army
and garrison combined.

Frederick Charles interposed between Orleans and the besiegers three full army corps, and he had the inner position. In the last week of November he was in touch with Aurelle; on December 1 and 2 he drove him back on to Orleans, and once more the Germans entered that city. Meanwhile the great sortie from Paris, timed to take place on November 30, so as to join hands with Aurelle from the Loire, was directed to the south-east and east, and after four days of heavy fighting the French fell back. Gambetta now dismissed Aurelle, and put in his place Chanzy and Bourbaki. Chanzy fought hard against Frederick Charles December 8 and 10, but could not break through. The Republican government was withdrawn from Tours to Bordeaux, and Chanzy circled round westwards to Le Mans to rest his men and organise for yet another effort. Bourbaki seemed to disappear out of sight southwards. Thus the concerted movement failed, though in all some 200,000 French of the new levies were brought into action.

In November also General Faidherbe was collecting an army in the north based on Amiens. Manteuffel, released from the siege of Metz, with two corps of the old First Army, had little trouble in pushing his way through; he captured Amiens and Rouen in succession, and overran Normandy up to the coast. Another centre of French resistance was Dijon in Burgundy. Garibaldi came hither to put his services at the disposal of the Republic, but he was far from being the old Garibaldi of 1849 and 1860; he lacked energy, and was accused, it may be with some truth, of intolerance and even persecution of priests and monks. The Germans invested Belfort in November, and to cover the siege a corps under General von Werder lay between the Vosges and Dijon.

Thus the main great operation, the siege of Paris, was being carried on without a break. As the autumn passed away the feeling of many neutrals in Europe began to change. Sympathy was felt for France now suffering for the sins of Napoleon, and holding out to prevent a loss of territory which she did not deserve. The energy of Gambetta, the heroism of Aurelle and Chanzy, the presence of Garibaldi, the thought of the great city, the intellectual and artistic capital of the world, now blockaded and within measurable distance of starvation, each made for sympathy. Thiers was making a tour through Europe to obtain help from neutrals, or to induce the four remaining Powers to concert to put pressure on Germany. Bismarck felt anxiety. In his own reminiscences published many years later, and in his talk as recorded by his Boswell Busch, he both resented the imputation against German *Kultur* and showed scorn of France. It was no crime, he protested, for Germans to stamp down resistance after the "not an inch of our soil nor a stone of our fortresses" proclamation; Paris had no real claim to be the "Mecca of civilisation," the *Ville Lumière* of literature and art, so that it should be exempted from the penalties of war; civilians were bound to suffer in all wars, even to the point of starvation, and if starvation why not bombardment? He was scornful of Thiers, cringing to foreigners for help, though he certainly foresaw trouble if a Concert of Europe should demand the relaxation of Germany's grip. What excited him most was English sentimentality about the bombardment which had not yet begun; the Crown Prince had an English wife, our Princess Royal, who was much influenced by Queen Victoria; the chief of his staff and other high-placed Germans were also married to Englishwomen; feminine sentimental interference, and English feminine interference at that, was hateful to the serious man of blood and iron. The worst of it was that King William himself was influenced. Moreover there was some tension between Bismarck and the military leaders. He writes as if they resented his being present at councils of war, and he was certainly vexed that they were not hurrying up the heavy siege-guns. Winter was near, and it was absolutely necessary to bombard so as to force a speedy surrender.

In November Bismarck found a powerful ally in Carlyle. The strong-minded Scot never swerved from his admiration for all things German, and his letter to *The Times* on November 18 was characteristic of him. He began by several references to past history to show how France had always been the aggressor; Henri II got Metz, Verdun, and Toul, "by fraudulent pawnbroking," and Louis XIV got Strasburg " by attorneyism...but not so much attorneyism and the long sword as the housebreaker's jemmy"; "no nation ever had so bad a neighbour as Germany has had in France." He honoured France for her First Revolution, which was an "Insurrection against Shams," but then she stopped short. "The further stage must be under better presidency than that of France....The German race, not the Gaelic, are now to be protagonist in the immense world-drama....Considerable misconception as to Herr von Bismark is still prevalent in England....Bismark, as I read him, is not a person of 'Napoleonic' ideas, but of ideas quite superior to Napoleonic; shows no invincible 'lust of territory,' nor is tormented with 'vulgar ambition,' but has aims far beyond that sphere; and in fact seems to me to be striving with strong faculty, by patient, grand, and successful steps, towards an object beneficial to Germans and to all other men. That noble, patient, deep, pious, and solid Germany should be at length welded into a nation and become a Queen of the Continent, instead of vapouring, vainglorious, gesticulating, quarrelsome, restless, and over-sensitive France, seems to be the hopefullest public fact that has occurred in my time." Archibald Forbes, the famous war-correspondent of the *Daily News*, expressed the same thing in different language; the Germans were to him hearty and honest comrades, who certainly drank good beer and wine, but were not sodden with cognac and absinthe; they did not requisition supplies beyond what was necessary, and paid for much that they took, nor did they loot systematically; their endurance in the bitter winter, their steadiness and patriotism, were admirable.

Were Carlyle and Forbes right? Were the Germans justified, or were they as in 1914 inhuman beyond the methods of most victors in war? This is the place to discuss such questions, because Carlyle's letter, appearing before the bombardment, while Thiers was making his appeal to neutrals and sympathy was being loudly expressed for France, both in England and in other countries, had a very great influence. We can hardly imagine that Gladstone in any case would have been forced by sympathy into war. But not only the public opinion of historians and intellectual leaders owed very much to Carlyle; he also touched the average man. It is fair to bracket the name of Forbes with his, for the practical man who was on the spot, watching the siege of Paris, had also an undeniable influence. They have this in common that, each in his own way, they followed the lead of Burke in putting into the foremost place a consideration of "Temper and Character." The present writer remembers very vividly how his elders, during and after the war, referred to Carlyle as the sage against whom there was no appeal, and quoted Forbes as a man of real insight above all journalists. They were the two men who counted, and we have to get at contemporary evidence rather than the legend created since 1870.

After more than forty years we can see the flaw in Carlyle's argument. The French seizure of the three bishoprics of Lorraine and of Alsace was unjust possibly, but possession had been confirmed by several international treaties, and finally by the Congress of Vienna; the happiness and prosperity of the inhabitants, and their wish to remain French, outweigh the wickedness of annexation; all nations have conquered what was not theirs, but very few have been the equals of France in winning the affection and loyalty of the conquered; Germany's own record in Poland, Schleswig, and Alsace, has been consistently bad. If France had been a bad neighbour to Germany, Bavaria and Prussia have at various periods been very bad neighbours to Austria[1]. Moreover the First French Republic

[1] We turn naturally to Carlyle's estimate of Frederick the Great. If Louis XIV used a burglar's jemmy at Strasburg, how did Frederick seize Silesia in 1741? Here is the answer in Carlyle's words. "Will not Europe, probably, blaze into general War; Pragmatic Sanction going to *waste sheepskin*, and universal scramble ensuing? In which he who has 100,000 good soldiers, and can handle them, may be an important figure in urging claims, and keeping what he has got hold of!......Hear Friedrich himself: 'It was a means of acquiring reputation; of increasing the power of the State.'......'Add to these reasons,' says the King, with a candour which has not been well treated in the History Books, 'Add to these reasons an Army ready for acting, Funds, Supplies all found, and perhaps the desire of making oneself a name.' 'Desire to make himself a name; how shocking!' exclaim several Historians. 'Candour of confession that he may have had some such desire; how honest!' is what they do not exclaim. As to the justice of his Silesian Claims, or even to his own belief about their justice, Friedrich affords not the least light which can be new to readers here.......'Just Rights? What are rights, never so just, which you cannot make valid? The world is full of such. If you have rights and can assert them into facts, do it; that is worth doing!'"

did much good to Germany by introducing first to her the idea of the rights of man, even though at the bayonet's point, and Napoleon I put new life into Saxony and Bavaria and his other allies, even if he spoilt his own work by his absurd love of conquest. But the strongest argument is that Carlyle could not foresee what would be the German ideal of Empire when, after his death, that Empire was founded in Africa; the treatment of the Hereros, for instance, was such that where an Englishman could go unarmed a German hardly dared to go with a strong fully armed escort; such is our answer to the jeer of the modern Germans that they have a right to Empire as much as ourselves. The moral deterioration of the "noble, patient, deep, pious, solid" Germans of 1870 into "these professors of brutality" of 1914 would have been such a shock to Carlyle, that he could hardly have been able to use any of his favourite phrases. All this simply means that we must wrench ourselves away from recent events if we wish to understand him and his influence. ἀρχὴ ἄνδρα δείξει. Time had not shown to Carlyle how the Germans would use their Empire.

One special thing has to be said about Bismarck; he was not in favour of the annexation of French soil. It was Moltke, and the German military leaders in general, who demanded Metz and Strasburg, so as to form a series of impregnable German fortresses over against France. Bismarck feared the result of annexing too much land where sympathies would always be in favour of France, partly it may be from fear of incurring odium in other countries, partly from a recognition of the difficulty of holding the population down with a strong hand. Therefore Carlyle was right so far in saying that Bismarck had no lust for territory.

The evidence of Forbes, and other evidence of which there is a good deal, is to the effect that, though there was a great deal of suffering in France at the hands of the Germans, it was not beyond bounds. Acts of brutality certainly occurred, but from what we are told there was not the systematic brutality as encouraged and even ordered by those in authority in the August and September of 1914. Requisitions were made, but Forbes distinctly states that German officers paid for much of what they took, and that the French were willing enough to sell. He gives instances of houses left untouched when the owners awaited the coming of the Germans instead of running away. On the other side the shooting of German troops by *francs-tireurs*, the horror felt at the employment of Turcos against Europeans, the haughty pride of the French Imperial officers at the beginning of the war, and the demoralisation of the rank and file in defeat, and in particular of the Parisians, must be acknowledged. Against this we put the wonderful recovery of the French since 1870, which is as remarkable as the deterioration of the Germans. We can hardly picture the soldiers of Napoleon I himself, or of Napoleon III if he had been victorious, plundering as systematically, and destroying in a manner as barbarous as the modern Huns; but they plundered in 1806 after Jena, and probably would have plundered in 1870 if they had had the chance. Hardly a Prussian family but had its tradition of suffering under Napoleon I. We must go back to the contemporary judgement on the fire-eating and loudly talking French officers of 1870, corrupted as they were by the Napoleonic régime, if we wish to try to understand German hatred of them, and must get out of our minds the honourable and clever generals of the regenerated France of to-day. Forbes did not see them;

he saw high-minded Germans quite unlike their prosperity-corrupted descendants. Lastly, of course all the French were not boastful or absinthe-sodden in 1870; but such were most in evidence.

A hideous feature of 1914 has been the wanton fouling of houses and even of churches, done so deliberately as to be beyond belief, and more utterly beyond belief because the Germans claim to be so artistic and literary and musical. Centuries ago Puritans defiled churches, partly through religious mania. But the peculiar grossness of the Prussian dirt-slinging, in an age when sanitation is a fine art, shows a deeper-seated vileness of mind. The evidence is not always clear, for people do not write much of such things. But an English officer who marched from Waterloo to Paris in the rear of some Prussians says that this horror occurred in 1815. Oral evidence says that it occurred in 1870. Perhaps in neither year was it committed so systematically as in 1914, especially on the altars of churches. So in 1870 the Germans drank, but no evidence accuses them of the orgy of drunkenness such as broke out when they were let loose, like weak-minded boys allowed for once to drink what is usually forbidden, in the cellars of Champagne in 1914. In 1870 they shot *francs-tireurs* and burnt villages which sheltered them; the Spaniards of the Peninsular War, many of Garibaldi's men, and the Boers, have fought without being in uniform, and probably often suffered for it; but the awful vengeance for free shooting in 1914, inflicted on a neutral country deliberately invaded and scorned, inflicted merely on a bare statement of Germans themselves who may be lying, has no parallel in 1870. The Crown Prince did not wish that Paris should be bombarded; his son's heart bled for what he was forced to do at Louvain!

The bombardment of Paris at last began late in December; some of the outer forts were ruined at once, though the strong Mont Valérien was not hurt; then some sections of the city were laid in ruins. Sorties were yet made occasionally. Chanzy made his last efforts against Frederick Charles in the neighbourhood of Le Mans south-west of Paris, and his army finally collapsed after January 12. Faidherbe came again into the field but was forced to give battle at Saint Quentin, and was finally beaten on January 19, falling back to the fortresses of Arras, and Lille, and other places on the Belgian border. A third move was made by Bourbaki, whose object was to raise the siege of Belfort and then push forward into South Germany or into Alsace to destroy the German depots of supplies, and generally to do as much damage as possible. This last of Gambetta's armies was formed into four corps and was tolerably well equipped with rifles and artillery, but the supply of boots was painfully insufficient, and there was no transport train. Manteuffel, detached from the north, had three army corps; one under Werder was immediately in line to head off Bourbaki, who was supported from Dijon by Garibaldi, and to cover Belfort; Manteuffel brought up the other two himself to press in when Werder had already held his ground with success. Between January 21 and February 2 the much smaller force of Germans, well fed and well supplied, turned Bourbaki off his line of attack and pressed him on to the Swiss frontier. Their object was to surround him and bring about a second Sedan. But this was just avoided, when on February 2, 80,000 French, starving and miserable, almost all without shoes in the bitter frost, straggled over the frontier into Switzerland and were there disarmed and kindly treated. Indeed the winter was unusually bitter.

Whilst English schoolboys were enjoying a solid five weeks of uninterrupted skating, to the bombardment of Paris and the plight of the relieving armies, which in any case would have been wretched, was added the extra misery of frost-bite. Hence the heroism of these last armies was lost, and Bourbaki's poor fellows crossed the frontier in a hopeless state of disorder[1].

Paris was actually surrendered under the terms of an armistice on January 28, while Bourbaki was yet fighting and Belfort was yet besieged. Of course it could only be an armistice at first, for the Germans required some security for a regular peace, such as a regularly constituted government could alone give; also the eastern district, where Bourbaki was still in arms, was excepted. Trochu indeed would have held out longer, and the Parisians themselves and the National Guard, who were quite at variance with the regular troops and the limited number of good mobiles that Trochu still commanded, called out for yet another sortie. But Favre negotiated the armistice. The forts were handed over, but the National Guards were allowed to retain their arms. An election was to be held at once. It took place

[1] The fate of Bourbaki's army is the best commentary on the wrongheadedness of the historians who created the republican legend of 1792. Michelet, who wrote his *French Revolution* in the fifties, was full of enthusiasm for the *volontaires* of '92 ready to fight for France and Republic 600,000 strong; "they only lacked guns and shoes and bread!" Ultimately these men, sorted out and trained with and by the old regulars of Louis XVI, carried everything before them on the Meuse and Rhine and Po, but in the first year without those regulars they were a mob. Ignorance of war on the part of such historians led Frenchmen to believe that republican ardour could beat disciplined troops, and France received a bitter lesson in 1870–71 when Bourbaki's men "only lacked shoes and bread" and training. One wonders what was the state of Michelet's mind when he wrote that "only."

on February 8, and the Assembly met at Bordeaux on February 12; Legitimists, Orleanists, and Republicans, each mustered 200 strong, and there were very few Bonapartists. The spirit of France had been cowed, and only a comparatively few extremists amongst the Republicans wished to follow Gambetta in prolonging a hopeless resistance. It has been noticed that in the Assembly were many noblemen and men of substance and few professional politicians, for the great number of the peasants and small proprietors who settled the election were afraid of Gambetta and the violence of his followers. That Alsace and north Lorraine would be surrendered was now a foregone conclusion. Thiers was chosen provisionally to be Head of the Executive, and Favre was by him made Foreign Minister. In the meanwhile Paris was being revictualled largely by help from England.

Peace was practically settled at Versailles on February 26, though it was finally ratified by the Treaty of Frankfort next May. The two points on which Thiers and Favre held out were the surrender of Belfort and the amount of the war indemnity. Bismarck consistently opposed Moltke so far as the German military chiefs insisted on the annexation of much territory and many fortresses; the Emperor himself settled the question by supporting Moltke. But France was allowed to retain Nancy, Lunéville, Verdun, and Toul, and therefore a very considerable portion of south Lorraine. After an acute controversy Thiers finally held his own and obtained Belfort for France. Also he got the Germans to reduce the indemnity from six to five milliards of francs; a milliard equals 1000,000,000 francs, therefore five milliards come to £200,000,000 of our money. The German troops were to be withdrawn from their positions on the south and west of Paris, and

their entire withdrawal from French soil would take place
when all the indemnity was paid.    The French prisoners
would be restored, but in the meanwhile in consideration
of the cession of Belfort and the reduction of one milliard,
the Germans were to march 30,000 troops into Paris.
Certainly France was humiliated, *saigné au blanc*, yet the
jeers of the Germans who found fault with the riotous
behaviour of a section of the Parisian mob during the days
of the formal entry of their troops March 1–5, are hardly
in good taste; if there is much suffering there is naturally
much resentment ; they claim credit for not having fired
upon this mob.    Forbes tells how he was badly mauled,
when he had been seen to shake hands with some German
officers, and then went to mix with the crowd; this again
is a matter of good taste.

It remains to notice the three chief consequences of
the great war.    Firstly we take the establishment of the
German Empire; it would be wrong to say the re-establishment, for it was utterly unlike the old Holy Roman Empire.
There were difficulties in the way.    William himself wished
to remain King of Prussia, though the Crown Prince was
in favour of the Empire.    The Kings of Bavaria and
Wurtemberg were strongly opposed to the idea, but the
Grand Duke of Baden favoured it.    So strong was the
feeling that Bismarck, however keenly he had been pressing
on towards his purpose in the past few years, might have
been unable to realise it if it had not been for the exceptional
circumstances of the case, the encampment of the German
army around Paris, and the situation of the royal head-
quarters at Versailles in the palace of Louis XIV with
its associations of French animosity against Germany.
The negotiations were going on at least in December, when
a deputation from the Prussian Chamber offered the title

to their King, or rather expressed their wish that he should take the title. How the Bavarian opposition was overcome is not known, but probably there was a fear that the minor states might take the matter into their own hands, and in any case the Bavarians, having had their full share, and it may be more than their fair share, in the fighting and losses during the war, could hardly turn now against Prussia, however angry they were at such a termination of their efforts. The ceremony of the proclamation took place at Versailles on January 18.

Secondly, Italy profited by the war. As in 1866 she obtained Venice, so in 1870 she obtained Rome. Of course the French troops were withdrawn, for they were wanted in France; Napoleon being the prisoner of Germany, there was no one left who wished to protect the Pope; Victor Emmanuel's soldiers entered Rome on September 20[1] after a slight resistance of the papal troops by way of remonstrance against force, and after the breaching by cannon of part of the old wall. The Italian Parliament and the Royal Court were ultimately transferred to Rome after the usual *plébiscite* had been taken amongst the inhabitants of the patrimony and city. The Pope excommunicated Victor Emmanuel and his officers, and by way of dignified protest withdrew with his court to the Vatican, his palace on the rising ground above the right bank of the Tiber adjoining St Peter's, which he never quitted.

Thirdly, Russia took advantage of the humiliation of France to repudiate the Treaty of Paris of 1856. The Russians and the Prussians can hardly be said to have been on good terms with each other, yet the rulers of each country had come to an understanding, and in such matters the wishes of monarchs count more than the wishes of

[1] Every Italian town to-day has its Via Venti Settembre.

nations.   Bismarck was willing to let Russia put forward
the repudiation, because he wanted Russia's help to keep
the Austrians from supporting France.   On their side the
Austrians, or at least Count Beust who was bitterly
anti-Prussian, are credited with having offered their
support to Russia on this question as the price of an understanding between the two nations to threaten Prussia.
Gortschakoff, the Russian Chancellor, issued a Circular
to the effect that it was within the rights of the Tsar
to repudiate the articles of the Treaty which bound
him not to maintain warships on the Black Sea, or to
erect any arsenal or place of arms on the coast.   His argument was that by the "Convention of the Straits" the
passage of the Dardanelles was to be closed to ships of
war only in time of peace, so that by the connivance of the
Sultan an enemy might send a force to the Black Sea in
time of war to the detriment of Russia; also Moldavia
and Wallachia, which by the Treaty ought to have separate
governments, had been united in 1861 into the Principality
of Rumania.   The Circular was handed in to our Foreign
Secretary, Lord Granville, on November 9.   The excitement
here almost counterbalanced excitement over the war in
France.   Earl Russell, who had been three years in retirement, urged our ministers to resist even at the risk of war;
he wrote a very naive letter, suggesting that our small
standing army could be reinforced by 100,000 militia, and
that the Rothschilds would probably be willing to advance
£100,000,000; it was certainly a strange attitude for the
minister responsible for the Schleswig fiasco in 1864.
Gladstone simply let the question slide; he had the
Alabama dispute on his hands, and did not feel called upon
to have trouble with Russia also.   It is quite possible
that, owing to the strong feeling that there was in America

against the British, of which the Alabama question was a symptom, Gladstone had some fear of a Russian-American combination against us. Our newspapers took vengeance on Russia by a bitter denunciation of the Circular, and that was all. Whether Russia would have persisted if faced by the possibility of war must remain uncertain. In the course of the next few years Sebastopol was re-created as a place of arms and a new Black Sea fleet was built. A reopening of the Eastern Question was foreshadowed, though hardly anyone expected this to occur within six years.

*Note to Second Edition.* The Prussians, warned by the inferiority of their artillery to the Austrian in 1866, paid special attention to that arm before 1870. Krupps turned out new iron field-guns which completely outdistanced the French, so that Prussian officers opened fire always just outside the French maximum range, and new siege-guns before which all forts, except the very strongest outside Paris and Metz, were powerless. The age of all-steel guns is the nineties.

TSARS; HOUSE OF ROMANOFF

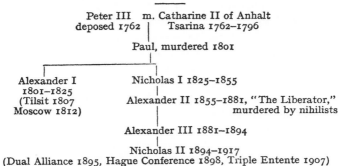

Peter III    m. Catharine II of Anhalt
deposed 1762 |    Tsarina 1762–1796

Paul, murdered 1801

Alexander I             Nicholas I 1825–1855
1801–1825
(Tilsit 1807        Alexander II 1855–1881, "The Liberator,"
Moscow 1812)                         murdered by nihilists

Alexander III 1881–1894

Nicholas II 1894–1917
(Dual Alliance 1895, Hague Conference 1898, Triple Entente 1907)

# CHAPTER VIII

## THE EASTERN QUESTION

The Franco-German War is, after the fall of the first Napoleon, the most momentous event of the 19th century. The nation which had led European thought was dethroned; would the nation which was now in the ascendant take its place as the leader of thought? Certain national aspirations were now realised; would the new "nations" prosper and do good to the world? Indeed they were as yet incomplete as nations, for the German Empire lacked Austria, and Italy was *irredenta* as long as part of the Adige valley and Trieste and the old possessions of Venice on the Dalmatian coast were under Austria. But, France being humbled, and new Germany requiring time to settle down to altered circumstances, to shake herself together, so to speak, and to see whether Bavaria and Saxony would be satisfied by the Prussian ascendancy, no troubles were destined to occur on "national" grounds, except in the Balkans, for a long time yet to come. There was no national cry indicating yearning after an ideal, now that Prussia had her ascendancy and Italy had Rome. Pan-Slavism had yet to be formulated.

Napoleon III overthrown, there was no personal disturbing element. The man was gone who might at any moment take up a national cause on behalf of a people under a foreign yoke, abandon the cause when it was half won, and yet seek to aggrandise France by claiming non-French land. There was nobody to champion a great many Poles, a few Danes, and a good many Frenchmen and Germans who wished to be Frenchmen, who were all forcibly held to be Germans. But a cause there still was which depended not on the vagaries of one man, the cause of the Roman Church, which prayed for deliverance from an excommunicated king, which hoped to have its temporal power restored to it by some legitimist king, and which claimed the allegiance of its German bishops. The "Ultra-Montains" of France, and of Germany likewise, were distinctly a disturbing element for some little time after 1871. The fierce opposition of the Republicans, led by Gambetta, destroyed their power in France, but at the cost of much bad feeling between clericals and anti-clericals; Bismarck uncompromisingly opposed them in Germany, the struggle being bitter while Pius IX lived, less bitter afterwards, and finally dying out.

The Concert of Europe was doomed by the events of 1870–71. Till then it had had influence at intervals, and afterwards it seemed to be revived to its full importance when the Congress met at Berlin in 1878. But the advancement of Prussia upset calculations, and the history of Europe after this decade is concerned with the formation of the Dual and the Triple Alliances; then Europe was divided into two armed camps, and at any moment a war might have broken out. The seventies, therefore, are the period of transition, and in it the questions were, What will be the future of France struggling to raise herself? how will Germany use her power? will the distant Power ever be able to assert herself as the centre of Pan-Slavism? will the island Power always remain insular? As the result, we find the Balance of Power becoming more important than the Concert, until at last, under new conditions and under the guidance of new men, Germany bound polyglot Austria-Hungary to her and thought herself strong enough to defy or overawe all the others; the decision of 1914 meant that whatever the Concert had tried to do at intervals was of no account, and that in the eyes of Germans only Germany counted. War songs are sufficient to show us that; in 1870 Germany was on the defensive to keep watch over the Rhine, in 1914 she is over all.

In the period of transition we start with the possibility of French recovery. The Assembly which met at Bordeaux in February 1871 had before it the question of the terms of peace and of nothing beyond. The deputies were largely monarchists,—it would be unfair to style them at such a crisis reactionaries,—but it was agreed by the "Bordeaux Compact" that the future constitution of France, whether Monarchy or permanent Republic, should be left undecided. Thiers was formally accepted as "Head of the Executive," and himself insisted on the addition "of the Republic" to show that the *de facto* accredited government was republican. Of course he was by his past history an Orleanist. Yet Favre and Simon were Republicans, and Gambetta, whose services he had to accept because of the man's superabundant energy, was *un fou furieux*, one might say a rabid Republican. The preliminaries of peace were signed at Versailles on February 26. The Assembly proceeded to sit at Versailles, when the German headquarters were withdrawn—the temporary German occupation of a part of Paris itself lasted only a few days, and then the Germans gave up the western and southern forts, preserving their hold only on the eastern and northern—on March 20.

The next question, before even any steps could be taken
to raise the money for the war indemnity, was that of the
Commune of Paris.    The National Guard, composed of the
city population, was still armed.    These men passionately
resented not only the cession of Alsace-Lorraine, but also the
German entry into Paris; they thought that they had been
despised by Trochu, not being allowed by him to take part
in the more serious sorties from Paris; their hatred of the
Germans was turned into a hatred of those who would not
let them fight against the Germans like the old triumphant
levies of 1792–93, that is to say honest Republicans who
carried all before them; they were offended because the
Assembly sat at monarchical Versailles, the place of memories of Louis XIV, and, more recently, of Kaiser William.
It was such men moreover whom the Germans mostly
despised, and accused of a rabidness at the time of the
entry which would have justified them in firing, and whom
Archibald Forbes especially denounced as noisy absinthe-
soaked undersized rowdies.    Against them the feeling in
the Assembly was distinctly strong; they were the Jacobins
of 1792–94 revived.    Now "Commune" has really nothing
to do with "Communism."    These Communards wanted
to set up a form of city government, or government by
communities; Paris would have its own municipal officers
directly elected and responsible to itself, federated to
similar communes in the other great cities, in which, not
the bourgeois and rich, but the working men would be able
to play the chief part.    Of course the main support of the
Assembly was to be found in the peasants, who always
suspected the townsfolk as likely to set up "Communism"
as we know it, the preliminary step to which would be
confiscation.    On March 18 troops sent by the Assembly
to take the guns which were massed in the suburb of

Montmartre were opposed by the Communards, and the
two generals commanding them were shot. Thus civil war
began.

The troops available for service under the Assembly
were prisoners of war released by the Germans with
MacMahon at their head; from their head-quarters they
were known as the Versaillais. After a couple of months
the troops carried one of the gates of Paris on May 21,
seized the enceinte wall, and proceeded to attack up the
wide streets. It took them a week to carry all the barricades,
the churches, such as the Madeleine, which had been converted into fortresses, and especially the Latin Quarter,
where many of the rabid students were desperate fighters.
The horrors of the strife can hardly be exaggerated. It is
always said that the Communards did not begin to take
hostages until the Versaillais began to shoot the leaders
who fell into their hands, and the cruelty was not all on one
side. When passions were thoroughly roused neither side
gave quarter. The Communards killed the Archbishop of
Paris and priests and policemen, and the women earned
a terrible reputation as *pétroleuses*, sprinkling oil over the
barricades and public buildings, so as to destroy themselves,
and the Versaillais, and Paris itself together; it seems
that rumour absurdly exaggerated the amount of damage
done by these harpies, though it remains that the Tuileries
and the Hôtel de Ville were burnt out, and it may be that
their intention was to burn the Louvre. On the other
hand the officers of the Versaillais, largely old Bonapartists,
who looked upon the mob as a gang of traitors, and were
especially sore at the insinuation that they could not fight
the Germans but took pleasure in killing their own country-
men, shot their prisoners without trial and without mercy.
After the Commune had been suppressed large numbers of

men and women were tried, and many thousands were sent to Cayenne or New Caledonia. Amnesty for these was not passed till 1879 on the motion of Gambetta, who indeed had himself withdrawn from public life during the actual civil war.

The next question was to find the money and so to bring about the withdrawal of the German forces from French soil. France herself raised the money, though at first a good deal of the coin had to be borrowed from England; even so France herself very soon was able to find food for the starving, though at first most of the supplies brought into Paris after the siege was over came from England. Europe was profoundly impressed by the promptness of the payments after all the miseries and the expenses entailed by the war. "The inexhaustible stocking of the countryman" solved the problem. It was not only that the French peasant was fond of actual hoarding; the agricultural banks founded by Napoleon III also played their part. But the peasant's thrift is undeniably the source of France's wealth, typified by, and probably often enough stored in, his hidden stocking. The government loan of June 28 of two milliards was covered twice over, and resulted in the evacuation of several departments. In June 1872 a loan of three milliards was covered fourteen times over. By July 1, 1873 only Verdun remained in German occupation, and the last soldier retired across the new frontier in September. Then the Assembly voted that Thiers, President of the Republic, had deserved well of his country. The interest on the loans was not met by income-tax, which indeed the French have always disliked. It was raised by indirect taxation on matches and stamps, and charges for the use of waste ground, as on the sea-shore at bathing resorts, and similar means.

Army reorganisation was of course necessary. It is difficult for us with our knowledge of Napoleon I to estimate the strength of the French dislike of conscription. It seems that the memory of the draining of the manhood of France by him endured so strongly that even his nephew relied on a long-service professional army; the attempt to modify the system in the later years of Napoleon III's reign failed through corruption, lack of determination to carry it through, and the fatal mistake of allowing substitutes. Now was created a national army, with five years in the ranks, and four in the reserve, followed by service in the territorials; it was of course the Prussian system extended. As it was impossible to train so many men at once, the conscripts were divided by lot into two sections, and the lucky ones in such numbers as were necessary served only six months. Substitutes were strictly forbidden, and there is little doubt that this regulation has been honourably carried out. Eldest sons of widows, clerics, and teachers were entirely exempt. At a later period, also in imitation of the Prussian system, educated men with qualifications were quit for one year's service. Later again, clerical students were forced to serve, but might be grouped together in the non-combatant branches. The five years were reduced to three, then to two, but shortly before 1914 raised once more to three.

In spite of his services an opposition was formed against Thiers, and he felt it necessary to resign in May 1873. The money once raised and France once more returned to the ways of peace, he fell between the proverbial two stools. The Conservatives were Monarchists, and the Republicans were Radicals. It was a monarchical majority which passed a resolution which he construed into a vote of censure; thus the ex-Orleanist retired from public life in

defence of Republicanism.   Europe certainly expected now
the restoration of the monarchy.   MacMahon was elected
President for seven years.   The work of creating a constitution was dragged out slowly and deliberately; in the
meanwhile the choice of mayors of communes, prefects of
departments, magistrates and officials, university professors
and so forth, was made a political affair, and reactionaries
were chosen just on the same lines as when Bourbon or
Bonaparte was actually on the throne.   The Roman
Catholic feeling came to a head, and the recovery of Rome
was openly proclaimed.   But it was the obstinacy of
"Henry V" that ruined the monarchy.   He was a no-
surrender Bourbon, and, as the last male of the senior line,
he refused to be restored except under the White Flag.
When he saw that he had ruined his own chances, and
surrendered his claim to the Count of Paris, grandson of
Louis Philippe, it was too late.   The only result of his
obstinacy was to give strength to the Republican war-cry
as voiced by Gambetta; "le cléricalisme, voilà l'ennemi!"
If it be thought that the Church and the royal family have
not received fair-play from the Republic, and that various
laws expelling princes of the blood, subjecting religious
houses to a state scrutiny of their revenues, and finally expelling monks and nuns and Jesuits, have been vindictive,
it can be argued on the Republican side that all the power
and resources of the Church were being devoted to the
restoration of monarchy and of privilege, not to mention
the temporal power of the Papacy, and that at a time when
France simply needed rest.

The permanent Constitution was very gradually settled
during MacMahon's presidency.   Power is vested in the
President, the Senate, and the Chamber of Deputies.
The President has no responsibility, but cannot govern

without the approbation of the Chambers which control
the ministers chosen by him.   He can dissolve the Chamber
with the consent of the Senate, with a view to obtain the
will of the nation upon some particular point, but from the
very first it was decided that never again should a *plébiscite*,
with its Napoleonic associations, be put before the nation.
The Senate is composed of 300 members, 75 of them for
life, and 225 elected for nine years, of whom 75 resign
and are re-eligible every three years; elections are in
the hands of committees of deputies and of municipal
and departmental councillors.   The Chamber of Deputies
is elected by manhood suffrage for four years, one deputy
to each division of a department or of a city.   When there
are many candidates the man at the top of the poll must
have a proportional majority, or else there must be a second
ballot, and in that case most of the useless candidates are
withdrawn.   Parties as we know them have never existed
under the Third Republic, but the most solid section of
deputies has been the "left centre," republicans and liberals,
yet not entirely extremists; whenever they unite with the
socialists[1] of the "left" they form a strong block to carry
some particular law, an anti-clerical law usually.   Both
Houses sat at Versailles till 1879, for fear of the influence
of Paris; their establishment in Paris that year, which
took place about the time when the Communards were
amnestied, was a blow for the monarchical and conservative
element; MacMahon resigned in January that year, Jules
Grévy was elected President, and Republicanism was
assured under the energetic influence of Gambetta.   But
still, when a President has to be elected, both Houses meet
together at Versailles, which is the last remaining sign of
a fear of mob rule; indeed, when at the height of the

[1] In France " collectivists " is the proper term.

Dreyfus excitement such an election was held, it was very lucky that Versailles was the place.

The Constitution of the German Empire was based on the practical control of the executive by the Emperor; he was the head of the army and navy, declared war and made alliances; his will alone was responsible for the choice of ministers. There was a Federal Council to which the special governments of the allied Imperial states contributed members; the sanction of this body was necessary to a declaration of war; it appointed the executive bodies in control of Imperial matters, army, navy, foreign affairs, tariff, commerce, railways, posts and so on. The popular House was the Diet or Reichstag, elected by manhood suffrage in proportion to the population of each state; its chief duty was to legislate on proposals submitted by the Emperor and to vote taxes; it was on this point that in recent years the Socialists showed their power, but all the attempts that were made to hinder the creation of a German navy, or the enormous expansion of the German army, failed, when once the spirit of domination, which necessitated a monster army and navy, had been drilled into the populace. But before the Socialistic party became strong, the main opposition against Bismarck came from the Roman Catholics; the laws of May 1873 decreed civil marriages, secular education, and a general control of priests and teachers by the Imperial authorities; Pius IX held out against this to his death in 1878; his successor Leo XIII came to terms with William I, after writing a personal letter to request a religious peace, and a compromise was arranged. Since then the Roman Catholic "centre" of the Reichstag has been a strong support to the Empire against Socialism.

The great problem of the early seventies was the attitude

of Germany towards the French recovery. The military authorities thought that France had recovered too quickly, that the speedy payment of the five milliards was a sign of prosperity, and the reorganisation of the army was a sign of strength, each of them dangerous as threatening a war of revenge. Moltke would have liked to have rushed into war and to have bled France really "to the white"[1] by inflicting this time a fine of ten milliards. The crisis arose in 1875, and it is generally acknowledged by historians to have been a very real crisis. The British and Russian governments, and Queen Victoria herself by a personal letter to William, did a great deal towards softening the aggressiveness of Germany. From this year it would seem that we must date German suspicions of Great Britain and Russia alike, being fanned constantly by the idea that our policy was dictated by jealousy, and Russia's policy by military ambition; a campaign was deliberately started against the feminine influence of Victoria and the Crown Princess, which came to a height at the time of the Crown Prince's illness, when he was attended by a British doctor. The suspicions of Russia quite upset Bismarck's foreign policy. He had always courted the sympathy of Russia, to counterbalance the possibility of an alliance between France and Austria; since 1871 he had worked up an understanding with the Tsar of Russia and the Emperor of Austria to form the Three Emperors' League, which can hardly be called a definite alliance, but which was close enough to an alliance to assure German ascendancy.

In 1875 therefore Germany and Russia fell apart, and Bismarck began to pay careful court to Austria; he had

---

[1] Professors taught their classes up to 1914 that next time they really would do it, 50 milliards, 500 milliards, and an occupation of France till payment of the last coin, etc., etc.

indeed treated Austria very leniently in 1866, and he now encouraged Francis Joseph to look to the Balkans and to become the rival of the Tsar, not so much as the champion of the distressed Christians, but as claimant to suzerainty. It had been no part of German policy to weaken the Sultan for the benefit of Slavs. Austria had been pushed by Germany into Balkan disputes so that she might be the opponent of Pan-Slavism, as if the national movement of the Slavs were a mere excuse for Russian aggressiveness. Indeed this was typically German, to boast loudly of German unity and yet deny to Slavs their right to con-federate under Russia. Austria was the instrument to be used, because millions of Slavs in that empire had to be kept down. Here is seen the influence of Hungary in the Dual Monarchy. In the seventies the Austrian Chancellor was the Hungarian, Count Andrassy, and the power of the Hungarian Diet was such as to dictate to Austria and enforce an anti-Slav policy. Russia had been the arch-enemy; Hungarians remembered, Austrians forgot, that the Slavs were anti-Magyars in 1848-49. Thus we can see that a Russo-French alliance would have to come in course of time, though it was slow in coming.

The Balkan problem came to the front in the autumn of 1875, but was not alarmingly acute before 1876. Since the Crimean War there had been very little to be said about Turkey or the Christians of Turkey. In 1860 we saw before that Napoleon III sent an expedition to save the Syrians. In 1862 the Greeks deposed their King Otto of Bavaria, profiting by his chance absence from Greece, and chose a son of Christian of Denmark, who reigned as George I; self-government was introduced amid much excitement, as though it would be the commencement of a new era of Greek prosperity and self-respect; in 1864

Palmerston's government, largely under the influence of
Gladstone, who was an ardent phil-Hellene, handed over
the Ionian Islands, which had been under the British
Protectorate, causing more excitement and self-congratu-
lation at the recognition of Greece as a civilised power by
the greatest of the free nations.   In Rumania a revolution
drove out the native prince—Moldavia and Wallachia were
supposed by the Treaty of Paris to have separate governments, and had solved the difficulty of union by both electing
the same man—and Prince Charles of Hohenzollern-Sigmaringen was elected Prince of a united Rumania.   In Serbia
a prince of the Obrenovich was ruling, and brought about
the expulsion of the Turkish garrisons in 1862.   He was
murdered in 1868 by the rival party, but his son Milan,
though quite a young boy, was chosen to succeed him.
Serbia, having followed the lead of Rumania in winning
independence, was imitated in turn by the Bosnians, but
they were suppressed by the Turks.   But more important
than these facts was the Russian repudiation of the Treaty
of Paris in the autumn of 1870.   It certainly presaged a
new aggression of Russia in the Balkans, when France was
not strong enough to interfere, and Britain, wedded to
insularity under the régime of Gladstone, was not likely
to interfere alone.   Yet the storm-cloud seemed to come
up with a rapidity that took Europe by surprise.   It may
be that Disraeli foresaw events.   Succeeding Gladstone in
1874 by the usual swing of the pendulum, Conservative
succeeding Liberal as if by the natural order of things
when our nation had had enough of peace and reform, he
began to show a tendency to imperialism by the act which
made Victoria Empress of India, and by his purchase of
the Khedive of Egypt's shares in the Suez Canal.

     It was in Bosnia and Herzegovina that revolt first

occurred, stirred up possibly by Russian agents in pursuance
of the new idea of Pan-Slavism, but certainly due in the
first place to the unbearable heaviness of Turkish rule.
One can hardly see how it could be considered a crime for
the Russians to entertain ideas of a union of Slavs, when
they saw united Germany and united Italy as established
facts; but the insinuation was that the Russians were
fomenting a revolt to have an excuse to declare war upon
the Turks.  The Chancellors of the three Emperors, still
connected informally by their league, though suspicious of
each other, drew up the Andrassy Note demanding Turkish
reforms in Herzegovina.    Disraeli, in a somewhat startling
manner, delayed the presentation of the Note as being
inopportune; it was just then that he purchased the Suez
Canal shares.    Of course he simply followed in the steps
of Wellington and Palmerston to maintain the integrity of
the Turkish Empire.    But he was more resolute than they,
and it would seem that he had a personal bitterness against
Russia, which it is hardly unfair to his memory to attribute
to his Jewish blood, for the Jews have always been treated
worse by the Russians than by the other nations—justly
so, it may be, if the money-lender and the vodka-seller,
who is the curse of the village, is usually a Jew against
whom the peasants are almost powerless.    Whatever was
the cause of Disraeli's animus against Russia, it was very
decided.    The Note, delayed by Disraeli, was presented
in February 1876.    The Sultan accepted it, but all Europe
knew that the acceptance by a Sultan meant nothing.    The
rebel Herzegovinans refused conditions; the Serbs and
Montenegrins were ready to help them.    An anti-Christian
outbreak at Salonica showed what the Turks thought.

In May 1876 the three Chancellors drew up another
paper of proposals known as the Berlin Memorandum, in

which the use of force against the Turks was definitely
threatened. The French and Italians accepted it; Disraeli
refused; more than that, the British fleet was sent to
Besika Bay just south of the Dardanelles. The excited
Mohammedans of Constantinople, especially the young
students, demanded a change of the Sultan's ministers,
and next the dethronement of the Sultan himself; he was
an Oriental despot of a low type, luxurious and selfish,
and unwilling to pay his officials, even his soldiers. Abdul
Hamid took his place. The events at Salonica and Constantinople indicated that the wild fury of Mohammedan
excitement, which may occur at any moment, was likely
to burst out. The same month it had already broken out
in Bulgaria, where there was a rising in imitation of the
Herzegovinans. Turkish irregular troops, known as Bashi-
Bazuks, many of them Circassians, were let loose in southern
Bulgaria, and there is distinct evidence that Turkish regular
troops were employed likewise. The horrors were not
known at first. When the truth was told there was an
outburst of passionate excitement in England such as is
extremely rare in our peaceably phlegmatic island. There
was good reason for it, for our fleet was near the Dardanelles
all the time giving support to the Turkish government,
our Prime Minister had gone against the Concert of Europe
in opposing the Berlin Memorandum, and our ambassador
at Constantinople approved of force being used by the
Turks in Bulgaria.

The Bulgarian atrocities roused party feeling in England
beyond anything of which later generations have had
experience, even the Chinese slavery agitation, or Lloyd
George's Budget proposals, or Home Rule. Disraeli's
supporters passionately declared that very few Bulgars had
been killed, and they were open rebels ; the integrity of

the Turkish Empire was still the key-stone of our policy
and was necessary to defend our interests; the Liberal
denunciation of the Sultan was only a political trick to
discredit Disraeli's ministry.   On the other hand the great
mass of the British were in very genuine anger, not only
Liberals; our responsibility for the crimes was painfully
clear; the heated imagination of some writers may have
exaggerated the number of the victims up to 30,000, but
very sober and impartial judges, such as Edwin Pears, a
barrister at Constantinople who wrote for the *Daily News*,
also some independent Americans, said 15,000; the force
of the feeling was far more real than any mere political
outcry could be.   Gladstone came out from his retirement
to put himself at the head of the movement, and expressed
himself strongly both in pamphlet and in speech.   He
demanded the withdrawal of the Turks, bag and baggage,
lest, always under cover of Disraeli's moral support, similar
massacres should occur in Serbia.   Whatever be thought
of Gladstone's political career in other respects, his Home
Rule bills of a later date in particular, he was a very
genuinely earnest man.   Disraeli's undoubted cleverness
could not hide his cynicism, which often showed itself in
bitterly sarcastic phrases, which have the appearance of
being designed simply to show his wit, as when he said
that Gladstone was "a sophistical rhetorician inebriated
with the exuberance of his own verbosity."   That the
country was not with Disraeli at this crisis is seen in the
reluctance of his own cabinet to follow him to the bitter
end;   Lord Carnarvon resigned in January, and Lord
Derby in March 1878, a long time after the Bulgarian
atrocities it is true, but they had restrained him from
going to war to help the Turks, and resigned when he seemed
to be on the point of going to war in spite of them; Lord

Salisbury and Sir Stafford Northcote stopped short of
resignation, but were equally against war ; and all this
means that they considered the Turks guilty of the
Bulgarian atrocities.    At the height of the excitement in
August 1876, Disraeli went up to the Lords as the Earl
of Beaconsfield.

The Serbians and Montenegrins were up in arms; the
Russians were deeply excited at the wrongs done to brother
Slavs, and thousands of them, with a Russian general,
volunteered help, yet the Turkish forces were too strong,
and the Tsar was simply forced to intervene when the
Serbians and Volunteers were being beaten.    He compelled
the Sultan to relax his grip, and told our ambassador that,
if the European Concert refused to act, he would have to
act alone.    The British proposed a Conference at Constantinople ;  this was to the good, if our Ministers really
meant to put pressure on the Turks.    But Disraeli seemed
to think that the nation was already forgetting the atrocities,
or else that the blessed word "exaggeration" was enough
to prove that the atrocities agitation was a party trick of
Gladstone, and in November he made a speech which nobody
could interpret but as a threat to help the Turks ; yet the
Tsar's words were studiously moderate, simply that the
Russians must end an intolerable state of affairs but would
not take Constantinople for themselves.

The Conference met at Constantinople in December,
Lord Salisbury representing us, and certainly he never
went the whole way with Disraeli as Turkey's friend.
Independence was demanded for the northern Balkan
states, guarantees for the decent government of the southern.
Then came a proclamation from the Sultan;  he would
grant a Constitution and summon a Parliament on western
lines, with responsibility of ministers and all the proper

paraphernalia; farce is the only word that can be applied.
The Conference broke up, and of it we need say nothing
except that Lord Salisbury said and did nothing to justify
the Sultan in expecting British help. A really honest
Turk, Midhat Pasha, was summoned to be Grand Vizier,
and he believed in reform and the possibilities of a Turkish
Parliament; his appointment having helped to delude the
Powers, the Sultan soon hustled him[1] out of Turkey as
being too honest to play his part in the farce. The Parliament met in March 1877, only to be dissolved when the
war began.

Alexander's hand was forced. No other action but
war was possible. The Concert had been thwarted by
Disraeli—though not by his cabinet—and fooled by the
Sultan. The Three Emperors' League was so far a reality
that Austria was satisfied that she would gain something
ultimately, and Germany stood by, reluctantly it may be,
yet conscious of being unable at this point to stop Russia.
It is quite possible that some revolutionary excitement
might have troubled Alexander at home if he did not
move. He already had a large force mobilised. A last
effort indeed was made; a Russian envoy went the round
of the courts of Europe, and one more note was drawn
up, accepted by all the Powers—even by Disraeli, probably
on the advice of his cabinet,—and rejected by the Sultan.
Nothing else could be done; so in April 1877, a military
convention being concluded with Rumania, the Russian
army moved.

The campaign deserves to be studied by civilians, if
only to show the difference between Russian and Prussian
methods. Twice Prussia attacked and carried all before

[1] It would have been dangerous to murder Midhat then. He
was lured back to Turkey and bowstrung at a later date.

her with a rush; once the enemy soon came to terms, and
there was no need to call up reserves; once the enemy
held out for another five months, reserves had to be called
up and were adequate; on both occasions Prussia was
quite ready, and had military bases near to the frontier,
besides more distant bases linked up by railways.    Now
Russia attacked, the Turks meekly surrendering the
initiative; the attack seemed to be carrying all before it;
suddenly it was held up, checked, and apparently spent,
as if it had been based on rashness rather than readiness;
the tug of war came when reserves were called up, arrived
by rail from long distances, slowly indeed, but arrived;
the Turks had no power of counter-attack in the interval,
but collapsed when the Russian reserves were there.    The
Russian commissariat was badly managed, but that of the
Turks was worse.    On both sides was seen a magnificent
power of endurance, but at the last pinch the Turks showed
less stamina.    Archibald Forbes, as hot a partisan of the
Russians as he had been of the Prussians, gave it as his
deliberate opinion that only one man, an Irishman, can
approach a Russian in endurance on a few biscuits a day;
it was this endurance that enabled the Tsar, in spite of
mistakes and probable corruption in some departments, to
pull through.    Also it was a war of improvised entrenchments after the first rush was checked; it showed the
enormous power of the breech-loader in defence, though
still a single-action rifle and using black gunpowder, and
not supported by machine guns; the Turks were marvellously cool under these conditions, but could not last
out, and their ideas of sanitation were barbaric, so that
typhoid was rampant and neutralised their enduring power.
The Russians showed higher qualities in the end, fit indeed
to put against the organised impetus of the Prussians.

War being declared in April, the Russians to the number of 200,000 moved into Rumania under the Grand Duke Nicholas.    There was trouble about the co-operation of the Rumans, because Prince Charles would not submit to subjection to Nicholas.    They approached the Danube. The Turks made not the smallest effort to forestall them by crossing to the north bank; perhaps this was a deep-laid plot of Abdul Kerim, their commander-in-chief, so that the Russians might lose men in the passage of the river and then be brought up against the quadrilateral of fortresses, Rustchuk and Silistria on the river, Shumla inland, and Varna on the coast.    But in 1853 Omar Pasha had crossed and greatly inconvenienced the armies of that day.    All that we know of the Turks points to their slackness in beginning, for they always lose their opportunities, unless indeed they are led by Germans.    In May and June the Russians were waiting for the water in the Danube to fall; towards the end of June they crossed in two places, low down into the Dobrudscha as a movement to distract the Turks, and at a point near Sistova in the north centre of Bulgaria; it was done successfully and without loss. Gradually the main army poured into central Bulgaria, while the main Turkish army was on their left flank towards the sea.    A forward dash was admirably executed by Ghurko, one of the smartest Russian generals of the war. Mountain warfare has to be studied from the campaigns of great men, of Napoleon in 1796-97, or of Wellington and Soult in 1813; passes must be watched, but need not all be defended in force, for then an enemy will concentrate his attack on one pass and the defenders of the others will be too far off to come in to help; above all, the defenders must keep their main force at the near foot of the range, ready to pounce on the attackers as they descend, or to

counter-attack at the particular pass where these have
concentrated. The Turks neglected all these precautions
from lack of study. Some of the Russian leaders at least
understood them. In July Ghurko's command seized a
rough neglected pass, and proceeded, being covered by
the Bulgarian peasants who prevented any information
from leaking through to the Turks, to create a track
along which at least light guns and waggons could go where
no track existed before. Then a cloud of Cossacks was
sent southwards to create an impression that an advance
was contemplated on Adrianople. But the main force
swung westwards, scattered some Turks, and proceeded
to establish itself at the southern mouth of the great
Shipka pass, the main crossing-place in the Balkan chain,
up to which ran the railway from Adrianople. Another
Russian force under the other and greatest hero of the war,
General Skobeleff, faced the Shipka from the north. The
defending Turks, thus cut off, beat back the first attack,
for it was difficult to time accurately the assaults on the
two faces; but, blockaded and abandoned and in danger
of starvation, they slipped away into the mountains. The
Russians now had their point in the Balkans and their
base on the Danube, thus holding a triangular area and
presenting two fronts, eastwards and westwards; but it
must be added, lest any one should read modern conditions
into their position, that they were not entrenched along
the whole of each front, and, being less than 200,000
strong, had not a fully continuous line.

The seizure of the Shipka pass was of enormous importance, for by it alone were the Russians able to maintain
themselves when the Turks made their rally. They were
not in sufficient numbers to hold their triangle, much less
to advance definitely on Adrianople. The possession of

the inner lines, and consequent ability to reinforce any point against a Turkish counter-attack, alone enabled them to hold on in the critical days now fast approaching. They were hardly in a trap; for that would imply that the Turks deliberately led them into it, defending the Danube badly, scouting badly, and guarding the Balkans badly, all of set purpose; also that the Turks, with two months for preparation, April to June, deliberately failed to concentrate and keep touch. Moreover a considerable Turkish force was being wasted in Montenegro and on the border of Serbia. Lastly, if their strategy was deliberate, it was grossly inefficient; they allowed the key-stone, the Shipka pass, to be built into the Russian position. The truth is that you never know what the Turks are going to do next. When they seem to be on the verge of collapse, they suddenly win, and *vice versa*. This hardly implies a reasoned plan. Rather the individual excellence of their infantry, cool and phlegmatic so as to get the utmost value out of their breech-loaders, and the clever initiative of one man, Osman Pasha, who knew how to seize a position, to entrench it quickly, and to get the utmost value out of these men, saved the Turks for the time in spite of the stupidity of head-quarters.

On July 19, the very day when Skobeleff and Ghurko occupied the Shipka, Osman Pasha seized Plevna on the Russian west flank. He had come from Widdin, high up the Danube at the corner of Serbia, where his army was quite wasted in the first two months. The Russian Krüdener had made a great mistake in not anticipating him in seizing Plevna, as he had plenty of time to do, and indeed he had been ordered to do. He advanced on Osman on July 20, and was at once repulsed. He gathered up a larger force for a more serious attack on July 31. But Osman had

used his ten days to fortify an amphitheatre of swelling
hills to the east of Plevna, and the deadly rifle fire of the
Turks was for the first time understood by all Europe;
one redoubt the Russians carried only to find themselves
under a more deadly fire from the next line; it was like
the British capture of the Redan, a position untenable
because open to and dominated from the rear. A typical
stolid Turk had known how to repulse trained troops with
great losses, proving that Turks could yet fight and reversing
all previous judgements—neither the British nor the French
had had any opinion of them in the Crimea, nobody had
expected them now to beat the Russians in pitched battle,
and the Russian advance of the past month only seemed
to confirm previous judgements,—but could he follow up
his success?

Abdul Kerim was cashiered, and Mohammed Ali was
put into the chief command with his post on the Russian
east flank and base at Shumla. Suleiman was brought
round from Montenegro, and with his army was carried
by rail to the south foot of the Shipka. Osman had his
rear open to Sofia by way of the Orkhanie pass, by which
he obtained for the time plenty of supplies and reinforcements, most of whom however were only *redifs* or second-
line militiamen; he also had a strong post at Lovtcha
between himself and the Shipka. Everything now depended
on a vigorous offensive upon the dismayed Russians, directed
by one master-mind, and timed in such a way as to prevent
any reinforcement of a weak point, by means of the possession of the interior lines, from one less threatened.
Meanwhile the Russian reserves were coming up by rail
from long distances, and an immediate relief was at once
given by Prince Charles and 50,000 Rumans whom the
Tsar in his anxiety could not afford to offend by putting

under the Grand Duke's command; in fact Charles took
over the chief command against Plevna.    But the Turks
once again had no notion of strategy.    Even Osman's excellence stopped short at a brilliant conception of defensive
tactics.    The only Turk who tried to attack was Suleiman,
and he attacked madly and blindly in the worst place and
in the worst manner, though as a matter of fact he was at
one moment within an ace of success.

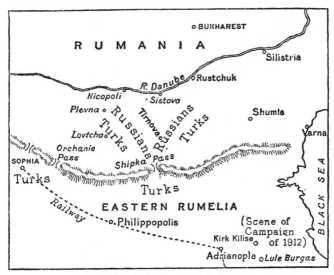

Bulgaria in the war of 1877.

Suleiman might have brought up his force by rail to
Sofia, and thence through the Orkhanie pass to Lovtcha,
thus isolating the defenders of the Shipka while a smaller
body blocked them to the south; or he could have used
a pass further to the east, thus joining Mohammed's left
flank and bursting in by Tirnova.    In either case he could

have helped to break in the head of the Russian triangle
and thus drive a wedge into the Russian centre. But he
simply hurled his men straight up from the south at the
main position on the Shipka. Quite a small force of
Russians were defending, but they held firm, and were
reinforced in time by light infantry brought up at full
speed on horseback behind Cossacks. The position was
saved, by a very narrow margin, but saved, August 24[1].
Next on September 3 Skobeleff seized the connecting
position at Lovtcha with considerable losses to the Turks.
It now seemed time for a third and final assault on Plevna,
for no counter-attack had come from this side, and Mohammed delivered but a series of most feeble blows from the
east. The Russians and Rumanians mustered 75,000 strong
on September 11. The attack upon the north of Osman's
semicircle of redoubts and trenches failed utterly; on the
east a joint Russian and Rumanian attack carried one
redoubt only; to the south-east the Russians were thrown
back with fearful losses; on the south only was an impression
made, for there Skobeleff was in command and he knew
how to bring on his lines in a series of waves instead of in
one great mass, besides that he knew how to appeal to his
men and get the most out of them by sheer force of character
and sympathy. But even the position won by Skobeleff
was lost next day by Osman's counter-attack with men
drawn from his other flank, where they were not wanted.
The Russians were quite right to attack all along the line,
so as to keep the whole of Osman's army busy; where they

---

[1] It was reported in London that the Pass had actually been
carried, and the revulsion of feeling next day, when the news was
contradicted, was extreme. The despatches of Forbes to the *Daily
News* were as greedily awaited as in 1870; he was as then by far
the cleverest and most trustworthy of the correspondents.

failed was in not having a strong reserve to break through at the one selected point when once successful there, so as to neutralise the Turkish efforts elsewhere and turn the whole position from the rear. It was an early period in the history of breech-loaders and entrenchments. Only Skobeleff had thought the problem out, and he had been left without a strong reserve to drive home his blow at the right point.

Once more the Tsar was in despair, and the Grand Duke proposed a retirement into Rumania, leaving only a fortified position on the south bank of the Danube. Luckily other advice was pressed on the Tsar. It was pointed out to him that neither Osman himself nor Mohammed had made a strong push between July 31 and September 11, and that they were not likely to make such a push now. Meanwhile the Shipka was safe, for Suleiman stuck to his mad policy of hurling attack after attack up-hill, simply dashing his head against a wall and losing his men. The great Russian reinforcements were yet arriving and would soon be available. Thus retreat was rejected. But the Tsar determined not to waste more lives by assault, but to call up the veteran Todleben to undertake a regular siege of Plevna. This news was received in London with much excitement; it seemed to show that the Crimean War of 23 years before was not so much ancient history as might have been thought in spite of the military developments which seemed to make Crimean tactics antediluvian. It has been thought that the Russian strategy was wrong, that it would have been better to have contained Osman and Suleiman, and to have delivered the main blow against Mohammed. Yet the decision to invest Plevna at least pinned down the Turks to a defensive; henceforward their main object was to feed Osman by way of Sofia and Orkhanie; Mohammed and

Suleiman could be safely left to show their incapacity, each in his own way. The Sultan indeed deposed Mohammed and put Suleiman in his place. The latter did nothing worthy of mention, except that he once made a point towards Tirnova; but he did not press the blow home, but dug himself in, passing from the extreme of a mad offensive to a stupid defensive, as if digging in was likely to stop the inflow of Russians in an opposite direction.

Todleben, with a force amounting to 120,000 Russians and Rumanians, gradually spread round Osman and shut him in by the end of October; here the phlegmatic Turk was seen at his worst, though the commander at Sofia did his best up to the end to send up food and reinforcements. Osman's own wish was to fall back on Orkhanie and Sofia, where he would still have had a strong position on the Russian flank. But the Sultan interfered and forbad retreat. The siege lasted about seven weeks. Typhoid broke out and damped the spirits of the defenders. Osman made a big effort on December 10 to break out to the south-west, failed to cut his way through, and capitulated at last with over 40,000 men, gaunt and hollow-cheeked with fever and starvation.

In less than a month the Russian armies were shaken up and reorganised for their advance, defying the winter weather. The moral result of the fall of Plevna was very great. Suleiman came round from the eastern flank to contest the passage of the Balkans. His plans were as badly devised as ever, and he scattered his forces in an attempt to hold all the passes at once. Early in January Ghurko dashed through the western Balkans, secured Sofia, and got well in on Suleiman's left rear. Simultaneously two Russian forces pushed through two side passes to right and left of the Shipka, and enclosed the whole of the Turkish army blocking the south of that pass. The avalanche burst through the mountains with so overwhelming an onslaught, that the Turks simply broke and fled as best they could to the sea-coast. Ghurko actually entered Adrianople on January 20.

The campaign in Asia was of secondary importance, and was carried on with very similar fortunes. The Russian general Melikoff had pushed through from the Caucasus, and actually laid siege to Kars. Then the Turks rallied under Mukhtar Pasha, and drove the besiegers back on the frontier. In their turn the Russians rallied, routed the Turks, laid siege again to Kars, and captured it in November. Then they advanced on Erzerum, but had not captured it when the armistice was concluded for Europe, which by implication included Asia, on January 31.

The Turks having collapsed the period of diplomacy began. Disraeli was obviously on the look-out to stop the Russian advance, but the completeness and suddenness of the overthrow was such that he had no time, even if his cabinet had given him a free hand, to interfere by force of arms. Of course troops could not be procured in a moment; even if they had been at hand, they could have done little more than rally a certain number of the scattered Turks who, clustered round them as a nucleus, might hold the lines covering Constantinople between the Black Sea and the Sea of Marmora. Obviously the terms of the Russians would not be the same now that they were victorious, as they had been a year earlier when the Tsar was still trying to bring about a peaceful solution only to be thwarted by Disraeli. The Tsar himself was now in Petrograd, whence he gave orders to stop the advance and grant an armistice. The Grand Duke and the military leaders in general wanted to advance, as was only natural after what they had endured

and done.    Of the strength of public opinion in England
it is impossible to state anything with any degree of
confidence.    There was an excited cry that "the Russians
shall not take Constantinople," the base of which was an
ostentatious and exaggerated claim that we had "fought
the bear before"; these are words from a music-hall song,
and betray the sublime ignorance of the uneducated, or
worse still the half-educated, author and audience, who had
not the remotest notion that we had fought the bear in
alliance with France, and that the most important part
of the fighting had fallen upon the French.    As the poet
of this doggerel appealed to "jingo" in confirmation of his
statement, any wild shriek for war with or without excuse
has been called jingoism, and the ignorant shriekers are
called jingoes.    Apparently the Bulgarian atrocities were
forgotten; the only thought in some quarters was that
at all hazards, even if we had actually to fight in defence
of the blood-stained Turks, the interests of our country in
the Mediterranean and in India demanded that on no
account should the Russians reach the Dardanelles.    On
the other hand the historian Freeman uttered his celebrated
phrase "Perish India"; common fairness demands that the
sense of the context should be added, "rather than that
our possession of India and our interests in the Suez Canal
should bind us to fight for a barbarous power."    But, an
unstable public opinion notwithstanding, it is very doubtful
if Disraeli had much of a following in his own cabinet.
On January 23 our fleet was once more ordered to the
Dardanelles.    At once Lord Carnarvon resigned.    Then the
order was changed, and it was not to advance into the
Dardanelles.    Meanwhile six millions were voted in parliament for military expenses.    Terms were being discussed
after the armistice of January 31; during the discussion

the Russians held the Marmora-Black Sea line; our fleet came through into the Sea of Marmora, yet did not enter into the Bosporus. All the other populations of the Balkans were at extreme tension, Greeks, Serbs, and Montenegrins. The Russians and Bulgarian insurgents were inflicting on Mohammedans the same misery which the Turks had, at intervals during many centuries, inflicted when they had the power; it is even said that these new atrocities rivalled those of eighteen months back. The Austrians were certainly alarmed, and were taking up the same situation which they had taken in 1854.

Now it is reasonably certain that the Russians were hardly in a position to undertake a new campaign in case Austria declared war, or in case Disraeli, set free by his previous opponents in his cabinet, should proceed to extremes though he only had a fleet on which to rely to back up threats. Russian administration and organisation always had a knack of breaking down just at the wrong moment, partly through corruption and selfishness in high places, partly through inability to carry out war far from home. In all probability Tsar Alexander understood this. Early in February Austria proposed a Conference; almost immediately a second proposal suggested a Congress to be held at Berlin; Bismarck, to use his own words, put himself forward as an "honest broker" to settle between his neighbours business matters which did not concern himself. Bismarck indeed rather over-acted his part, especially when he declared that the whole Eastern Question was not worth the bones of one Pomeranian grenadier. But it was a fine thing that the Concert of Europe should be revived, though it would have been a finer if it had been effected before the war. The alteration of Conference into

Congress meant that Chancellors and Prime Ministers would attend in place of Ambassadors.

But before the Congress could meet the Tsar published in March 1878 a treaty made by him and the Sultan at San Stefano near Constantinople. Very little territory was claimed for Russia, just a small portion south of the Caucasus to include Batum and Kars. Very little was to be given, as a reward for all their services in 1876 or 1877, to Rumania or Serbia or Montenegro. But a large new Bulgaria was to be created, extending from the Danube and across the main Balkans to the coast, so as to take in Adrianople, Kavalla, Salonica, and Monastir; that is to say, all the debateable ground, where Turks and Greeks, Serbs and Bulgars, lived in inextricable confusion, was to be definitely Bulgarian, and therefore under Russian influence. And, worse than this palpable slighting of Ruman and Serbian claims, was the insult to the Powers; for how could there be a Congress if the Russians had already settled with the Turks? In fact, the Tsar had not played his cards cleverly.

Disraeli looked on this treaty as almost a defiance. Freed by the resignation of Lord Derby who had always been a check on him, and calling in Lord Salisbury to be his new Foreign Secretary, he made preparations for war, ordered some troops from India to Malta, and called up reserves at home. But the doubt as to whether the nation would support him or not was never put to the test. As the spring and early summer advanced, the Russians outside Constantinople, invincible as they had seemed to be in the cold weather, were collapsing fast in the heat, all the faster because of the tremendous efforts that they had then made. The Turks had rallied; stiffened by British and sepoy regiments, and backed by our fleet, they could have retaliated on their conquerors. Alexander could not have afforded to renew the fight. Moreover, the attitude of Austria was decidedly hostile, and behind Austria was Germany, in spite of Bismarck's overdone expressions of indifference. Consequently, Salisbury and Gortschakoff discussed what arrangements could be made between Britain and Russia so that they could meet each other; the San Stefano treaty was practically annulled, and everything was to be resettled at Berlin.

The Congress met in June. The three Imperial Chancellors were there, Bismarck, Andrassy, and Gortschakoff; Disraeli went over himself, attended by Salisbury; M. Waddington represented France, and Signor Corti Italy. The final settlement was that Russia was to have the same region in Asia, the land round Batum and Kars. Rumania was to cede Bessarabia to Russia, but to receive the Dobrudcha. Serbia and Montenegro were to have some territory and full independence. Bosnia and Herzegovina were to be put under the protectorate of Austria. Greece was to wait for a rectification of her frontier. Bulgaria was to be limited to the country between the Danube and the Balkans, plus a piece jutting out to the south-west to include Sofia, and was to be self-governed under a Christian prince[1] chosen by the Powers, yet nominally under the suzerainty of the Sultan; but Eastern Rumelia— and this was the point for which Disraeli made his strongest effort—was to be, though under a Christian governor, an integral part of Turkey, so that the southern outlets of the Balkan passes should be held by Turkish troops.

The disappointment of the Russians must have been bitter. Being left alone by the Powers to coerce the brutal

[1] Alexander of Battenberg, a morganatic relative of the reigning family of Hesse Darmstadt, was chosen.

Turk and having made incredible efforts, they had got very little for themselves, yet saw their Austrian rivals definitely recognised as protectors of two large districts. Moreover it seemed to be insinuated that they had not been sincere in their professions as champions of the Christian races. There is little wonder that Disraeli's admirers, believing that they always were and always would be our hereditary enemies, welcomed him warmly on his return from Berlin as bringing "Peace with Honour." It seemed as if he had been the protagonist against Russia. Yet the profit was to Austria. Meanwhile Bismarck in the background must have been chuckling to himself; the old understanding between himself and Russia had come to an end, and there was jealousy between the conquerors of the French and the conquerors of the Turks; meanwhile he had got Austria to be his catspaw, and the immediate result was a deep hatred of Russia against us under cover of which Germany's interests were assured. That he pulled the strings, and let Disraeli have both the glory and the hatred, seems clear enough to us now. A dozen years later William II will get rid of him as too old-fashioned, but he was already giving to Germany the chief voice in Balkan affairs.

# CHAPTER IX

## AFTER THE BERLIN CONGRESS

Granted that Disraeli honestly thought that Russia was the arch-enemy that should be checked, he certainly acted cleverly and quickly to forestall her designs in Asia. With finances in disorder, with nihilists rampant, as ever has happened when she has felt the strain of war, she was not in a position to take up his challenge on the north-west frontier of India. He struck at once to secure for us "a scientific frontier" towards Afghanistan. Thanks to Roberts, whose name then first became familiar to our ears, and to the new Amir, Abdur Rahman, whose loyalty to our raj was great, he gave us an assured influence over the country so as to make it a buffer-state against a Russian advance, 1878–80. Alexander II was murdered by nihilists in 1881; Skobeleff's great campaign against the Turkomans did not take place till 1883, and then he died with his dream of a Russian invasion of India unfulfilled; and it was only in 1885 that the Russians approached the northern frontier of Afghanistan. Gladstone, after Disraeli's fall from power in 1880 and death in 1881, made a settlement with Alexander III. Thus with a barrier erected against her in the Balkans, and a new barrier to the north-west of India, the waters of Russia's ambition flowed over towards Siberia and the coasts opposite to Japan, and her expansion proceeded, not by the trans-Caspian, but by the trans-Siberian railway. Yet for several years to come Russian intrigue and threats of invasion vexed our statesmen in India.

In this same period France entered upon a series of colonial ventures. William I and Bismarck restrained the eager war-party in Germany, probably because they had their sufficiency of glory, and were content that Germans should adapt themselves to the works of peace. It seems as if they scornfully allowed France to colonise so that there might be trouble between her and us, while they would look on and profit; should the trouble come, the French and British fleets would weaken each other, while just then the German fleet was negligible. Thus Jules Ferry in 1881 took Tunis under the protectorate of France, and henceforth French expansion in Africa was the national aim. A Dual Control over Egypt was established by France and Britain. But in 1882 Mohammedan excitement, roused by the war of 1877 and already seen in action in Afghanistan, blazed out in Egypt. Arabi Pasha demanded "Egypt for the Egyptians," and denounced the Western Powers who were exploiting the country and the canal for their own benefit. Of course his supporters were but an aristocratic military faction, who, like Mohammed Ali and Ibrahim before, wanted to domineer and cared nothing for the fellahin or peasants. He had to be suppressed. France, naturally enough, was not anxious to entangle herself so that Germany might seize the chance of threatening her. Therefore the British fleet alone bombarded Arabi's forts at Alexandria in June, and a British army was landed to save the canal and break his power at the battle of Tel-el-Kebir in August. We took over the protectorate of Egypt. But the Mahdi, the fanatical Mohammedan of the interior,

our government left to misrule the Sudan after our failure
to save Gordon and Khartum in 1885.

Ferry lost his power; and Gambetta, the ever rabid
enemy of Germany, who hated to see France diverted into
colonial paths away from her plain duty of concentrating
her strength on *la revanche*, succeeded him.  But suddenly
Gambetta died, and at the same time died Generals Chanzy
and Gallifet who were marked as the leaders in any new
German war.  Ferry came back to continue colonial
expansion.  Intensely sore that the British protectorate
was established over Egypt, the French kept their eyes on
Africa, also on Madagascar, and, in Further India, on
Tonquin and Siam.  Almost at any moment a rupture
might have occurred.  As this was the period of Russian
bitterness against us, it followed that France and Russia
drew closer to each other, not only as against Germany,
but also as against us.  Committed by Disraeli to an anti-
Russian policy, and by sheer bad luck to an Egyptian
policy which offended France, our statesmen and nation
did not see that the rulers of Germany were all the time
unfriendly to us, that already they were jealous of our
sea-power and empire as beyond the reach of their proud
army.  However in the eighties the Germans as a nation
had not yet been drilled to look on our nation as their
natural enemy and destined prey.  Thus we continued to
believe in Germany as Carlyle had taught us, and to think
slightingly of France.

In 1885 Germany, already allied to Austria, made overtures to Italy.  Thus was formed the Triple Alliance.  The
Italian navy was of value to the mid-Europe Powers, and
Italy was jealous of French control of north Africa; moreover
the years 1859–60 and 1870 were still too recent for the
soreness between France and Italy to have been soothed.

Also in 1885 there was excitement in the Balkans. Eastern Rumelia, inhabited largely by Bulgars, declared for incorporation with Bulgaria under Prince Alexander of Battenberg. Serbia made this a *casus belli*, but was badly beaten by Alexander's joint force of Rumeliots and Bulgars. The Powers allowed the incorporation, and Lord Salisbury was a consenting party; yet it had been thought to be a triumph for Disraeli that he had at the Berlin Congress kept the two provinces apart so that the Turks might still control the main Balkan passes, and Salisbury was thought to be Disraeli's ardent disciple. Tsar Alexander III, however, strongly resented it; it seems clear that he looked upon Prince Alexander as his servant who had no right to strike out a policy for himself without Russia's help. There were various intrigues, and Prince Alexander was on one occasion kidnapped, though ultimately he was restored. Finally he resigned, and his place was taken by Ferdinand of Saxe Coburg. The Russian policy strikes us as having been unwise. Hence forward the Bulgars, offended by Russian imperiousness which cancelled their sense of gratitude, began to look to Austria for support.

Kaiser William I died in 1888, peaceful and tolerant towards France to the end. The Crown Prince became the Emperor Frederick, but, stricken by mortal disease, he died before he could be formally crowned. He had been attended by a British doctor, against whom there was a wild outcry in Germany; and his wife, our Princess Royal, was distinctly unpopular. Yet our eyes were not yet open to mark the signs of anti-British feeling in Germany. William II succeeded, and in 1890 got rid of Bismarck. For a long time yet to come we could not understand the new Kaiser. He seemed to be erratic and impulsive, and yet he was bent on getting all the power into his own hands.

His grandfather and Bismarck had had enough glory; he himself, too young to fight in 1870, had none. Yet year after year went by without an outbreak, and we began to believe that he was really pacific, at least towards us, and that he even needed our sea-power on his side to balance the French and Russian navies. Now Alexander III stopped short of a formal engagement with France; but Russian loans, especially those for the completion of the trans-Siberian railway, were being placed in France; finally in 1895 Nicholas II definitely announced the Dual Alliance. When once it had been formed, with France and Russia both angry with us because of Egypt and Afghanistan, surely, we all thought, the Kaiser's dislike of his mother's country meant nothing.

The keynote of the new Kaiser's policy, as we see it now, was to get control of German over-seas interests. Bismarck had not taken steps to bind to Germany all those German emigrants, who, driven abroad by overpopulation, naturalised themselves in foreign lands and were thus lost to the fatherland; Bismarck had not cared for colonisation, or for the creation of a colonial empire; therefore he had to go. Then William II put himself at the head of a gigantic scheme of "peaceful penetration," by which colonists in new German colonies,—in the scramble for Africa Germany got a great deal of land, and Lord Salisbury bartered away our island Heligoland in consideration for German acknowledgement of our control over Zanzibar,—German traders in Italy, Spain, Denmark, Holland, Russia, and even France, and settlers in the United States and Latin America, should be protected and financed by German state-controlled banks, should be nursed to prosperity, and made to see that patriotism was a paying quality. Britain and the British Empire were overrun by Germans; not only waiters

and hairdressers and clerks to whom we were accustomed
already, who had seemed hitherto to be good naturalised
British subjects, or who returned home having learnt our
language; but also shopkeepers of many kinds, merchants,
bankers, company-promoters, who got a grasp over our
vitals; all this under cover of our free trade and traditional
welcome of foreigners, and under the protection of our navy.
To mature the scheme time was required, and it would also
take time to create a German navy. Meanwhile it was
politic not to drive the French to desperation by new threats
of war.

There was a natural revulsion of feeling for a time in
France against Ferry's colonial policy; the colonies were
expensive, and were distracting her from her higher duty
of *revanche*; the loss of life in the tropical climates was
great. Yet she still pushed inland, southwards from Algeria,
eastwards from Senegal, and put the finishing touch by
occupying Timbuctoo and the upper and middle Niger;
thence she looked across to the upper Nile. Meanwhile
we were extending our lower Nigerian protectorate on the
one side; and, having pacified and regulated lower Egypt,
were ready to strike up the Nile, avenge Gordon, occupy
Khartum, and civilise the Sudan, on the other. Friction
between the two expanding nations was liable to cause a
blaze at any moment in the last half-decade of the century.
Siam caused trouble in another direction. Russia was
steadily laying down the trans-Siberian railway by means
of French loans, so as to threaten our trade supremacy in
the Far East; and all the time the Russian threats against
India by way of the trans-Caspian railway never ceased.

French domestic politics require a word. The Third
Republic had to live down several unsavoury scandals;
the Grévy scandal, when the President himself was forced

to resign because his son-in-law sold the decorations of the Legion of Honour; the Boulanger trouble, when an incompetent war-minister posed as the soldiers' friend, and pranced before the people on a fine black horse to show that he was their destined leader against Germany; the Panama scandal, when a company formed under M. de Lesseps to cut the Panama canal went bankrupt, partly owing to the expense of labour and to mosquito-bred fevers, but largely also because of bribery among politicians and journalists; the unending civil strife between Catholics and anti-Catholics; and, on top of all, the Dreyfus scandal, when a Jew, a captain in the army, was condemned for trying to sell the secret of the new field-gun, and there was a scare of war at any moment if the Kaiser's name were but mentioned, and, whatever truth there may have been in the original charge, false evidence was manufactured in support later. Of course the Socialistic movement was also strong in France; so it was in Germany, but in free countries it has been more deadly than in the Kaiser-ridden country where national prosperity, belief in the national army, and excitement in the creation of the new national navy, were cleverly used to distract Socialists from becoming internationalists[1]; that is to say, German Socialists may have been strong, but they have not thrown in their lot with the workers of other nations against their own government, as those of democratic France and Britain have often seemed ready to do.

In 1894 the Far Eastern Question was first opened; hitherto an occasional interference by some Western Power had merely led to the acquisition by Britain of Hongkong,

[1] The "International" was founded in 1862 by a German, Karl Marx. But recent events have shown that only a small number of Germans prefer internationalism to the fatherland.

to the opening of treaty ports, and to the forcing of our trade on the Chinese; but in this year Japan startled the world. We suddenly discovered that the Japanese had a disciplined army, and a small but up-to-date fleet. It was an absolutely unique phenomenon, like the rise of a new planet. They overpowered the Chinese and obtained territory at their expense. Then we heard the phrase "The Yellow Peril." Would Easterners, a yellow race, be a match for Europeans? William II promptly combined with France and Russia, and forced the Mikado to give up his newly won Port Arthur and its peninsula. Thus for a moment it seemed as if the three Great Powers could really be friends. In 1897 Germany demanded the cession of Kiaochow on the excuse that two of her missionaries had been murdered by Chinese; thus she obtained a naval base. Russia followed by seizing Port Arthur. Our government obtained Wei-hai-wei and stood out for the "open door," *i.e.* free trade, but without success; Germany and Russia cared only for German and Russian trade monopoly.

The constant revolts in Cuba and the inability of the Spanish conscript army to repress them made the United States interfere in 1898. The U.S. navy was vastly superior to the Spanish, and the war ended by the freedom of Cuba under U.S. control; also the lesser island of Porto Rico, and the Philippines in the Pacific, were annexed by the Americans, and thus for the first time they had to "take up the white man's burden." This meant that they must have an even more up-to-date navy, large as well as scientifically efficient. It also meant that they must shorten the distance between the Pacific and Atlantic, and themselves complete the Panama canal; this was promptly assured by a convenient revolt of Panama against the "United States" of Columbia, when they supported the

rebel and in return received a canal concession. Scientific
tackling of the mosquito and fever peril, businesslike
tackling of labour problems, and clever engineering, at
last made the canal a reality. It remains that the United
States and Japan as rival Pacific powers may have troubles
in the future.

In 1898 Nicholas II proposed an all-world Peace settlement. The division of Europe into two armed camps owing
to the Triple Alliance and the Dual Alliance was producing
an intolerable stale-mate. Therefore the suggestion was
welcomed, and a Conference was held at the Hague.
Nothing indeed came of it as far as disarmament, or even
reduction of armaments, was concerned; but Germany at
once saw her opportunity to weaken our natural advantages
for enforcing a blockade by sea, while she never gave any
sign of abating her military or naval preparations. Yet by
general agreement a standing Arbitration Tribunal was
founded for international disputes. This was so far to the
good.

The critical years for England were 1898 to 1902. Lord
Salisbury's government, now that lower Egypt was decently
governed and prosperous under our protectorate, was
making steps to put an end to the horrors of the Khalifa's
rule in the Sudan; the Khalifa was the Mahdi's successor.
Helped by a railway, Kitchener's expedition could move
more rapidly than the Gordon relief force. The Arab
resistance was broken down, Khartum occupied, and
Gordon avenged, in 1898. But the French had been
working across from west-central Africa to the upper Nile,
being covered by Kitchener's advance which diverted
the Arabs towards us. Major Marchand had reached
Fashoda, 400 miles above Khartum. French bitterness
against our continued occupation of Egypt very nearly led

to a criminally disastrous war, but wiser counsels prevailed and Marchand was withdrawn. Then came the Boer war of 1899–1902. That the French and Russians should applaud the Boers and gloat over our preliminary disasters was natural. But we were hardly prepared for an equally fierce outbreak of anti-British feeling in Germany, and indeed in every country of Europe except Italy and Greece.

The Boer war was yet in progress when the Boxer rising occurred in China. The six European Great Powers, the United States, and Japan, sent troops to save the Legations at Pekin. This was the occasion when William II ordered his Germans to behave like Huns so as to cow their enemies by the frightfulness of their severity; and nobly they obeyed him, looting and beating and killing peaceful villagers as well as Boxers, as eye-witnesses among our officers have testified. Yet, in spite of the apparent unanimity of eight countries, the old-fashioned and natural belief in a Balance of Power ultimately prevailed in Far Eastern politics as in European. Lord Salisbury drew near to Japan, and in 1902 was concluded the Anglo-Japanese Alliance by which, if either ally was ever attacked by two Great Powers, the other ally was to join in.

At this crisis the British nation began seriously to ask why we were hated and reviled. We could understand French and Russian ill-will; but why were other nations, in spite of our traditional welcome of foreigners to our island and in spite of our generous treatment of them by our system of Free Trade, so persistently hostile? We were not conscious of undue pride, nor had we gloated over our neighbours' disasters. The answer is to be found in our insularity. We had always been free from invasion, we had gained commercial advantage and had established our Sea Power under cover of every great war, we had

extended our Empire, while posing as the champions of
liberty in Europe as against a Louis XIV and a Napoleon.
The palpable benefits of our 19th century Free Trade to
other nations never destroyed the old catch-words of which
Napoleon had made good use; we were "a nation of shop-
keepers" and "the tyrants of the sea." Above all, not
only had we never suffered the horrors of war at home, but
we had fought, whenever we did fight, with but a small
"mercenary" army; yet our older history books had
implied that we alone had beaten Napoleon to his knees
and had "fought the bear" at Sebastopol. French writers
had always pointed out that *le côté fort de la politique
anglaise* was to get some ally or allies to do our work, to
subsidise all Europe against Napoleon I, to use Napoleon
III to check Russia at one period, and to rely on Austria
to keep watch on the ramparts against Russia at another.
Meanwhile all other national armies were really nations in
arms; we alone had no conscription, only a contemptibly
little paid army. There was just enough truth in such
arguments to be galling to us. The Japanese alliance
seemed to our enemies to be another example of our
readiness to obtain some foreign power to promote our
interests.

The result of our new outlook on the general situation
was the *entente* in 1904 with France. It seemed to come
about with surprising quickness, and at first it was thought
that it was chiefly due to the personal influence of our new
king, Edward VII, who during his mother's life had had
no opportunity to take part in politics. But there were
various reasons why it was readily accepted. The very
fact of the intensity of French bitterness about Egypt and
the nearness of war on the Fashoda incident made both
nations, as well as serious politicians, acknowledge the

wrongness of perpetual rivalry. Our control of lower Egypt was admittedly a benefit to civilisation, and our reconquest of the Sudan was already promising equal results. In other parts of the world disputes could be settled without war, which indeed would be a crime rather than a blunder. Thus the quickness of our understanding was proof of its reasonableness.

The value of the *entente* was at once put to the test. The Russian government, scorning to come to terms with Japan so as to define their respective spheres of interest in Manchuria and Korea, provoked a war. William II, as if deliberately wishing to cause a general conflagration, called upon the Tsar to protect civilisation against "the yellow peril." But, as France did not move to support Russia, we were not called upon to take up the cause of Japan. Even when Russian war-ships fired upon our fishing boats in the North Sea under the delusion that they were Japanese torpedo craft disguised, the matter was submitted to arbitration under the Hague scheme.

Russian defeats at the hands of Japan led to the usual turmoil, industrial revolution and nihilism. Of course Kaiser William, having previously done his best to goad Russia to war, now in her period of humiliation abroad and civil strife at home took advantage of her weakness to hector France. In 1905 he himself landed at Tangier to assert Germany's rights in Morocco, and he demanded the dismissal of M. Delcassé, the French Foreign Minister. This was a direct challenge to the Anglo-French *entente*; would it bear the strain of resistance to German dictation, now that Russian cooperation was out of the question? M. Delcassé voluntarily resigned, and the French assured William that German trade should not suffer from any monopoly of theirs in Morocco; but otherwise they held firm, and our government stood by them. A Conference was held at Algeciras on Spanish soil near Gibraltar. Thus war was averted. The reason why William did not proceed to extremities is to be found in Germany's weakness at sea. He received the solid support of Austria at Algeciras. But Italy was not at all keen, and he had reckoned hitherto on the Italian navy while his own was in the making. Moreover we had just built H.M.S. Dreadnought, the first of the new heavily-gunned monster ships which seemed to make all her predecessors obsolete. Thus having seen that we were in earnest to support France, he preferred to wait patiently until in ten years' time he should have enough up-to-date Dreadnoughts and other craft in proportion; such an advance in naval architecture means that all Powers start equal, and success will attend those that can stand the strain of steady building on the new lines.

In 1907 an Anglo-Russian agreement was made, so that at last the Triple Entente was a solid fact. Yet one wishes that it had come about earlier, at least before the Japanese war; the seven years 1907–14 were hardly long enough to convert into a hearty ally the power that we had opposed for thirty years previously, and that we had applauded Japan for defeating. Even in the recent war it was insinuated that we only cared to have on our side "the steam roller"—pestilential phrase—so that it might flatten out Germany for us when our obstinate refusal to prepare for war brought about its own punishment. Also the agreement, now that it was unnecessary to maintain a strong force on the north-west frontier of India, gave an excuse to the authorities at Simla to practise a false economy and starve the Indian army. Yet German intrigues in Turkey, and especially the German control of the railways of Asia Minor and the Euphrates, might have taught even these civilians that it was not wise to undo the work of Roberts and Kitchener.

The Turks made no effort to reform after 1878. We did not care, and were not stirred by the Armenian "atrocities." We even joined with the other Powers in a naval blockade of Crete in 1896, when the Christian insurgents were actually bombarded in their camp by the guns of our ships. In 1897 the Greeks took up the cause of Crete and were badly beaten by the Turks; it must be remembered that ever since the Hellenic revival which led to their War of Independence, and especially since their expulsion of their Bavarian king in 1862, the Greeks considered themselves to be the champions of all their kinsfolk scattered through the Turkish empire, and claimed that they, not the Russians, had the right to hold Constantinople. Though beaten now they were saved by the Powers from Turkish revenge. Crete soon came under their protection, and the Mohammedan garrison and landowners evacuated the island.

But, while the other Powers were undecided and could not strike out a strong line for or against the Sultan, William II saw his opportunity. He would make German interests supreme in Turkey, reorganise the army under German officers, penetrate into Asia Minor and link up with Mesopotamia by railways financed by German capital. Paying a visit of ceremony to the Sultan he treated him as a civilised monarch and the equal of Christian kings. But time was required for the development of his policy even as for the creation of the German navy, and the dénouement was not yet.

In 1908 the Young Turks revolted and deposed the Sultan. Complacently we said that now at last there would be good government in the Balkans so that we had

no call to interfere. The Austrians, prompted obviously
by William who stood by them "in shining armour,"
declared their protectorate of Bosnia and Herzegovina to
be at an end and definitely annexed the two provinces.
Then Prince Ferdinand pronounced himself as an independent sovereign, and took the title of Tsar of Bulgaria.
Rumania and Serbia and Montenegro were much upset,
being thus surrounded by enemies and powerless unless
Russia helped them.

That remarkable man Venizelos, a Cretan, becoming
Prime Minister of Greece by sheer merit, seemed at one
time to have produced a better state of affairs.  He has
been termed a "demagogue," a convenient term to sling at
a man who has risen and overshadowed the local aristocracy.
But he has voiced Hellenic aspirations, and has had an
unexampled influence over the Greek peasants and people.
He created a Greek-Montenegrin-Serbian-Bulgarian league
before which in 1912 the Turks collapsed; and yet we all
thought that under German training the army, at least, of
the Young Turks had been transformed.  But when each
ally had been victorious, the Greeks winning Salonica, the
Bulgarians Adrianople and Kavalla, the Serbians Monastir,
and the Montenegrins Scutari, they fell out.  The Bulgarians, anticipating as it seems a Greek-Serbian league
against themselves, tried to get in the first blow; both
Greeks and Serbians beat them, the Rumanians threatened
them in the rear, the Turks rallied and regained Adrianople.
Stories of atrocities of each against each were spread through
Europe.  Yet the dreaded European war did not break
out, for the Kaiser had not given the word.

Of course, as we work up to the outbreak in 1914, we
see that the central fact is the solidity of the German-
Austrian alliance.  Though Prussia had been so consistently

a bad neighbour to Austria up to 1866, Francis Joseph was tied to William by a close bond. He supported Germany both in Morocco and in the Balkans. When William complained that he was being shut in by a ring of Entente Powers, when Italy was becoming cold owing to the peaceful penetration of her industries by German traders and capitalists, Austria stood staunchly by him. In fact it would seem that William's ideal of a Middle Europe, based on the superiority of the Teuton over both Slav and Latin, fascinated the Germans of Austria proper. And it appealed to Hungarians also. Whatever remained of the old bitterness between Austrian and Hungarian disappeared gradually after the compromise of 1867 when the Dual Monarchy was created. Thus the amazing ingratitude of Francis Joseph is explained. In 1848–49 he owed his salvation to the loyalty of his Slav subjects in Croatia and to his alliance with the Slavs of Russia who crushed Hungary for him.

But needing since 1867 the support of Hungary to consolidate his empire, and especially needing the cooperation of Hungary to carry out William's anti-Slav policy, he sacrificed Slav to Magyar, allowing the Magyar language to be imposed officially on all non-Magyars of the Hungarian Kingdom and Magyars to hold all important offices. In the Balkans he played the rôle of a conqueror, not of a champion of distressed Christians. And finally it came to pass in the capital of Bosnia that tyranny led to the assassination of his heir and grand-nephew.

# INDEX

For EU product safety concerns, contact us at Calle de José Abascal, 56–1°,
28003 Madrid, Spain or eugpsr@cambridge.org.

www.ingramcontent.com/pod-product-compliance
Ingram Content Group UK Ltd.
Pitfield, Milton Keynes, MK11 3LW, UK
UKHW012328130625
459647UK00009B/151